Analyzing Crime Patterns

This book is dedicated to the men and women
of the New York City Police Department.
The successful reduction of crime in New York
demonstrated the power of automated crime mapping
and made this book both possible and necessary.

Analyzing
Crime
Patterns
Frontiers of Practice

Victor Goldsmith

Philip G. McGuire

John H. Mollenkopf

Timothy A. Ross

Editors

Sage Publications, Inc.
International Educational and Professional Publisher
Thousand Oaks ■ London ■ New Delhi

For information:

Sage Publications, Inc.
2455 Teller Road
Thousand Oaks, California 91320
E-mail: order@sagepub.com

Sage Publications Ltd.
6 Bonhill Street
London EC2A 4PU
United Kingdom

Sage Publications India Pvt. Ltd.
M-32 Market
Greater Kailash I
New Delhi 110 048 India

Printed in the United States of America

Library of Congress Cataloging-in-Publication Data

Main entry under title:
   Analyzing crime patterns: Frontiers of practice / edited by Victor Goldsmith,
Philip McGuire, John Mollenkopf and Timothy A. Ross.
      p.   cm.
   Includes bibliographical references (p.   ) and index.
   ISBN 0-7619-1940-6 (cloth: perm. paper)
   ISBN 0-7619-1941-4 (pbk: perm. paper)
   1. Crime analysis—United States.   2. Criminal statistics—United States.
3. Spatial behavior—United States.   I. Goldsmith, Victor.
   HV7936.C88 A53   1999
   364′.042′0973—dc21   99-6533

This book is printed on acid-free paper.

00   01   02   03   04   05   06   7   6   5   4   3   2   1

Acquiring Editor:	Kassie Gavrilis
Editorial Assistant:	Anna Howland
Production Editor:	Sanford Robinson
Editorial Assistant:	Karen Wiley
Typesetter/Designer:	Lynn Miyata
Indexer:	Molly Hall
Cover Designer:	Michelle Lee

Contents

Foreword

The genesis for this book stems from one of the first Locally Initiated Research Partnership grants funded by the National Institute of Justice (NIJ) in 1996. This grant program challenged applicants to form partnerships between research entities and law enforcement agencies to conduct research or evaluate a program of mutual interest to both parties. The City University of New York's Center for Applied Studies of the Environment (CAPSE) and the Center for Urban Research (CUR) submitted a proposal in partnership with the New York Police Department (NYPD) to examine various crime-mapping methods in support of the NYPD's then newly adopted COMPSTAT process.

NIJ was impressed with the interdisciplinary research team of CUR and CAPSE staff, representing political scientists, sociologists, geologists, and geographers, as well as the practical application of the project. One of the noteworthy elements of the CUR/CAPSE/NYPD project was that the grantees identified the top researchers in the area of the spatial analysis of crime to draw on their expertise and knowledge. The researchers were invited to a meeting in New York at which they presented papers based on analyses of a geocoded data set of New York City crime. The papers presented at that meeting became the chapters that comprise this book.

Coincidentally, at the same time that the CUR/CAPSE/NYPD grant was awarded, NIJ established its Crime Mapping Research Center. This fortuitous timing brought many of the same people who attended the meeting in New York to a meeting in Washington, D.C., just a few weeks later to help advise NIJ on how its new center could best meet the needs of the criminal justice research and practitioner communities. These meetings marked the beginning of a new and ambitious research and programmatic effort that today is represented by $11 million in NIJ grants for research involving the spatial analysis of crime and an annual conference that in 1998 drew close to 800 participants.

Analyzing Crime Patterns exemplifies this renewed interest in the spatial analysis of crime and criminal behavior, offering some of the best work in the field to date. The chapters herein present findings and methods that range from practical applications to the exploration of discrete measurement issues. This book is truly a frontier in practice—one recommended to anyone interested in the spatial analysis of crime.

—Nancy G. La Vigne
Director, Crime Mapping Research Center
National Institute of Justice

Acknowledgments

As with any book, the number of people to thank is enormous and the space to do so is inadequate. We could easily use a page outlining the contributions of each of the people in the following paragraphs.

Jeremy Travis and Nancy LaVigne at the National Institute of Justice funded the conference at which papers for this book were first conceived and they provided continued support for the partnership between the City University of New York (CUNY) and the New York City Police Department (NYPD). The research reported in chapters 2, 7, 9, and 13 of this volume was supported by the National Institute of Justice under grant 97-LB-VX-K013. Robert Langworthy provided valuable advice while at NIJ. Sally Goodgold at the Police Foundation also facilitated the CUNY-NYPD collaboration.

The NYPD provided data, technical support, and invaluable advice. We thank Police Commissioners William Bratton and Howard Safir, Deputy Commissioners Michael Farrell and Michael Amarosa, and Inspector William Batista. Police Officer Steve Quinn from the Management Information Systems Department deserves a special acknowledgment for having the foresight to make the original connection between NYPD and CUNY. Also from the NYPD, we thank John Yohe from the COMPSTAT Unit and Rachel Jacobovitz, John Eterno, William Chimento, and Edward Alexander from the Office of Management and Planning.

Timothy Ross acknowledges the help of Kassie Gavrilis, Karen Wiley, Anna Howland, Sanford Robinson, Lynn Miyata, Janelle LeMaster, and Terry Hendrix at Sage Publications. Victoria Allen, Jennifer Holdaway, Tom Kamber, and Charles Swartz were helpful colleagues at the Center for Urban Research. At CUNY's Center for Applied Study of the Environment, Colin Reilly and Alicia Fierer provided invaluable help.

The editors also thank family members for continued support, including Irma Birnbaum, Chris McGuire, Kathleen Gerson, and Lori Urov.

INTRODUCTION

Operational Imperatives and Intellectual Cautionary Tales

Part I provides an overview of mapping and geographic information systems in crime analysis. The first two chapters are written by practitioners, and the latter two contributions are from academics. Combined, they seek to give readers a thorough background in the uses and vocabulary of crime mapping.

Chapter 1, by Philip Canter, outlines the type of data that need collecting and then categorizes several methods used to analyze spatial crime data. Canter makes important distinctions between tactical and strategic mapping. Tactical mapping is used for short-term operations, whereas strategic mapping addresses longer term policy planning. Canter also distinguishes between descriptive and analytic mapping. Canter points out that the types of data and the method used to analyze data are driven by the types of questions that need to be answered.

Chapter 2, by Philip G. McGuire, discusses the integration of crime mapping into the much-heralded COMPSTAT process used by the New York City Police Department. He asserts that although the crime mapping aspect of COMPSTAT receives most of the attention, COMPSTAT is primarily a managerial tool that co-incidentally incorporates crime mapping as an integral part of executive oversight. McGuire suggests that for mapping to reach its full potential, it must be integrated into the standard operations of law enforcement rather than be kept separate as a specialized unit.

In Chapter 3, Keith Harries argues that crime data alone rarely provide enough information for an adequate understanding of criminal problems. Both census data and data from city agencies illuminate underlying trends that may be useful to policymakers. Harries also suggests that digital orthophotos generated by aerial photography will be the next wave in crime mapping.

Charles Swartz's review of academic crime literature in Chapter 4 indicates that the spatial analysis of crime has broadened our understanding of criminal activity, but it has also generated many continuing controversies. Swartz shows that researchers have identified a vast number of factors that are associated with crime but need more refined and focused techniques to make academic studies more relevant to real-world situations.

Together, these chapters show that although crime mapping appears to be a highly technical and specialized field, it has a wide range of applications. Mapping can not only lead to more effective and efficient policing but also improve and refine theoretical understandings of crime.

CHAPTER 1

Using a Geographic Information System for Tactical Crime Analysis

PHILIP CANTER

This chapter discusses the uses of a geographic information system (GIS) for tactical crime analysis. A tactical crime analysis GIS is built on the assumption that police managers and line officers need access to timely and accurate information for problem solving, community policing, crime prevention, and enforcement activities. The goal of using a GIS system is to address some of the shortcomings of traditional policing, such as reactive responses prompted by 911 calls for service.

Police in the United States have a well-established practice of using crime statistics to help manage operations. Spelman (1988) notes that Chief August Vollmer of Berkeley, California, was the first police manager to use crime records for short- and long-term planning in 1909. The Bureau of Justice Statistics (1994) reports that crime analysis is frequently used by police departments to provide general management information and to provide tactical and strategic support. Accreditation standards for law enforcement agencies require police departments to use crime analysis information for supporting management and operations.

The use of maps to examine the spatial distribution of crime also has a long history as evidenced by the work of Guerry (1833) and Quetelet (1842/1973), who noted that crime was not evenly distributed across geographic areas in France (Brantingham & Brantingham, 1981). Studies in England by Plint (1851) and Mayhew (1862/1968) also noted the spatial variation in crime, as did research in the United States by Lottier (1938a, 1938b), Shannon (1954), Schmid (1960a, 1960b), and Harries (1971). Comparative studies, most notably the work of social ecologists of the Chicago school of sociology during the first half of the twentieth century, found that high delinquency rates corresponded to communities with other social problems (Shaw, 1929). Comparing the spatial distribution of crime with other data on an area's inhabitants contributed to the development of several criminological theories. Social disorganization theory developed from the work of Shaw and McKay. Brantingham and Brantingham (1981) noted that early comparative mapping studies were used to support arguments about criminal etiology made by social positivists during the early twentieth century. Examining various aspects of crime within a geographical context has contributed to a better understanding of offender travel patterns (Gabor & Gotthell, 1984; LeBeau, 1987; Pyle, 1974; Rengert, 1972; Rossmo, 1995), the built environment (Jeffery, 1971; Newman, 1972; Taylor, Sumaker, & Gottfredson, 1985), and social ecology (Harries, 1980; Sampson & Groves, 1989; Schuerman & Kobrin, 1986; Shaw, 1929; Shaw & McKay, 1942, 1969).

CRIME ANALYSIS

Crime analysis involves the collection and analysis of data pertaining to a criminal incident, offender, and target. Police managers recognize that competent analysts provide important information to decision makers. One of the most important purposes of crime analysis is to identify and generate the information needed to assist in decisions regarding the deployment of police resources to prevent and suppress criminal activity. In addition, crime analysis can be used to evaluate the effectiveness of programs such as community policing and crime prevention, develop policy through research, justify budget requests, and help identify or define a problem.

Data are an important part of any crime analysis function. Although an agency should collect the best data possible with a minimum resource expenditure, it is critical that data be relevant, reliable, accurate, and timely. *Relevant* data will be guided by an agency's crime analysis function and any research that identifies data elements important to an agency's operation. At a minimum, an agency involved in crime analysis should collect incident data on the type of crime, location, time, date, target, suspect, property stolen, and modus operandi. The data should conform to standard codes and definitions to allow comparisons and to perform pattern and linkage analysis. *Reliability* suggests that multiple data sources and procedures are in place to ensure the continued collection and processing of data. Some agencies may want to supplement data from their 911 system with information collected by investigating officers to reduce data entry costs or to lessen the data collection workload of investigators. Redundant systems should be in place in the event that data collection methods are interrupted. To ensure *accuracy,* records should be sampled and compared against written reports. If possible, source reports used to collect data should be reviewed by line supervisors, a formal report review unit, and analysts using the data. Crime data must be *timely* because the chances of apprehending an offender responsible for a series of cases depends on quick identification of the crime pattern. Agencies may rely on the electronic transfer of data, laptop computers transmitting data through radio frequencies, or scan forms to ensure receipt of timely crime data.

Crime analysis has two broad functions: tactical and strategic. Although the focus of this chapter is tactical crime analysis, the use of GIS for strategic crime analysis should be noted.

Strategic Crime Analysis

Strategic crime analysis usually involves the collection and study of data covering a period of several years. It is generally more research oriented, involving inferential and multivariate statistics. Strategic crime analysis includes crime trend forecasts, resource allocation, and situational analysis.

Crime trend forecasting uses time series to estimate future crime based on past trends. Methods vary, but they often include linear techniques, exponential smoothing models, and autoregressive integrated moving average methods. By identifying discrepancies between predicted and observed crime rates, time series analysis can help determine if an outside influence, such as a crime prevention program, may be influencing criminal activity. Time series can also be used to determine seasonality, such as an increase in no-force burglaries during warm-weather months, so that a department can plan and not react to anticipated changes in crime. For example, Harries, Stadler, and Zdorkowski (1984) found that some low-status Dallas, Texas, neighborhoods were more susceptible to heat stress-related assault because they did not have the resources to protect themselves from high temperatures and humidity. Although most police would admit there is little they can do about climatic conditions, a GIS could identify low-status neighborhoods for possible intervention at the outset of anticipated heat waves.

Resource allocation involves the distribution of personnel in response to changes in service demand. A typical example involves the design of police posts or sectors in response to changes in workload during a 24-hour period. A GIS can adjust post boundaries in response to temporal and geographical changes in workload. Modifications performed within a GIS can often be exported as a file directly into a computer-aided dispatch system.

Situational analysis is used to describe details about a particular area, such as a community's inhabitants, type of land use, built environment, and crime history. It allows analysts to examine the spatial interrelationship of criminogenic factors. Examinations of crime in taverns and liquor stores (Block & Block, 1995), abandoned buildings (Spelman, 1993), public housing (Roncek & Francik, 1981), and high schools (Roncek & Lobosco, 1983) are examples of situational analysis. The information resulting from the overlaying of multiple databases in a GIS can provide new perspectives on crime and crime interdiction strategies.

Tactical Crime Analysis

Tactical crime analysis involves pattern detection, linkage analysis for suspect-crime correlations, target profiling, and offender movement patterns. The main difference between strategic and tactical crime analysis is the timeliness of the data. Strategic crime analysis usually involves data covering at least a year-long period, whereas tactical crime analysis uses data collected during several days.

Pattern detection occurs when offenses reported during a short period of time have common attributes, such as type of crime, modus operandi, and type of weapon used. A crime pattern could occur over a large geographic region, or it may occur in a relatively small area. A crime pattern occurring in a relatively small area is called a "hot spot" or cluster. Sherman (1995) defines a hot spot as "small places in which the occurrence of crime is so frequent that it is highly predictable, at least over a 1 year period" (p. 36). Block (1990, 1994) notes that hot spot areas are defined by clusters of events or locations. The high concentration of cases and the greater probability of future cases occurring within the same area make it a suitable target for crime-suppression strategies. The ability of a GIS to map one or more attributes associated with reported offenses makes it an invaluable tool for pattern analysis. Analytical methods available for identifying hot spot areas include using point locations in a GIS to construct contour maps, standard deviational ellipses, and k means clustering.

Linkage analysis correlates a suspect to one or more criminal incidents. It requires matching information maintained in a suspect database, such as modus operandi or physical description, against the same attributes associated with criminal incidents. The objective of linkage analysis is apprehension and case clearance. Some studies (Pyle, 1976; Rand, 1986; Rengert & Wasilchick, 1985) have found that suspects tend to travel within a predictable range to commit a crime. Linkage analysis can narrow search areas by identifying known criminals or other suspects who reside within a certain distance from incident locations.

Target profiling identifies locations that may have an unusually high likelihood of victimization within an active pattern area. Within a large geographic area, offenders tend to target certain types of locations rather than others, especially for crimes influenced by the location of commercial or service-oriented activity, such as convenience stores or banks. A GIS can assist in target profiling by mapping the location of all potential targets, such as fast-food restaurants, relative to actual incident locations.

Developing a profile for potential targets within a hot spot area sounds simple, but a hot spot area for residential burglary may contain thousands of potential targets. Profilers catalog the common features of actual targets located within a hot spot area, and then they identify all targets sharing these features. Often, these features may not be collected as part of a crime analysis database but may be maintained as part of another agency's database files. Detailed information about the physical structure of dwelling units, for example, is usually available from tax assessment files. Information about guardianship may be available from alarm company registrations or bureaus licensing dogs, and the number of targets, such as retirees, is available from the decennial census. A GIS can select and match features obtained from files maintained by outside agencies with incident locations. A GIS can then identify potential sites within a target area that contain the same unique features.

Offender movement pattern analysis ties at least two or more points to one or more criminal incidents. One example is the theft location and recovery site of a stolen motor vehicle. Connecting the two locations, theft and recovery, may help identify the roads used by an offender after stealing an automobile. Similarly, relating an offender's last known residence to an arrest location such as an open-air drug market can identify roads used by dealers to transport drugs. Intelligence information collected on individuals seen in a known drug market can be linked to their place of residence or other locations, such as place of employment or recreation, and subsequently associated with a crime pattern occurring within that individual's activity space.

GEOGRAPHIC INFORMATION SYSTEMS

The ability of a GIS to relate and synthesize data from a variety of sources enables analysts to examine various aspects of criminal activity, including the built environment, crime risk and opportunity measures, and offender search patterns. Several examples of the uses of a GIS for both strategic and tactical crime analyses have previously been cited.

The utility of a GIS depends on (a) the accuracy of the data; (b) the data attributes associated with each incident; and (c) the database, mapping, and analytical capabilities of the GIS. The purpose of this section is to summarize the important mapping features of a GIS as they relate to tactical crime analysis. Specifically, a GIS has two broad applications that can be used for tactical crime analysis: descriptive mapping and analytic mapping.

Descriptive Mapping

Descriptive mapping displays thematic information assigned to a point location or boundary. The thematic display is based on one or more attributes associated with the mapped object. Examples include burglary locations color coded by day of week and a thematic map showing the number of robberies per week by census block group. Another type of descriptive map assigns multiple attributes obtained from different databases to a point or boundary. For example, an analyst may wish to determine the location of residential burglaries by assessed value of the targeted dwellings over time. The analyst may then be able to determine whether an offender is targeting dwellings within an assessed dollar range or if a relationship exists between the assessed value of a structure (and presumably the value of property stolen) and the length of time between successive cases. Descriptive mapping can also relate geographic information such as the size of a census block group to the number of crimes reported in the respective census block group. The resulting crime density map attempts to compensate for variations in the number of reported crimes that might result from differences in a boundary's land area.

Descriptive mapping is similar to automated pin mapping used by crime analysts. The ability to query databases to select point locations based on specified case attributes is helpful in detecting crime patterns. Examining the spatial distribution of crime may contribute to an understanding of an observed pattern, and by describing the spatial distribution of crime one may anticipate or predict future activity. The interpretation of mapped information remains subjective, however, given that a point pattern or thematic boundary map is not being compared to a hypothetical distribution.

Analytic Mapping

Analytic mapping describes spatial patterns associated with two types of distributions: discrete and continuous. Discrete spatial distributions are defined at certain locations, such as an incident address or a census tract. Spatially discrete point patterns can be examined relative to a study area using quadratic or distance methods or relative to each other using measures of arrangement. A spatially continuous distribution varies over a surface and can be measured only by sampling at discrete locations.

Analytic mapping can test hypotheses about the spatial distribution of discrete patterns. Crime locations identified as points on a map, or grid cells containing the number of reported crimes during a period of time, can be compared against an expected randomized spatial pattern. Point distributions that are not random, and by inspection appear to be clustered as opposed to dispersed, suggest an unusual amount of criminal activity. Note that the pattern depends on time and space, and both dimensions are defined by the analyst according to study objectives. It assumes that accurate and timely information on crime is being collected for analysis.

In the absence of any detailed information about a crime incident, analysts can still identify a crime pattern based on the number of incidents occurring within a given time period and study area. In this situation, the crime analyst can identify high concentrations of criminal activity taking place during a short period of time. Pattern detection suggests that (a) a greater than expected number of crimes are being reported for a given area, (b) it is likely that the pattern will continue without intervention, and (c) the same criminally active area may contain a high amount of unreported crime. Pattern detection and analysis can be used to efficiently manage police operations by deploying resources to criminally active areas and may increase the rate of apprehension, reduce or displace crime, and assist in identifying other factors that may contribute to criminal events.

CONCLUSION

Several methods that have potential use for tactical crime analysis were discussed in this chapter. Crime analysts and researchers are making substantial progress in identifying high crime activity areas and predicting future target locations. It is clear that descriptive and analytic mapping will be an important part of strategic and tactical crime analysis efforts.

REFERENCES

Block, C. R. (1990, December). *Hot spots and isocrimes in law enforcement decision making.* Paper presented at the conference on Police and Community Responses to Drugs: Frontline Strategies in the Drug War, University of Illinois at Chicago.

Block, C. R. (1994). ASTAC hot spot areas: A statistical tool for law enforcement decisions. In *Proceedings of the Workshop on Crime Analysis Through Computer Mapping.* Chicago: Illinois Criminal Justice Information Authority.

Block, R. L., & Block, C. B. (1995). Space, place and crime: Hot spot areas and hot spot places of liquor-related crime. In J. E. Eck & D. Weisburd (Eds.), *Crime prevention studies: Vol. 4. Crime and place* (pp. 145-154). Monsey, NY: Criminal Justice Press.

Brantingham, P. J., & Brantingham, P. L. (1981). *Environmental criminology* (pp. 7-26). Prospect Heights, IL: Waveland.

Bureau of Justice Statistics. (1994). *Demonstrating the operational utility of incident-based data for local crime analysis. Reporting systems in Tacoma, Washington, and New Bedford, Massachusetts* (pp. 14-15). Washington, DC: U.S. Department of Justice.

Gabor, T., & Gotthell, E. (1984). Offender characteristics and spatial mobility: An empirical study and some policy implications. *Canadian Journal of Criminology, 26,* 267-281.

Guerry, A. M. (1833). *Essai sur la statistique morale de la France.* Paris: Crochard.

Harries, K. D. (1971). The geography of American crime 1968. *Journal of Geography, 70,* 204-213.

Harries, K. D. (1980). *Crime and the environment.* Springfield, IL: Charles C Thomas.

Harries, K. D., Stadler, S. J., & Zdorkowski, R. T. (1984). Seasonality and assault: Explorations in inter-neighborhood variation, Dallas 1980. *Annals of the Association of American Geographers.*

Jeffery, C. R. (1971). *Crime prevention through environmental design.* Beverly Hills, CA: Sage.

LeBeau, J. L. (1987). The journey to rape: Geographic distance and the rapist's method of approaching the victim. *Journal of Police Science and Administration, 15,* 129-136.

Lottier, S. (1938a). Distribution of criminal offenses in sectional regions. *Journal of Criminal Law, Criminology, and Police Science, 29,* 329-344.

Lottier, S. (1938b). Distribution of criminal offenses in metropolitan regions. *Journal of Criminal Law, Criminology, and Police Science, 29,* 37-50.

Mayhew, H. (1968). *London labour and the London poor: Vol. IV. Those that will not work, comprising prostitutes, thieves, swindlers and beggars.* New York: Dover. (Original work published 1862)

Newman, O. (1972). *Defensible space.* New York: Macmillan.

Plint, T. (1851). *Crime in England.* London: Charles Gilpin.

Pyle, G. F. (1974). *The spatial dynamics of crime* (Research paper No. 159). Chicago: University of Chicago, Department of Geography.

Pyle, G. F. (1976). Spatial aspects of crime in Cleveland, Ohio. *American Behavioral Scientist, 20,* 175-198.

Quetelet, M. A. (1973). A treatise on man and the development of his faculties. In *Comparative statistics in the nineteenth century.* Bergstrasse, Germany: Gregg International. (Original work published 1842)

Rand, A. (1986). Mobility triangles. In R. M. Figlio, S. Hakim, & G. F. Rengert (Eds.), *Metropolitan crime patterns.* Monsey, NY: Willow Tree Press.

Rengert, G. F. (1972). *Spatial aspects of criminal behavior: A suggested approach.* Paper presented at East Lakes Division, Association of American Geographers annual meeting. Philadelphia: Temple University, Department of Geography.

Rengert, G. F., & Wasilchick, J. (1985). *Suburban burglary.* Springfield, IL: Charles C. Thomas.

Roncek, D. W., & Francik, J. M. A. (1981). Housing projects and crime. *Social Problems, 29,* 151-166.

Roncek, D. W., & Lobosco, A. (1983). The effect of high schools on crime in their neighborhoods. *Social Science Quarterly, 64,* 598-613.

Rossmo, D. K. (1995). Multivariate spatial profiles as a tool in crime investigation. In C. Block, M. Dabdoub, & S. Fregly (Eds.), *Crime analysis through computer mapping* (pp. 65-97). Washington, DC: Police Executive Research Forum.

Sampson, R. J., & Groves, W. B. (1989). Community structure and crime: Testing social disorganization theory. *American Journal of Sociology, 4,* 774-802.

Schmid, C. (1960a). Urban crime areas, Part I. *American Sociological Review, 25,* 527-543.

Schmid, C. (1960b). Urban crime areas, Part II. *American Sociological Review, 25,* 655-678.

Schuerman, L., & Kobrin, S. (1986). Community careers in crime. In A. J. Reiss Jr. & M. Tonry (Eds.), *Communities and crime.* Chicago: University of Chicago Press.

Shannon, L. W. (1954). The spatial distribution of criminal offenses by states. *Journal of Criminal Law, Criminology, and Police Science, 45,* 264-273.

Shaw, C. (1929). *Delinquency areas; A study of the geographic distribution of school truants, juvenile delinquents, and adult offenders in Chicago.* Chicago: University of Chicago Press.

Shaw, C. R., & McKay, H. D. (1942). *Juvenile delinquency and urban areas.* Chicago: University of Chicago Press.

Shaw, C. R., & McKay, H. D. (1969). *Juvenile delinquency and urban areas* (Rev. ed.). Chicago: University of Chicago Press.

Sherman, L. W. (1995). Hot spots of crime and criminal careers of places. In J. E. Eck & D. Weisburd (Eds.), *Crime prevention studies: Vol. 4. Crime and place* (pp. 35-52). Monsey, NY: Criminal Justice Press.

Spelman, W. (1988). *Beyond bean counting. New approaches for managing crime data* (pp. 1-2). Washington, DC: Police Executive Research Forum.

Spelman, W. (1993). Abandoned buildings: Magnets for crime. *Journal of Criminal Justice, 21,* 481-495.

Taylor, R. B., Sumaker, S. A., & Gottfredson, S. D. (1985). A neighborhood-level links between physical features and local sentiments deterioration, fear of crime, and confidence. *Journal of Architectural and Planning Research, 2,* 261-275.

CHAPTER 2

The New York Police Department COMPSTAT Process

Mapping for Analysis, Evaluation, and Accountability

PHILIP G. McGUIRE

GENESIS

In 1994, the recently elected Giuliani administration instituted a new managerial command and control system within the New York City Police Department (NYPD). The system grew out of the need to manage, monitor, and assess the impact of the administration's new crime control strategies and soon became known simply as "COMPSTAT" (computerized crime statistics).

By 1996, the results attributed to the NYPD's new management philosophy would make COMPSTAT a familiar term in criminal justice circles. New York City's annual Federal Bureau of Investigation Uniform Crime Statistics recorded a cumulative reduction of more than 41% from 1993 to 1997, giving the COMPSTAT process national exposure (Table 2.1). New York's reduction in murder and nonnegligent manslaughter was particularly striking, decreasing from 1,946 in 1993 to 770 in 1997—a decline of more than 60%. Reductions were recorded for every index crime category. In 1995, New York accounted for approximately 70% of the reduction in the nationwide total index crime. Reductions were recorded for every major felony crime category and in each of the city's neighborhoods. Between 1993 and 1997, all New York City's 76 precincts (Figure 2.1) recorded reductions in total felony crime, ranging from 30% to 56%. These trends continued in 1998. No other major American city has recorded as significant or sustained a reduction in crime during so short a period, or any comparable period, in the modern crime-reporting era.

AUTHOR'S NOTE: All of the tables and figures to which this chapter refers can be found on the World Wide Web at http://www.urbanresearch.org

TABLE 2.1 Crime Reduction in New York City, 1993-1997

Crime	1997	1993	±%
Homicide and nonnegligent manslaughter	770	1,946	−60.4
Forcible rape	2,157	2,818	−23.5
Robbery	44,707	86,001	−48.0
Aggravated assault	45,229	62,778	−28.0
Burglary	54,099	99,207	−45.5
Larceny theft	157,039	235,132	−33.2
Motor vehicle theft	51,892	112,464	−53.9
Total index crime	355,893	600,346	−40.7

THE PROCESS

Approximately once every 4 weeks, on Wednesday or Friday, precinct commanding officers from one of the seven borough commands travel to police headquarters in Manhattan to participate in a COMPSTAT crime strategy meeting. The managerial philosophy embodied in these meetings has given the department the ability to successfully adapt its tactics to continuously changing crime conditions. This philosophy can be expressed as four simple rules:

Accurate and timely intelligence

Rapid deployment

Effective tactics

Relentless follow-up and assessment

During the COMPSTAT meetings, commanders brief department executives on the results of crime-control initiatives undertaken since their last COMPSTAT meeting. Commanders are expected to be well versed in their precinct's crime and disorder conditions as well as in the characteristics of both resident and transient populations and the performance and morale factors associated with the precinct's staff. They are questioned by members of the executive staff about how they have dealt with their responsibilities and how their efforts affected major crime in their precincts.

Commanding officers from Housing Bureau Police Service areas, Transit Division districts, and specialized operational and tactical units also attend the meetings. They participate in the briefing to the extent that a precinct's problems occur in city housing projects or transit facilities. Also, they are involved in the precinct's crime-control initiatives. Members of the Housing Bureau and the transit division

Figure 2.1. New York City Police Precincts

participate in periodic COMPSTAT meetings specifically dealing with their jurisdictions and subordinate commands, police service areas, and districts.

The following criminal justice agencies send representatives to the meetings: the district attorneys from each of the five boroughs, the New York State Department of Parole, the City Probation Department, and the City Corrections Department. Other city agencies, such as consumer affairs, social services, and environmental protection, may also attend if the problems or strategies to be discussed require inter-agency coordination and cooperation.

Questioning of precinct commanders can be intense. The effectiveness of commander actions and decisions are frankly and openly evaluated by the executive staff. A commander's success at the meeting requires a detailed and careful study of precinct conditions, an understanding of the success or failure of recent tactics, and the ability to use this insight to respond to questions and present appropriate plans for the next period.

THE TOOLS

At the first COMPSTAT meetings in 1994, precinct commanders were required to bring and be prepared to discuss selected crime incident maps. The maps were of the classic "pin map" variety, varying in size depending on the maps available from each department's cartography unit (most required an easel for display). Command-ers were required to separately map robberies, murders, shootings, and narcotics arrests, and they were strongly encouraged to map any other conditions or crimes that were likely to be considered a major problem for their command.

During the summer of 1994, staff from the Office of the Chief of Depart-ment's COMPSTAT unit began to investigate the feasibility of electronic pin map-ping. Their interest was not only to determine the usefulness of electronic mapping software but also to resolve the logistical issues of acquiring timely incident data and securing the appropriate hardware to prepare and present the mapped data at COMPSTAT meetings.

With the assistance of the department's Management Information Systems Division, selected information on the major felony crimes reported to the police was collected via a mainframe-based computer network. The information recorded in-cluded initial classification and descriptive data, time of occurrence (when avail-able), and the location of the incident. The software used to collect the data was a reworked version of earlier test software for a proposed mainframe network based on the on-line complaint system (OLCS). This system was replaced in the fall of 1996 by a data transfer link from the department's new local area network (LAN)-based OLCS phased into citywide operation during 1995.

After the major crime data for the past 4 weeks are downloaded from the mainframe to the COMPSTAT unit each Monday, preparatory work for the Wednes-day and Friday meetings begins. Crime incidents are geocoded, a process that links each location with a latitude and a longitude and allows the mapping software to display the incident on a precinct's electronic base map. Maps for all the major crime categories, typically by tour, are produced and saved for display. The geocod-ing and mapping tasks are performed using a small network of Pentium-class PCs in the COMPSTAT unit.

Overlays of other significant sites, such as housing projects, transit stations, bus stops, and schools, are used in conjunction with the incident displays to provide

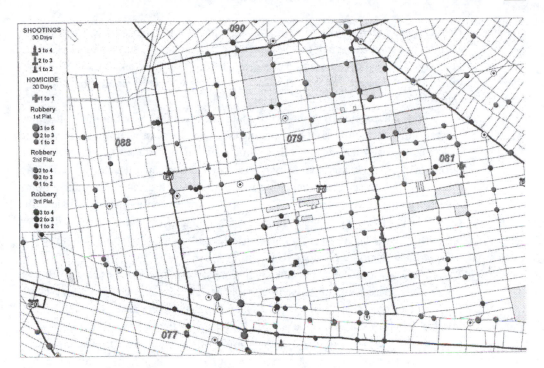

Figure 2.2. Sample COMPSTAT Map

additional information. Indicators such as enforcement activity (arrests and summonses), auto theft recovery locations, and parole residences have also been used. Maps and overlays are projected on large screens overlooking police headquarters' command and control center, as precinct commanders review crime and disorder conditions under their command and discuss their plans for the next review period (Figure 2.2).

Display modes other than that for mapped crime data are also used to review a precinct's public safety indicators. The COMPSTAT unit routinely prepares extensive tabular data providing week-to-date, month-to-date, and year-to-date volumes, differences, and percentage changes in major complaint and arrest crime categories (see Appendix A). Graphical data, such as standard line, bar, and pie charts, are also used to examine the timing of arrest activity versus crime occurrence times, to identify precincts making the largest contribution to recent increases or decreases in crime, and to specify the proportion of a command's patrol officers making specific numbers of arrests during a particular time period (see Figure 2.3 on web site).

IMPACT

The routine availability of electronically mapped crime data and related overlays has both an amplifying and catalytic effect on the weekly crime strategy meetings. The maps provide a much more intimate view of a command's crime problems.

Crime-prone locations are identified by graduated dot density displays. Multiple crime types can be overlaid to investigate their spatial distribution and association. Overlays identifying fixed sites make possible the identification of associations between crime clusters and specific types of sites, such as transportation hubs and schools.

The visualization of crime in this manner also indicates potential deployment target zones in which a variety of existing enforcement or prevention strategies and tactics can be used. The displays also stimulate discussions of new tactics and evaluations of previous crime-control measures carried out since the last COMPSTAT meeting. The impact of the mapping tools has been so great that initially many observers in the media and the criminal justice community identified the COMPSTAT process synonymously with the mapping tools themselves. COMPSTAT, however, is a management technique that can exist without mapping, although it is believed that mapping greatly aids the process.

The knowledge of where and when crimes occur in any one of New York's 76 precincts is shared with all those in attendance at the weekly crime strategy meeting, including members of the NYPD's executive staff. The discussions frequently involve details of specific crime patterns and ongoing investigations that previously would not have been brought to the attention of top management. The result is a familiarity and knowledge of week-to-week operational results at the executive level that helps flatten the organizational pyramid—an accomplishment that many thought impossible before COMPSTAT.

Both success and failure play an important role in COMPSTAT's effectiveness. Word of performance at COMPSTAT spreads rapidly via the exposure given to a command's results, good or bad, at every meeting. The necessity of formulating a plan to maintain or improve on past success and to learn from disappointing results keeps the entire process focused relentlessly on the future.

The obvious value of electronic pin mapping to the weekly crime strategy meetings led to the deployment of PC-based mapping software for use at the borough commands by mid-1995 and of LAN-based software for precinct crime analysts' use by early 1996. Increased federal funding supported the purchase of computer hardware for the implementation of precinct mapping in the 76 patrol precincts and seven borough commands. Software development was guided by the department's Office of Management Analysis and Planning with the assistance of staff from the COMPSTAT unit and the Management Information Systems Division. The Vera Institute of Justice also provided key programming assistance during the development of both borough and precinct software.

The software tools provide crime analysts with easy access to complex mapping software via a graphical user interface using standard police terminology to specify maps for virtually any time period and set of incident characteristics. The new precinct tools provide commanders with the ability to map and analyze their own crime complaint data for day-to-day decision making and in preparation for their COMPSTAT briefing. Borough commands are able to access the same select incident data used by the COMPSTAT unit for use by their crime strategy coordinators and pattern identification modules.

MAINTAINING THE PROCESS

The COMPSTAT process reestablished the importance of two powerful management concepts—accountability and analysis. New technology, in the form of computerized mapping, provided a highly effective way to identify local crime problems, closely monitor the implementation of any proposed tactical response, and quickly measure apparent impact. Technology, therefore, played a key role in realizing managerial concepts as best practice. The NYPD's commitment to (and dependence on) the new mapping technology raises many important maintenance and support issues that the department continues to engage.

TRAINING

The training of staff to use the new mapping technology and to support the COMPSTAT process has been extended to include as many of the department's staff as is practical and productive given resource and time constraints. One way to reduce training costs is to make user interfaces as simple as possible. Programming standard simple interfaces that produce easy to use but effective mapping tools allows department members to perform their jobs without becoming overly involved with the detailed settings and options provided by complex mapping software. Only a few users need to be fully conversant with the technical details of the software, but this core group must be maintained to effectively respond to complex analysis assignments and manage the day-to-day technical support problems that occur.

MANAGING TECHNOLOGY

Managing the growth and improvement of the COMPSTAT process is challenging, especially in regard to technology and software changes. Computer hardware, operating systems, and mapping software change at a very rapid pace. The department does not adopt every software revision and operating system upgrade, but eventually some changes must take place; new hardware may not support older software, and vendors may discontinue technical support for their older products. An ongoing assessment of changing technology and its impact has become a routine part of managing the COMPSTAT process.

Data quality and maintenance are also concerns. Incident data, the city base map used to geocode data, the fixed-site databases used to create overlays of schools, public housing developments, and transit stops, and other databases all must be maintained and occasionally improved. Unmapped areas within the city may need mapping if incident levels are high enough and precise incident location might lead to more effective strategies, tactics, or assessments. Other department databases may provide new insights when mapped alone or in conjunction with the crime complaint incidents. The integration of computer-aided dispatch data, warrant data, and perhaps investigative follow-up information into the appropriate analysis may be particularly helpful.

ACCESS AND COOPERATION ISSUES

The NYPD deals with four types of access and cooperation issues: interunit, interagency, interdepartmental and public. Interunit exchanges of crime incident data, mapping technology, and related data analysis tools are increasing. Initially, the selected complaint data used in the COMPSTAT process was made available to other commands via floppy diskettes. Downloading COMPSTAT data from a secure bulletin board was introduced as another option. Eventually, COMPSTAT data may also be shared over a department-wide intranet. The department's precinct LANs will become part of a wide area network, allowing adjoining precincts to access each other's incident data.

The COMPSTAT process has been the catalyst for interagency cooperation on problems that directly involve multiple city agencies. These alliances may also provide the means to access other agency information that can be mapped or included in the department's mapping analysis as overlay data characterizing a specific place or area. Cooperative efforts of this nature are most likely to succeed if the agencies involved can all benefit from the merged data or the operational impact derived from the new information.

As the success of the COMPSTAT process and its use of automated mapping technology has become more widely known, the department has received an increasing number of external requests for information and assistance. Although the NYPD believes in the dissemination of law enforcement techniques, it does not have the resources to assign staff to individual requests. In addition to written materials, the department responds to inquiries by holding conferences and allowing observers to attend COMPSTAT meetings. The NYPD spring conferences held in 1997 and 1998, each attended by representatives of more than 300 agencies, prominently featured workshops on the technical details of the process and crime strategy development. Many conference participants attended an actual COMPSTAT meeting, although the demand for seats at COMPSTAT far outstripped the supply.

Training, managing change, and access and cooperation issues are likely to increase in complexity in the future. COMPSTAT's continued success depends in part on addressing these issues while maintaining the focus on crime reduction and not technology.

CONCLUSION: FUTURE DEVELOPMENTS IN THE NYPD'S CRIME MAPPING STRATEGY

The introduction of automated mapping technology into the COMPSTAT process demonstrated that complex incident maps, once difficult and time-consuming to prepare, could be produced "on demand." Rapid production of complex crime maps, although an important achievement, will not provide an analysis or make an assessment. Crime analysts must still visually identify patterns and concentrations, make period-to-period judgments about changes, and decide if crimes are occurring disproportionately in certain areas or types of locations. The initial automated mapping accomplishments of COMPSTAT are likely to be only the first steps in automating the analysis and assessment process.

In the future, automated systems will classify and analyze clusters of crime incidents ("hot spots") in a manner already in use in many industrial and scientific settings. Automated hot spot identification would allow comparisons of crime concentrations and support searches of incident databases for the highest concentrations of incidence by time, type of crime, and virtually any other incident characteristic deemed important. The ability to compare hot spots over time can also help in the assessment of enforcement interventions or other changes in the environment. Comparisons of current concentrations with prior long-term concentrations and interventions may provide some understanding of future patterns.

Maps portraying comparative concentrations and other incident trends are likely to be computationally complex and require clear presentation. Once tested and refined, the technical sophistication of new analysis techniques can be kept in the background by allowing the automated process to present the results rather than the computational details. Visualization techniques, borrowed from other fields and from those tailored specifically for crime data, are likely to become increasingly important, particularly as the complexity of the information conveyed to both analysts and superiors increases. Pictorial and symbolic representations, perhaps even animation, may aid in interpreting, understanding, and presenting results. Software implementing these techniques must, however, be unobtrusive and easy to use. Crime analysts should spend their valuable training time learning to analyzing crime and not learning to use complicated software. The analytic software tools used within the current COMPSTAT process have been developed with these principles in mind.

The mapping technology used in the COMPSTAT process will continue to evolve, and law enforcement will have a role in this evolution. The NYPD has collaborated with researchers at the City University of New York to develop enhanced mapping analysis techniques. The Justice Department's National Institute of Justice (NIJ) is funding the research. As a result of the growth in use of GIS technology by law enforcement agencies, the Justice Department established the Crime Research Mapping Center within NIJ. The center disseminates information on GIS technology, provides training, and encourages research of interest to the criminal justice community. Research that improves support for management, deployment decisions, and operational assessment will be of special interest to law enforcement agencies.

The NYPD's experience with the COMPSTAT process demonstrates that to obtain the most significant impact from technological innovation, the technology must be integrated into the agency's mission and operational strategies. The COMPSTAT process is a management tool for quickly identifying problems, developing strategies and tactics, evaluating impact, and expanding and enhancing successful aspects of the program. GIS technology continues to be used within the COMPSTAT process because electronic mapping makes a very important contribution to the process.

WEEKLY CRIME/COMPLAINT COMPARISON REPORT

REPORT COVERING THE WEEK OF 07/14/97 THROUGH 07/20/97

Date Prepared 07/21/97

WEEK NUMBER 29
PRECINCT

CRIME COMPLAINTS

	WTD 1997	WTD 1996	% Change	28 Day 1997	28 Day 1996	% Change	YTD 1997	YTD 1996	YTD 1995	% Change	2yr % Change	3yr % Change	4yr % Change
MURDER	1	1	0.00%	1	2	-50.00%	13	20	15	-35.00%	-13.33%	-56.67%	-61.76%
RAPE	1	1	0.00%	3	7	-57.14	45	51	36	-11.76%	25.00%	-2.17%	-19.64%
ROBBERY	17	19	-10.53%	76	98	-22.45	503	614	735	-18.08%	-31.56%	-50.88%	-58.70%
FEL.ASSLT	15	13	15.38%	62	81	-23.46	454	511	492	-11.15%	-7.72%	-19.07%	-30.58%
BURGLARY	8	14	-42.86%	33	42	-21.43	306	337	314	-9.20%	-2.55%	-38.80%	-32.00%
GR.LARCENY	12	10	20.00%	41	41	0.00%	226	256	335	-11.72%	-32.54%	-51.71%	-53.78%
G.L.A.	5	5	0.00%	19	31	-38.71%	154	213	225	-27.70%	-31.56%	-57.46%	-53.47%
TOTAL	**59**	**63**	**-6.35%**	**235**	**302**	**-22.19%**	**1,701**	**2,002**	**2,152**	**-15.03%**	**-20.96%**	**-43.13%**	**-47.37%**
SHOOT VIC.	2	7	-71.43%	8	17	-52.94%	45	74	74	-39.19%	-39.19%	-56.31%	-73.53%
SHOOT INC.	2	7	-71.43%	8	17	-52.94%	41	68	67	-39.71%	-38.81%	-57.29%	-74.38%
RAPE 1	1	1	0.00%	2	6	-66.67%	32	39	28	-17.95%	14.29%	-17.95%	-31.91%

ARREST STATISTICS

	WTD 1997	WTD 1996	% Change	28 Day 1997	28 Day 1996	% Change	YTD 1997	YTD 1996	YTD 1995	% Change	2yr % Change	3yr % Change	4yr % Change
MURDER	1	0	......%	4	1	300.00%	22	25	21	-12.00%	4.76%	4.76%	37.50%
RAPE	0	1	-100.00%	0	6	-100.00%	13	19	10	-31.58%	30.00%	-13.33%	8.33%
ROBBERY	5	10	-50.00%	31	31	0.00%	229	238	288	-3.78%	-20.49%	-22.37%	-27.30%
FEL.ASSLT	13	16	-18.75%	49	71	-30.99%	325	336	245	-3.27%	32.65%	41.92%	76.63%
BURGLARY	2	2	0.00%	11	19	-42.11%	94	103	90	-8.74%	4.44%	-4.08%	27.03%
GR.LARCENY	4	4	0.00%	18	9	100.00%	70	58	51	20.69%	37.25%	89.19%	29.63%
G.L.A.	3	3	0.00%	6	7	-14.29%	46	44	70	4.55%	-34.29%	-48.31%	-45.24%
TOTAL	**28**	**36**	**-22.22%**	**119**	**144**	**-17.36%**	**799**	**823**	**775**	**-2.92%**	**3.10%**	**1.91%**	**8.12%**
GUN ARR.	3	3	0.00%	5	9	-44.44%	59	78	96	-24.36%	-38.54%	-64.24%	-73.89%
NARC ARR.	24	43	-44.19%	73	159	-54.09%	785	1080	956	-27.31%	-17.89%	-26.77%	21.33%
PSB ARR.	63	55	14.55%	267	220	21.36%	2080	1713	1702	21.42%	22.21%	60.99%	69.66%
OCCB ARR.	46	42	9.52%	115	176	-34.66%	1156	766	258	50.91%	348.06%	514.89%	609.20%
D.B. ARR.	22	16	37.50%	65	73	-10.96%	435	363	238	19.83%	82.77%	215.22%	330.69%
H.B. ARR.	9	27	-66.67%	61	102	-40.20%	435	849	962	-48.76%	-54.78%	-66.51%	-19.44%
T.B. ARR.	28	17	64.71%	90	69	30.43%	688	591	899	16.41%	-23.47%	7.84%	53.91%
ALL ARRESTS	**170**	**159**	**6.92%**	**605**	**642**	**-5.76%**	**4,888**	**4,411**	**4,080**	**10.81%**	**19.80%**	**36.42%**	**95.68%**

SUMMONS ACTIVITY

	WTD 1997	WTD 1996	% Change	28 Day 1997	28 Day 1996	% Change	YTD 1997	YTD 1996	YTD 1995	% Change	2yr % Change	3yr % Change	4yr % Change
PARKING	439	651	-32.57%	2198	2761	-20.39%	14020	22617	20059	-38.01%	-30.11%	......%	......%
MOVING	146	410	-64.39%	892	1589	-43.86%	6915	14777	10662	-53.20%	-35.14%	......%	......%
CRIMINAL	131	113	15.93%	442	620	38.13%	2402	1808	1908	32.85%	25.89%	......%	......%
ECB	2	0	......%	12	4	200.00%	38	698	22	-94.56%	72.73%	......%	......%

FIGURES ARE PRELIMINARY AND SUBJECT TO FURTHER ANALYSIS AND REVISION

Appendix A. COMPSTAT Statistical Page From "The COMPSTAT Process" Booklet

APPENDIX "B"

PRECINCT COMMANDER PROFILE

			PRECINCT
Rank:	CAPTAIN	C.O. Prev. Commands: NA	
Years in Rank:		Current Eval:	Date Assigned C.O.
Appointment Date:		Date of Promotion:	
Education:		Resident Pct:	
Other Training:			

Precinct Demographics

Total:	32978
White:	78.65%
Black	6.07%
Hispanic	6.07%
Asian	8.10%
Amer. Ind	0.24%
Other	0.14%

Precinct Personnel

	pre-safe	1996	1997	%Change	%CW
Uniform	162	202	204	0.99%	-16.2
Civilian	27	22	19	-13.64%	-23.1
RAM	No	**	**	****	****
Dom Viol	***	1	1	0.00%	****
Youth Off	***	3	3	0.00%	****
SNEU	***	0	0	****%	*****
AvTime Cmd 4 yrs. 8 mons		CW 4 yrs 3 mons			
AvAge Cmd 31 yrss 8 mons		CW 31 yrs 2 mons			

Precinct Non-Crime

	1996	1997	%Change	%CW
RMP Acc.	15	8	-46.67	-24.57
Arr O/T	$29548	$36757	24.40	-0.95
Oper O/T	$15200	$18774	23.51	-15.32
Total O/T	$201220	$125682	-37.54	0.65
Park Sum.	22743	13256	-40.53	-42.09
Mov Sum.	5732	3494	-39.04	-39.68
Crim Sum.	742	828	11.59	27.67
ECB Sum.	497	250	-49.70	-63.12

Uniform Absence (Avg. Days YTD)

1996	cw96	1997	cw97	LOD96	cwLOD96	LOD97	cwLOD97
3.09	2.33	2.01	2.14	0.46	1.04	1.24	0.73

Domestic Violence (1997)

Radio Runs	DIR's	%Compliance
82	135	164.63

Integrity Monitoring

	1996	1997	%Change	%CW	96ratio	97ratio
Bribery Arrests	1	0	-100.00	-100.00	1:202	1:***
Tot CCIB	9	2	-77.78	****	1:22.44	1:102.0
Force	4	0	-100.00	****	******	******
Abuse	4	1	-75.00	*****	******	******
Discourtesy	4	1	-75.00	*****	******	******
Off. Lang.	0	1	******	*****	******	******

10/84 Compliance

Pct	Boro	C/W
67.09%	67.06%	68.63%

Avg. Response Time

Pct	Boro	C/W
8.13	7.39	9.23

Unfounded Radio Runs

	1996	1997	%Change	%CW97	%boro97	%Tot97	%Tot96	%T CW97	%T Bo97
Tot. Runs	17839	13815	-22.56	-26.42	-22.38	19.17	12.71	14.47	13.02
Unif.Runs	3419	1456	-48.64	-49.40	-43.47				

Housing

PSA:	
C.O.:	
Facilities:	

Transit

District:	
C.O.:	
Facilities	

City Council Members:

State Senator(s):

10/98

Appendix B. COMPSTAT Commander's Profile From "The COMPSTAT Process" Booklet

CHAPTER 3

Filters, Fears, and Photos

Speculations and Explorations in the Geography of Crime

KEITH HARRIES

Crime patterns may be analyzed by specialists in several disciplines, and the most powerful methods for one area of study may not be particularly useful for another. Historians, for example, focus on longitudinal trends and changes in social dynamics behind the changes. Sociologists, who examine processes and relationships in the hope of teasing out causes of particular types of crime, focus on different factors than do criminologists. Each discipline has its own perspective, and the tools used for achieving that perspective vary. Even if the tools are similar, they are often used in different ways.

The most powerful techniques for the spatial analysis of crime are quite specialized and tend to emphasize the importance of real-time views to ensure timely responses. For example, police agencies are not usually interested in crime patterns that occurred in a neighborhood 10 years ago; it is the pattern during the past shift, day, week, or perhaps month that commands attention. Law enforcement usually wants to know the location of hot spots, how patterns are changing, and what interventions might reduce crime. Police officials may have some curiosity about the previous 10 years of crime patterns, but such analysis is usually a luxury few police departments can afford given the limited resources and crisis-driven atmosphere that often pervade these organizations.

In this chapter, I discuss both time-honored and innovative approaches to the spatial analysis of crime data. As the title suggests, emphasis is first on the filtering of data to select very specific subsets of a database, next on the emotion of fear and

AUTHOR'S NOTE: All of the tables and figures to which this chapter refers can be found on the World Wide Web at http://www.urbanresearch.org

TABLE 3.1 Bronx, New York: Selected Census Tract Indicators (1990)

Census Indicator	Value
Total population	1,203,789
Black population	449,399 (37%)
White population	430,077 (36%)
Other (not Indian or Asian)	282,682 (24%)
Males	555,154
Females	648,635
Male-female ratio	0.85
Median age (mean of the medians)	31.6
Median home value (mean of the medians)	$134,000
Median rent (mean of the medians)	$399
Median household income (mean of the medians)	$23,204
Per capita income (mean)	$10,781
With some graduate education	36,112 (<3%)

SOURCE: 1990 census.

how it might be mapped, and finally on the possible application of orthophotography in crime analysis. A description of the Bronx may be helpful in understanding the following discussion.

THE BRONX

Knowing only that the Bronx has a history as a troubled borough, an analyst should research its social history and geography before embarking on an analysis of Bronx crime data. I tapped two sources: an article by Wallace (1990) that discusses public health and violence in the Bronx and data from the 1990 census. Wallace, a medical geographer, focuses on the "systematic and continuing denial of municipal services—particularly fire extinguishment resources—essential for maintaining urban levels of population density and ensuring community stability" (p. 801). Although the causes of the Bronx's decline are hotly debated, the area, especially the South Bronx, has become legendary for its extraordinary social stress and general decline. Although an in-depth examination is beyond the scope of this chapter, Wallace postulates that an "overburdening of New York's criminal justice system" was due to "the increasing social disorganization of poor communities initiated and continued in considerable part by government policy" (p. 809), with strong parallels between inadequacies in both the medical and criminal justice delivery systems.

The 1990 census provides additional insight into the characteristics of the Bronx (Table 3.1). The population of the Bronx is large, about twice that of Washington, D.C., or Baltimore. The largest population groups are African American

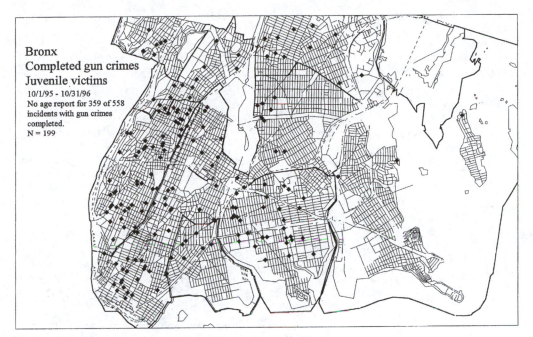

Figure 3.1. Bronx Completed Gun Crimes, Juvenile Victims

(37%), white (36%), and "other" (presumably Hispanic) (24%). This division suggests a potential for interethnic tension and conflict. The "missing male" phenomenon is also pronounced, with the male-female ratio a low 0.85, suggesting many males are undercounted, incarcerated, in the military, or prematurely deceased. Other attributes are unremarkable, with the possible exception of the small percentage of the population with some graduate education (<3%). These cursory data suggest a typical inner-city context with the usual set of accompanying pathologies, including crime.

FILTERS: SORTING INCIDENTS BY SPECIFIC CRITERIA

The most frequent application of geographic information systems (GIS) in crime analysis involves choosing a crime type, a time period, or other attribute to detect "hot spots" or to measure change in some way. Assuming that crime hot spots are also typically political hot spots, hot spot detection is a valuable police department tool.[1] Figure 3.1 is typical in that it has filtered for completed gun crimes with juvenile victims and mapped them in the context of precinct boundaries. As the legend notes, however, 359 of 558 reported completed gun crimes contained no age report for the victim, effectively removing the majority of the incidents from the data set. This example reinforces the principle that maps are only as good as the underlying data.

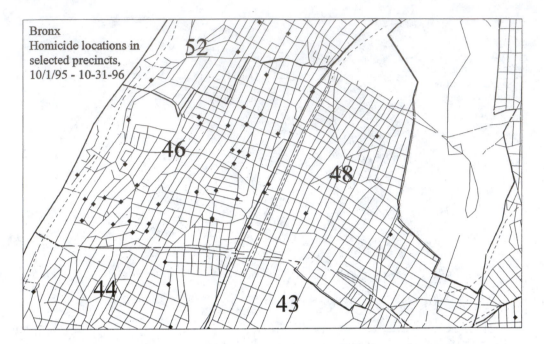

Figure 3.2. Homicide Locations in Selected Precincts

Figure 3.2 maps homicides for the 13-month period between October 1, 1995, and October 30, 1996. The 46th Precinct is an outlier, at least in terms of violence. A map such as that shown in Figure 3.2 is uninformative because it is an answer without a question. More interesting is the integration of crime and other databases. Citywide data integration has the potential to provide answers for several agencies without each having to reinvent the necessary data. Figure 3.3 (on web site) shows a more interesting use of GIS. It shows a census tract map of a powerful predictor of delinquency—the number of female-headed households with children under 18—with an overlay of 13 months of homicide data. The map suggests that most incidents occurred in tracts with high rates of female-headed households.

From a public policy perspective, a map of this genre could be used to help document the need for youth programs, increased surveillance of youth, longer hours for public schools, other programs to reinforce positive male role models, and related initiatives. Although this is not purely a law enforcement application, it emphasizes the point that no social problem is an island, treatable in isolation from the world around it. In effect, this map is a community policing tool that relates crime to an underlying social problem in a visual context, ideally enabling all interested parties to see relevant spatial relationships. It might be preferable to develop a multivariate index as a community underlay, with the weights in the index determined through a Delphi-like technique administered to a group of key people, including police, social workers, public health professionals, and firefighters.

Figure 3.4 (on web site) shows a map of homicide per 100,000 people. The map demonstrates an absurdity that can develop when population-based rate maps are produced for small areas. Rates relate incident locations to census or other geographical boundaries in choropleth maps, "pinning" the incident on the area whether or not a resident committed the crime. This becomes preposterous when the area has little or no population but experiences some crime: The small denominator produces high rates. This is exemplified by Tract 360050435.00, which includes most of Van Cortland Park in the 50th Precinct. It had a population of 58 in 1990 and one murder—a rate of 1,724/100,000. Although population-based rates are the norm in the social sciences including epidemiology, they diminish in usefulness as units of observation decline in size and the probability of areas with zero or near-zero populations increase. Raw frequencies are often more useful because they represent "the primary problem" from a policing standpoint.

Figure 3.5 (on web site) shows the murder distribution by population density. There is controversy concerning whether density generates or deters crime. Ignoring the objection that murder is often unpreventable, both arguments have merit, depending on the context. Theoretically, higher density results in a greater number of both victims and offenders. Potential personal crime could be seen as the square of the area's population in that each person could commit a crime against all other persons. It is also argued, however, that high density acts to deter some kinds of crime because it increases surveillance of homes, streets, and other public spaces. In effect, density generates countervailing forces of crime potential and surveillance coexisting in an uneasy imbalance, constantly moderated by underlying social conditions. Social conditions are important: A high-income high-rise apartment building with a doorman and a low-income public housing high-rise without security may have the same population densities, but the "crime outcomes" may be quite different.

Because data are filtered and visualized in alternate ways, it is worth noting that cartographic products are both art and science. A given data set may be mapped in a virtually infinite number of ways. Even the representation of point locations can be symbolized in different ways, and decisions about scale affect the perception of all map components including hot spots. At a very small scale, for example, a city crime map may appear as a blur of overlapping points. At a very large scale, all hot spots disappear, with the possible exception of those at single addresses. This begs the question of how to deal with multiple incidents at the same address, which without special treatment appear as single points.

FEARS: ESTIMATING THE GEOGRAPHY OF FEAR

What the "fear surface" looks like in a city is an intriguing mystery. Fear refers to the apprehension that people feel when crime has occurred, or may occur, in their own experience, in their neighborhood, or in their imaginations. The geography of fear can be visualized as a three-dimensional surface, with the city in x-y space and some fear metric as the z axis. Fear is the corollary of threat, and both generally decay with distance. Although many people identify inner-city environments as more fear-ridden compared to their suburban counterparts, there are peaks and valleys of fear in the inner city that correspond to hot spots of violence. By bounding and blurring hot spots, a "fear district" can be demarcated.

Fear is not usually accorded the attention it deserves. Fear not only affects the mental health of its victims but also provokes behavioral changes that can have devastating consequences for the community. The clichéd example, of course, is that people become "afraid to go out at night." The social dynamics, however, are much more complicated. Children may be kept home and prevented from normal socialization, and empty streets invite drug dealing, prostitution, and other undesirable behavior. Over time, the prevalence of such activities can diminish property values and may lead to housing abandonment and depopulation. Furthermore, police officers experience fear, as do probation officers and other community workers who habitually traverse dangerous terrain. Fearful officers may resort to lethal force more quickly and with less provocation than their colleagues in less feared areas. Community workers and other service providers may reduce the time they spend in fear-inducing neighborhoods.

Can the fear surface be visualized? Work of this sort has been done elsewhere (Smith & Patterson, 1980), but it has been the product of survey research. Given that surveys are expensive, it makes sense to try to approximate the spatial distribution of fear without recourse to a survey. One possible approach is to use the buffer tool in GIS software to create zones of assumed fear around crime events. These buffers could then be regarded as stand-alone fear zones or could be joined at their peripheries to make fear districts. Crime incidents could be weighted (murder counts more than burglary) using the weights from the *National Survey of Crime Severity* (Wolfgang, Figlio, Tracy, & Singer, 1985a, 1985b), with buffers shaded according to their "fear intensity" level. A fundamental problem is to determine a radius (or radii) for the buffers to represent the distance at which the intensity of fear "distance-decays" to insignificance. If we assume that the fear surface for each person is somewhat unique, the problem of assigning standard fear parameters to crime events is not trivial. Any fear map would require some restrictive assumptions, although different parameters could be applied to different communities.

Figure 3.6 represents a first step toward operationalizing the fear zone concept. Buffers with a radius of 200 yards were generated around all homicide events in the 13-month study period. The 200-yard radius covers an area of about 26 acres, or about 0.04 square miles. At the least, the fear buffers add a "pseudodimension" to the map of point data, and they form the skeleton for a map of at least one aspect of community mental health. Two redline areas in Figure 3.6 demarcate tentative fear districts, aggregated up from zones. The boundaries are sketched in by hand and are debatable in that they include what some might view as homicide incident outliers.[2] Including parts of the 46th, 50th, and 52nd Precincts, the two fear districts merely redefine and add another layer of meaning to what is essentially hot spot data. Treating the areas only as crime hot spots elicits considerable attention from

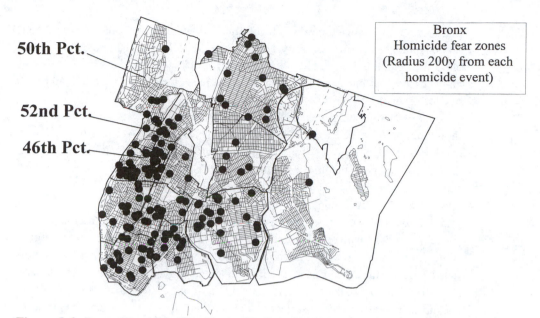

50th Pct.

52nd Pct.

46th Pct.

Bronx
Homicide fear zones
(Radius 200y from each
homicide event)

Figure 3.6. Bronx Homicide Fear Zones (Radius: 200 Yards From Each Homicide Event)

the police department whose mission is to apprehend and prevent crime. The public policy response, however, often does not include consideration of the fear dimension and its destructive ramifications. The recognition of fear districts could help structure a policy response going beyond the limited reactions of existing institutions.

There is a depth of meaning latent in spatial information about crime. It is tempting to cut intellectual and fiscal corners in a rush to the immediate answer to the immediate problem, but this carries with it the risk of overlooking those layers of meaning that can inform longer term public policy. One analogy might be found in our corporate culture and its obsession with quarterly dividends. The emphasis on short-term results is quite deeply embedded in our culture and tends to pull us toward short-term, often superficial, fixes.

PHOTOS: THE NEXT STEP FORWARD

Several police departments, including those in New York City and Baltimore County, are exploring the feasibility of using aerial orthophoto coverages in place of linear street base maps in the mapping and analysis of crime patterns. The rationale underlying this work is that photographic images provide a "real-world" context for the study of crime data and contain more accurate and meaningful data for the various audiences using the maps. When crime data are layered over a digital base map of "stickform" streets, an enormous amount of information is lost in the course of that transformation of the real world into an abstract set of connected lines. An orthophotograph, in contrast, reveals detailed land uses, such as open spaces, homes, and industrial plants, and other geographic data, such as slopes, planimetrics (building footprints, fence lines, sidewalks, and other physical features; Antenucci, Brown, Crosswell, Kevany, & Archer, 1991; Huxhold, 1991), and elevation (including those of taller buildings). Stick streets increasingly represent an excessive and unnecessary loss of information, given today's storage and processing technology.

Several problems prevent the rapid introduction of orthophotography, although all of them are surmountable. The first is availability. Currently, there is no available orthophotography for the Bronx. The U.S. Geological Survey offered LANDSAT imagery, but the resolution is far too low for crime analysis. Even SPOT imagery is inadequate. It might seem to be a simple matter to obtain and scan orthophotographs (or obtain digital orthophotos directly) and then bring the raster image into a GIS and layer the crime data of choice over the top. In practice, the process is more involved due in part to differences in projections between digital orthophotos and crime data. The former are often projected using state plane coordinates, whereas the latter use latitude/longitude, making a conversion step necessary.

Two other problems make the direct use of aerial photographs problematic. Elevation differences on the surface of the earth mean that some areas are closer to the camera than others and hence are at different scales (higher elevation = larger scale). Second, the camera lens at any given moment is unlikely to be perfectly perpendicular to the ground, thus distorting the image. In practice, orthogonal rectification is needed to create an image representing ground truth. These rectified images are referred to as orthophotos (Huxhold, 1991). In an experiment, a U.S. Department of Agriculture Soil Conservation Service aerial photo of part of Baltimore City was scanned and registered to an overlay of digital street maps. The registration process failed to bring the digital image and street maps into proper alignment, confirming that a more sophisticated orthogonal rectification is indeed necessary.

A demonstration project in the Middle River and Essex communities in Baltimore County plans to assess the practicality of substituting orthophotos for the stick base maps commonly used in crime analysis. An additional component will involve equipping selected patrol units with global positioning systems to enhance the accuracy of spatial data from the field, particularly in contexts such as shopping malls, parks, schools, and public housing complexes with spatially nebulous addresses. Depending on the addressing system used, crime incidents may occur half a mile or more apart and yet still have the same nominal street address.

RELEVANCE TO NEW YORK CITY

Much of this chapter is pedagogic and speculative rather than prescriptive in nature and is not directly relevant to the New York City Police Department (although the elements dealing with community policing and community mental health are worth further investigation). Whether the benefits of adopting any particular method outweigh the costs must be determined locally. At least with respect to base map technology, advances in imaging methods combined with the general usefulness of digital orthophotography in several realms of local government suggest that the days of "stick" street map are numbered. It is possible that larger police agencies with substantial resources will migrate to photographic coverages, whereas small agencies, hitherto without spatial analysis capabilities, will begin their use of GIS with stick maps. No doubt, the New York City Police Department will move toward the adoption of orthophoto coverage as a natural part of the evolution of GIS technology.

NOTES

1. Other fear districts could have been demarcated; the two drawn are not definitive.
2. Orthophotography could be used for environmental monitoring, open-space planning, construction permitting, and a variety of other applications.

REFERENCES

Antenucci, J. C., Brown, K., Crosswell, P. L., Kevany, M. J., & Archer, H. (1991). *Geographic information systems: A guide to the technology.* New York: Van Nostrand Reinhold.

Huxhold, W. E. (1991). *An introduction to urban geographic information systems.* New York: Oxford University Press.

Smith, C. J., & Patterson, G. E. (1980). Cognitive mapping and the subjective geography of crime. In D. Georges-Abeyie & K. Harries (Eds.), *Crime: A spatial perspective.* New York: Columbia University Press.

Wallace, R. (1990). Urban desertification, public health and public order: "Planned shrinkage," violent death, substance abuse and AIDS in the Bronx. *Social Science and Medicine, 31,* 801-813.

Wolfgang, M. E., Figlio, R. M., Tracy, P. E., & Singer, S. I. (1985a). *The national survey of crime severity.* Washington, DC: U.S. Department of Justice, Bureau of Justice Statistics.

Wolfgang, M. E., Figlio, R. M., Tracy, P. E., & Singer, S. I. (1985b). *Sourcebook of crime severity ratios for core-item offenses* (Microfiche No. NCJ-96329). Washington, DC: U.S. Department of Justice, Bureau of Justice Statistics.

CHAPTER 4

The Spatial Analysis of Crime

What Social Scientists Have Learned

CHARLES SWARTZ

This chapter reviews macrolevel and microlevel spatial research concerning social and physical environments and discusses the applicability of this research to actual police activity. Due to the volume and diversity of studies on this topic, an attempt has been made to select a representative subset of each domain of analysis. This chapter attempts to provide a comparison between macrolevel research and microlevel research in an effort to answer the following question: What information does each type of research contribute, and how can all this information be used to reduce crime?

MACROLEVEL CRIME RESEARCH

Ecological Analysis

For more than 150 years, crime researchers have sought to explain geographic variations in the rate of crime (Eck & Weisburd, 1995; Weisburd, Maher, & Sherman, 1992). Despite these efforts, there is little agreement on the causes of spatial variation of crime. In the early 1900s, the emergence of the Chicago school of sociology brought much attention to this topic by focusing on the characteristics of neighborhoods instead of the characteristics of offenders. Specifically, Shaw and McKay (1942), taking an "ecological" approach to the study of crime, postulated that a general atmosphere of social disorganization leads to high crime rates. Although the details of this important theory are discussed later, readers should note that it continues to have a large impact on all areas of crime research, even in the 1990s.

In an ecological analysis of crime, the researcher analyzes the social and economic characteristics of high- and low-crime neighborhoods (Katzman, 1981), cities (Harries, 1976), or regions (Dienes, 1988) to determine the variables that impact crime rates (Rengert, 1981). Ecological analyses represent the most common spatial analysis technique, probably because the creation of "neighborhood size" census tracts make gathering social, economic, demographic, and crime rate information easy. Data are often subjected to a regression analysis, and significant variables are identified. A distinction has been made between macrolevel research focusing on neighborhoods, cities, and countries as the unit of analysis and microlevel research focusing on the immediate physical environment, such as a street corner and individual building (Nasar & Fisher, 1993). Therefore, an ecological analysis of crime will be referred to as a macrolevel analysis. Microlevel research will be discussed in the following section.

In a review of "crime area research," Dunn (1980) notes that most ecological studies assessing the relationship between crime and social variables focus on socioeconomic status, family structure, and race. Thus, areas characterized by low socioeconomic status, a high percentage of single parents, and a large African American population tend to have the highest rates of crime. Using information from the British Crime Survey, a nationally representative victimization survey of more than 10,000 residents, Sampson (1987) found that the percentage of primary individuals (people who live alone) correlates positively with all residents' risk of burglary. People living alone spend more time away from home, thus increasing the probability of being the victim of a burglary.

Simcha-Fagan and Schwartz (1986) assessed neighborhood characteristics believed to affect the individual delinquency rates of adolescents. The neighborhoods included in the study were chosen according to their level of neighborhood family disorganization (percentage children in intact families) and neighborhood social rank (economic level). In-depth interviews of adolescents and their mothers provided important individual-level crime data and neighborhood-level "disorder" information. Results indicate that levels of officially recorded delinquency correlate positively with community economic level and level of community disorder. Also, age has a strong positive relationship with delinquency; older adolescents were much more likely to commit crimes. The authors note that the inclusion of individual-level information severely reduces the observed effects of neighborhood characteristics. Therefore, macrolevel research that omits individual-level information may statistically exaggerate the effect of the neighborhood on crime.

Using aggregated census tracts as his unit of analysis, Block's (1979, p. 49) study of Chicago found that "rates of both victimization and offense are consistently higher for blacks than for whites." Areas with a large African American population (>75%) had a homicide rate of 51 per 100,000 people, whereas areas with a small African American population (<25%) had a homicide rate of 6 per 100,000 people. Despite the correlation between race and homicide victimization, two other variables had an even greater impact on crime rates—percentage of residents from the South (a variable highly correlated with percentage of African Americans) and the residential proximity of poor and wealthy families (a measure of relative deprivation). Block (1979, p. 52) concludes that "it is clear that neighborhoods in which poor and middle-class families live in close proximity are likely to have higher crime rates than other neighborhoods." Proximity accounted for 56% of the variance in homicide rates and almost 40% of the variance in robbery and assault rates. Block believes that it reflects the unequal distribution of income in some neighborhoods and "the extreme racial segregation of housing units in Chicago" (p. 55).

In a similar study of adolescent delinquency, Johnstone (1978) calculated the neighborhood social rank (based on occupational and educational characteristics) and a measure of family status (based on household occupation and education information) to examine the effects of neighborhoods on delinquency versus the effects of individual family characteristics. He found that individual family characteristics accurately "predict" violent crime and property crime, whereas some types of violent crime seem to be the result of the addition of both neighborhood and family characteristics. The best fitting model, however, went against conventional wisdom. Many theories predict that low-status youth living in low-status areas will have high offender rates. Within the low-status group, however, those who lived near high-status areas committed more crimes than those who did not, a finding similar to Block's (1979). Johnstone believes that the absolute status of the adolescent is not as important as a youth's social status relative to the surrounding population, as hypothesized by relative deprivation theory. A situation in which "have-not" populations come into contact with "haves" appears to increase the frustration associated with poverty due to the constant reminder of inequalities. Routine activity theory and opportunity theory, however, also account for these results: Living in close proximity to wealthy individuals increases opportunities to steal valuable goods.

Sampson and Groves (1989) conducted a macrolevel analysis of crime using data from the British Crime Survey to test the social disorganization theory of Shaw and McKay. They found that the level of unsupervised teenagers in a neighborhood had the largest effect on all forms of victimization. Low organizational participation, high levels of urbanization, and high numbers of divorced and single-parent families all increased the risk of crime, as did an overall lack of friendship networks. Surprisingly, socioeconomic status and ethnic diversity did not have a significant relationship with crime after controlling for the previously mentioned variables. Sampson and Groves believe that this study highlights the importance of including all relevant variables when doing an analysis: Each missing variable reduces the overall validity and usefulness of the research.

In a study of suburban crime, Katzman (1981) found that, for property crime, the characteristics of surrounding neighborhoods are a better predictor of crime than are the economic characteristics of a neighborhood's local population. Furthermore, violent crime was influenced by local poverty more than surrounding economic conditions. Katzman (1981, p. 132) concluded that "while a neighborhood's local demographic composition provides a good statistical explanation of violent crime, property crime is better understood in terms of the demographic composition of surrounding neighborhoods." These results are related to differences in criminal mobility between property crime and violent crime offenders; property crime offenders travel greater distances when committing a crime, so characteristics of surrounding neighborhoods will have a greater effect on local property crime rates.

Using block-level data, Roncek (1981) studied the relationship between social characteristics of residential areas, physical features of the residential environment, and crime rates in Cleveland and San Francisco. He found that the most dangerous city blocks had high concentrations of primary individuals (one-person households), African Americans, apartment buildings, and population and were large in area. Roncek believes that such areas have decreased levels of social interaction and social control, and residents have more difficulty identifying "outsiders" who may commit crimes. He also found that the social and environmental characteristics of city blocks combine to affect the probability of victimization, and "environmental effects were more important for property crime than for violent crime" (p. 90), most likely due to the emotional characteristics of violent crime.

Gottfredson, McNeil, and Gottfredson (1991) combined research at the macrolevel with research on individual characteristics. The authors believe that spatial variation in crime rates could be caused by "contextual mechanisms," in which the social organization of an area influences the people who live there, or by "compositional mechanisms," in which spatial variations occur as a result of crime-prone individuals "choosing," or being forced due to economic circumstance, to live in certain areas of the city. The study involved 3,729 adolescents in four cities who were administered detailed questionnaires. Using census data at the block-group level (approximately 10 city blocks), Gottfredson et al. calculated the affluence level and level of disorganization (percentage single parents, families on welfare, poverty, divorce, and unemployment) of each teenager's neighborhood. Results showed that the levels of affluence and disorganization of the neighborhood are slightly but significantly related to delinquency. Overall, individual-level characteristics had a larger effect on rates of reported delinquency than macrolevel data.

Sampson (1985) assessed the relationship between the social, economic, and physical characteristics of neighborhoods and crime using the National Crime Survey, a victimization survey with data from more than 100,000 people in the United States. Results indicate that economic inequality did not affect crime, whereas racial composition, residential mobility, and structural density significantly affected crime. Both residential mobility and structural density had larger effects than racial composition, and in urban regions structural density explained more variation in crime than poverty level and race combined. Family structure (percentage divorced and percentage female head of household) also had a highly significant impact on crime, accounting for five times more variance than racial composition. An analysis using the three strongest predictors of crime—family structure, residential mobility, and structural density—revealed that family structure and structural density had large effects on theft, whereas residential mobility had the largest effect on violent crime. Sampson concluded that past ecological models were misspecified due to the omission of family structure; past findings that race affected crime may have been due to the association between family structure and race and not to a direct relationship between race and crime.

In a similar study, Sampson (1986) found that poverty, racial composition, high structural density, high levels of urbanization, and age of victim all had significant effects on rates of theft and violent crime. Surprisingly, age of victim, level of urbanization, and structural density accounted for the most variation in crime rates, whereas racial composition and poverty, two of the most widely studied variables in the literature, had the smallest effects. Sampson also assessed the interaction effects of these variables on crime to better understand the complexity of the relationship between macrolevel information and crime. He found that in highly urban areas poverty has a greater effect on theft than in suburban or rural areas; poverty exacerbates the effects of structural density on theft (the effect of multiple unit structures on crime is greater in poor areas), and urbanization interacts with structural density to predict rates of violent crime (structural density has less effect on violent crime rates in urban areas).

The previous review of macrolevel research highlights the major findings of ecological researchers and provides a glimpse of the size of the task facing ecological researchers in the future. Researchers must identify relevant variables from a large list of possible candidates and better specify the relationship of ecological research to individual-level research. Ecological research, however, provides important guidance to law enforcement and policymakers in terms of the deployment of manpower and resources and where future criminal activity might intensify. In addition, city planners should take note of the impact of structural density and concentrated poverty. Although law enforcement alone cannot tackle structural problems such as poverty and family dysfunction, effective policing can mitigate harmful effects.

Macrolevel Research on the Physical Environment and Crime

Macrolevel research on the relationship between the physical environment and crime differs methodologically from most ecological research in one important way: The research includes environmental variables, not just socioeconomic and demographic variables, in the spatial analysis. Some of the large-scale analyses that have attempted to better understand this important relationship are discussed in this section. Much of the microlevel research on the physical environment and crime will be discussed in the next section. It should be noted that the distinction between macro- and microlevel research, especially physical environment research, is blurry; therefore, some of the research discussed in this section is also applicable to the discussion in the following section and vice versa.

In one of the earliest spatial analyses, White (1932) assigned the location of felonies to census tracts and then analyzed the characteristics of the tracts to uncover patterns. He found that the rate of crime decreased as one traveled away from the central business district, but he identified two census tracts removed from the center of the city that had high rates of crime. He concluded that high crime rates in these two tracts cannot simply be attributed to the predominately black population; the proximity of railroad yards and a factory to these census tracts also contributed to crime.

Roncek (1981), in a study of crime in Cleveland and San Diego, found that blocks with large populations, high population densities, and many apartment buildings had high rates of crime. Physically large blocks had more crime than smaller blocks, and high vacancy rates were associated with increased crime in Cleveland but not in San Diego. Roncek also found that "environmental effects are more important for property crime than for violent crime" (p. 90), most likely because of the importance of personal relationships in the occurrence of violent crimes, and environmental variables had a greater effect on crime rates in Cleveland than in San Diego. Furthermore, Cleveland had higher rates of crime than San Diego, and the "slum blocks" of Cleveland were larger in area and population than those in San Diego. This suggests that environmental variables interact with socioeconomic and demographic variables in the creation of high crime areas. Roncek concluded that "the environmental features of residential areas are important for explaining where crimes occur" (p. 91).

Sampson (1983, p. 279) hypothesized that high structural density (the percentage of housing units in buildings with five or more units) "impedes environmental social control," reduces surveillance, and increases opportunities for successful criminal activity. Using data from the National Crime Victimization Survey, Sampson grouped households with similar levels of structural density (low, medium, or high structural density) and compared the assault and robbery victimization rates of these three groups while controlling for the race, age, and gender of the victim. Results indicated that "for all but one population subgroup, black females aged 12-20, rates of both robbery and assault victimization increase [steadily] as neighborhood structural density increases" (p. 281). Furthermore, this relationship was stronger for robbery than for assault, most likely because of the emotional characteristics of assault; robberies are usually motivated by a wish to acquire property, whereas assaults are often spur of the moment emotional reactions. In general, structural density positively correlated with crime in urban, suburban, and rural areas, although the relationship between victimization and structural density was most powerful in rural areas. Unfortunately, Sampson did not conduct a statistical analysis of the data; therefore, due to multicollinearity, we cannot truly understand the relationship between structural density, age, race, gender, and victimization. For example, after controlling for the age, race, and gender of the victim, structural density of a neighborhood might not be significantly related to victimization. Also, Sampson omitted important control variables, such as income and marital status.

In response to these criticisms, Sampson (1986) used a more statistically rigorous approach. His results indicated that structural density, when controlling for level of urbanization, poverty, age of victim, and racial composition, did have a significant effect on victimization. In fact, structural density accounted for more variance in theft and violent crime than both poverty and racial composition combined. Age of victim was the most powerful predictor of violent crime, followed by structural density. The level of urbanization had the strongest effect on theft, followed by structural density. Also, "structural density tends to have a greater effect in rural areas than in suburbs or central cities" (p. 16). He attributes these results to the already high levels of structural density in cities. Conversely, small variations in structural density in rural areas have much larger effects on crime due to the relative lack of apartment buildings in these areas. Finally, Sampson found that structural density has a greater effect on crime in poor areas, most likely due to an increased amount of guardianship (e.g., doorman, alarm, and security cameras) in high-income areas.

Greenberg and Rohe (1984) identified three pairs of high- and low-crime neighborhoods in Atlanta in their assessment of defensible space theory and opportunity theory. They matched neighborhoods according to racial composition, economic status, and physical adjacency, and they gathered information on the physical environment (street width, land use, street lighting, fences, parking facilities, etc.) and social characteristics (neighborhood social ties, informal surveillance, and neighborhood attachment) of each neighborhood. The authors theorized that the physical environment affects crime "through the intervening variable of informal social control" (p. 48). Greenberg and Rohe essentially set up a test between defensible space theory, which focuses on social factors, and opportunity theory, which emphasized features of the physical environment. The authors found more support for opportunity theory. They found that "physical characteristics distinguished between high- and low-crime neighborhoods to a much greater extent than did differences in informal social control" (p. 58). Low-crime neighborhoods had smaller streets, low rates of nonresidential land use, fewer public parking lots, and more single-family dwellings. In other words, low-crime areas were more isolated from outsiders and contained fewer public activities and parking facilities, thus decreasing the supply of potential offenders to the area.

White (1990, p. 59) believes that neighborhood permeability, defined as "the number of access streets from traffic arteries to the neighborhoods," influences the number of potential burglary offenders (and thus actual burglaries) coming into contact with an area. Controlling for neighborhood economic level, structural density, and residential mobility, the author found that permeability had a significant effect on burglary rates. White also found that areas with high burglary rates had low levels of structural density and not high levels as reported by Sampson (1986). In a similar study, Beavon, Brantingham, and Brantingham (1994, p. 138) found that "all other things being equal, opportunities have a greater likelihood of being exploited if they are on relatively accessible and frequently traveled streets."

Brantingham, Brantingham, and Wang (1991) believe that transportation affects crime by introducing potential offenders to potential targets, shaping travel times and destinations, determining travel paths, and influencing the types of crimes that occur at a location. They conclude that researchers must better understand the effects of different types of transportation, such as cars, buses, and trains, on the spatial distribution of crime.

MICROLEVEL CRIME RESEARCH AND "HOT SPOTS"

Many researchers have turned away from ecological studies in an effort to better understand the immediate spatial area surrounding high-crime locations. Although ecological research masks variation within the neighborhood, microlevel research focuses on criminal activity at the block level or lower (Sherman, Gartin, & Buerger, 1989). "The ecological tradition in criminology has been confined to relatively large aggregations of people and space, which may mask important variation and causal properties within those aggregations" (Sherman et al., 1989, p. 28). Instead of aggregating data within neighborhoods, microlevel research, also known as "environmental criminology" and "situational crime prevention," emphasizes the disaggregation of the neighborhood into distinct individual elements, focuses on individual locations, and attempts to explain the relationship between site-specific physical features, social characteristics, and crime (Bennett, 1986; Weisburd et al., 1992). Hot spots, the new "catchphrase" of crime research, represent locations with high concentrations of criminal activity, such as a high-crime street corner, tavern, crack house, or public housing complex (Block & Block, 1995).

Eck and Weisburd (1995, p. 3) assert that microlevel locations "can be as small as the area immediately next to an automatic teller machine, or as large as a block face, a strip shopping center, or an apartment building." Also, whereas neighborhood research focuses on the development of offenders, microlevel research focuses on the crime event. Block and Block (1995, p. 146) stress the distinction between "places," points in space at which events take place (a house, street intersection, bus stop, etc.), and "spaces," larger areas containing places and events (a census tract, census block, police district, city, etc.). They believe that researchers must recognize the reciprocal and transactional relationship that exists between places and their surrounding space. The combined characteristics of places affect and define the surrounding space, whereas the space surrounding specific locations affects and defines each place (similar to the relationship between words and sentences). "Focusing on variation across smaller spaces opens up a new level of analysis that can absorb many variables that have previously been [ignored]" (Sherman et al., 1989, p. 28).

Sherman et al. (1989), in an examination of calls for service data from the Minneapolis Police Department, found that more than half of the 323,979 calls for service in 1 year were concentrated in 3.3% of addresses and intersections. For example, a large discount store accounted for 810 calls for service, whereas a public housing apartment building accounted for 479 calls. The authors also found that certain crimes were even more concentrated, with all robberies occurring at 2.2% of places, all auto thefts at 2.7%, and all rapes at 1.2%. The data also suggest that, even within high-crime neighborhoods, large variations in crime rates exist at the place level.

As crime researchers turn away from traditional ecological research (Brantingham & Brantingham, 1993),

> there is a growing awareness that, because of the high variability in what is called a crime, in the people who commit crimes, and in the sites and situations in which criminal events occur, solutions to crime problems will often have to be focused and specialized. (p. 5)

In this new era, each individual situation becomes the unit of analysis, and site-specific solutions become the desired goal of crime research. Therefore, microlevel research has become a necessity because if concrete and effective anticrime measures are to be identified, we must attempt to understand the complex relationship between individual places and crime. Within this microlevel framework, it makes sense to focus our efforts on "cold spots" in addition to hot spots. Although no one will dispute the importance of understanding the characteristics of high-crime locations, we must also understand the sheltering qualities of low-crime locations. Due to the variety of microlevel research, specific discussions and examples of other research papers using this level of analysis are also presented in the following section.

MICROLEVEL RESEARCH ON THE PHYSICAL ENVIRONMENT AND CRIME

In microlevel research on the physical environment and crime, researchers examine the site-specific physical characteristics believed to influence victimization. Instead of census tracts, the individual building, street block, or university campus becomes the area of study. Instead of aggregated crime data, disaggregated information concerning the location of each individual crime points to specific physical features of the environment that help or hinder criminal activity.

In a study assessing the impact of street lighting on fear of crime and victimization in two British neighborhoods, Ditton, Nair, and Phillips (1993) interviewed adults at their homes, observed pedestrian traffic, and interviewed pedestrians both before and after the addition of superior street lighting. Results indicated that improving the quality of street lighting reduced the level of victimization from 16 to 7 victimizations in one town and from 19 to 0 in the other. Also, after the installation of improved street lighting, pedestrian traffic increased at night, people moved at a more relaxed pace through the area, and women felt more confident when walking through the area.

Painter (1994), in a similar study on the effects of street lighting in three neighborhoods in London, found that incidents of victimization and disorder decreased in all three neighborhoods after the introduction of superior street lighting. This decrease was large in two neighborhoods (from 21 to 3 incidents and from 18 to 4 incidents) and small in the third (from 2 to 0 incidents). The author believes that these benefits extended beyond the study area in at least one neighborhood. Improved street lighting also reduced fear of crime, improved people's image of the area, increased pedestrian street usage at night, and decreased fear among the elderly. Street lighting can decrease crime and fear by (a) improving visibility, thus deterring potential offenders who worry about being identified; (b) encouraging street usage, therefore increasing the number of "eyes on the street," informal surveillance, and "guardians"; and (c) improving residents' image of the area, thus psychologically encouraging and improving social control and neighborhood pride.

Nasar and Fisher (1993) identified three site-specific features that they believe affect fear and crime: concealment, blocked prospect, and blocked escape. Places that conceal potential offenders, hinder visibility, and prevent quick escape increase crime and fear of crime. Naser and Fisher noted, "Features such as alcoves, evergreen trees, or tall, dense shrubs that block prospect into places of concealment should be desirable for attackers, frightening for passersby, and difficult for police to secure" (p. 191). Places with many "nooks and crannies," blind spots, and poor lighting also apply. The authors tested their hypothesis using The Wexner Center, a building located on the Ohio State University campus designed to look disturbing and "produce a sense of instability" (p. 192). Eight areas of the building were rated by 20 graduate students to determine site-specific levels of prospect, concealment, and escape, and students who used the building were interviewed. An analysis revealed that areas of the building characterized by moderate concealment, low prospect, and blocked escape elicited the highest fear levels. Also, The Wexner Center experienced a disproportionate amount of outdoor crime, and 76% of these outdoor crimes occurred in areas with blocked prospect and high concealment.

In a test of defensible space theory, Taylor, Gottfredson, and Brower (1984) hypothesized that physical features have a direct and indirect effect on violent crime and fear. The environment directly influences offenders' perceptions of accessibility and probability of apprehension. It also indirectly influences the formation of social networks and territorial functioning; residents who feel protected and safe will use neighborhood space more often, thus increasing contact with other residents, and territorial boundaries will increase residents' feelings of control over their environment. The authors tested these hypotheses on 63 blocks in Baltimore using household surveys, calls-for-service police data, and measures of defensible space features. Results showed that defensible space features—real and symbolic barriers—slightly, although significantly, decrease violent crime, whereas levels of territorial responsibility and social ties strongly affect violent crime. Taylor et al. were not surprised by the small impact of physical features on crime because "it is inevitable that the size of the direct effects should diminish as relevant mediating social and territorial variables [such as territorial functioning and size of social networks] are carefully measured and incorporated into the model" (p. 325). Thus, the physical environment affects crime through the mediating variables of social networks and territorial functioning.

Perkins, Wandersman, Rich, and Taylor (1993) also examined the relationship between defensible space features of the physical environment and crime. Forty-eight blocks in three New York City neighborhoods were selected. Data consisted of (a) assessments of the physical environment; (b) a telephone survey of residents' perceptions of block conditions, demographic information, and social control; (c) a 15-month follow-up survey; and (d) police records of major and minor crime complaints. Results varied according to the equation used, but overall the authors believe that "the objective built and transient physical environment significantly and independently related to street crime and delinquency" (p. 44). The existence of nonresidential property (such as schools and stores), wide streets, and low visibility from building interiors to the street significantly increased rates of perceived crime problems. High residential mobility, large block populations, wide streets, nonresidential property, more crime prevention signs, and high rates of reported social control significantly increased rates of official FBI Part I crime complaints.

DISCUSSION

Both macrolevel and microlevel studies discussed in this chapter provide researchers and police officials with valuable information on the spatial distribution of criminal activity. Individuals interested in using this research, however, must be aware of the positive and negative aspects of the different levels of analysis. Politicians interested in allocating financial resources might not be interested in microlevel research in one specific neighborhood; politicians need an overall picture of crime using meaningful geographic units to allocate resources. A precinct commander interested in the best way to deploy a police force of 100 individuals might not be interested in the fact that census tracts with a high number of single parents also tend to have high rates of crime. The precinct commander already knows the high- and low-crime areas within his or her precinct, and he or she will be interested only in information that adds to this knowledge.

Macrolevel research (a) provided a general understanding of the demographic and physical differences between high- and low-crime neighborhoods and census tracts, (b) provided tools for researchers to develop and test hypotheses concerning the relationship between specific variables and crime, (c) helped criminologists identify high-crime cities and neighborhoods, and (d) was a necessary first step in understanding the spatial distribution of criminal activity. The existence of census tracts and excellent census data makes ecological analysis an inexpensive, relatively simple procedure. Also, the aggregation of crime data to the census tract level conceals the identity of any single crime event, eliminating the ethical questions raised when researchers have knowledge of specific crimes at specific addresses.

Macrolevel research can be used by individuals or organizations seeking general information on patterns of criminal activity at many different units of geography (e.g., city, county, community district, police precinct, and census tract). As stated previously, governments depend on data at politically meaningful levels of analysis to make allocation decisions. For most decisions, areas at least the size of census tracts must be used, making macrolevel crime research and analysis a necessary part of many public policy activities. Furthermore, knowledge of the most important variables related to crime could potentially be used to implement "indirect" anticrime initiatives. Instead of focusing directly on criminal activity, these initiatives could address the social and physical conditions that contribute to criminal activity. These activities could include improving neighborhood social ties and social control through the formation of block associations, providing after-school and evening activities for unsupervised teenagers, and providing job counseling, training, or both in poor areas.

Due to innovations in desktop mapping software and personal computers, the use of computers by police departments to record incident information, and the willingness of police departments to provide data on individual incidents, researchers have increasingly focused their efforts on microlevel analyses. Such research uses block-sized (or smaller) geographic units to better understand the site-specific, place-level characteristics of high-crime areas. The total study area could be as large as a neighborhood or as small as an individual building—a level of analysis that necessitates the use of very specific crime data and complicates the use of data collected at the macrolevel, such as census data.

Microlevel research can be used by local governments, grassroots organizations, block associations, and local police officials such as precinct commanders to better understand the spatial distribution of crime within a small geographic area. This research can provide valuable information concerning local hot spots, including data on the social and physical characteristics of these areas that contribute to localized criminal activity. The solution to the problem might be as simple as improving street lighting or reducing the concentration of taverns or as complex as improving the living conditions of local residents. Although macrolevel research points to troubled neighborhoods, microlevel research points to the troubled spots within these neighborhoods and offers important real-world solutions to police officials and policymakers at the local level. By using macrolevel research to identify areas requiring greater resources and attention, microlevel research could then be used to identify how to use these resources in the most useful and beneficial manner.

REFERENCES

Beavon, D., Brantingham, P. L., & Brantingham, P. J. (1994). The influence of street networks on the patterning of property offenses. In R. Clarke (Ed.), *Crime prevention studies* (Vol. 2). Monsey, NY: Criminal Justice Press.

Bennett, T. (1986). Situational crime prevention from the offenders perspective. In K. Heal & G. Laycock (Eds.), *Situational crime prevention: From theory into practice.* London: Her Majesty's Stationery Office.

Block, R. (1979). Community, environment, and violent crime. *Criminology, 17,* 46-57.

Block, R., & Block, C. (1995). Space, place and crime: Hot spot areas and hot places of liquor-related crime. In J. Eck & D. Weisburd (Eds.), *Crime prevention studies: Vol. 4. Crime and place.* Monsey, NY: Criminal Justice Press.

Brantingham, P., & Brantingham, P. (1993). Nodes, paths, and edges: Considerations on the complexity of crime and the physical environment. *Journal of Environmental Psychology, 13,* 3-28.

Brantingham, P., Brantingham, P., & Wong, P. (1991). How public transit feeds private crime: Notes on the Vancouver "skytrain" experience. *Security Journal, 2*(2), 91-95.

Dienes, L. (1988). Crime and punishment in the USSR: New information on distribution. *Soviet Geography, 29*(11), 793-808.

Ditton, J., Nair, G., & Phillips, S. (1993). Crime in the dark: A case study of the relationship between streetlighting and crime. In H. Jones (Ed.), *Crime and the urban environment.* Brookfield, NY: Avebury.

Dunn, C. (1980). Crime area research. In D. Georges-Abeyie & K. Harries (Eds.), *Crime: A spatial perspective.* New York: Columbia University Press.

Eck, J., & Weisburd, D. (1995). Crime places in crime theory. In J. Eck & D. Weisburd (Eds.), *Crime prevention studies: Vol. 4. Crime and place.* Monsey, NY: Criminal Justice Press.

Gottfredson, D., McNeil, R., & Gottfredson, G. (1991). Social area influences on delinquency: A multilevel analysis. *Journal of Research in Crime and Delinquency, 28*(2), 197-226.

Greenberg, S., & Rohe, W. (1984). Neighborhood design and crime: A test of two perspectives. *Journal of the American Planning Association, 50,* 48-61.

Harries, K. (1976). Cities and crime. *Criminology, 14*(3), 369-386.

Johnstone, J. (1978). Social class, social areas and delinquency. *Sociology and Social Research, 63,* 49-72.

Katzman, M. (1981). The supply of criminals: A geo-economic examination. In S. Hakim & G. Rengert (Eds.), *Crime spillover.* Beverly Hills, CA: Sage.

Nasar, J., & Fisher, B. (1993). "Hot spots" of fear and crime: A multi-method investigation. *Journal of Environmental Psychology, 13,* 187-206.

Painter, K. (1994). The impact of street lighting on crime, fear, and pedestrian street use. *Security Journal, 5*(3), 116-124.

Perkins, D., Wandersman, A., Rich, R., & Taylor, R. (1993). The physical environment of street crime: Defensible space, territoriality and incivilities. *Journal of Environmental Psychology, 13,* 29-49.

Rengert, G. (1981). Burglary in Philadelphia: A critique of an opportunity structural model. In P. J. Brantingham & P. L. Brantingham (Eds.), *Environmental criminology.* Beverly Hills, CA: Sage.

Roncek, D. (1981). Dangerous places: Crime and residential environment. *Social Forces, 60,* 74-96.

Sampson, R. (1983). Structural density and criminal victimization. *Criminology, 21*(2), 276-293.

Sampson, R. (1985). Neighborhood and crime: The structural determinants of personal victimization. *Journal of Research in Crime and Delinquency, 22,* 7-40.

Sampson, R. (1986). The effects of urbanization and neighborhood characteristics on criminal victimization. In R. Figlio, S. Hakim, & G. Rengert (Eds.), *Metropolitan crime patterns.* Monsey, NY: Criminal Justice Press.

Sampson, R. (1987). Does an intact family reduce burglary risk for its neighbors? *Sociology and Social Research, 71,* 204-207.

Sampson, R., & Groves, W. (1989). Community structure and crime: Testing social-disorganization theory. *American Journal of Sociology, 94*(4), 774-802.

Shaw, C., & McKay, H. (1942). *Juvenile delinquency and urban areas.* Chicago: University of Chicago Press.

Sherman, L., Gartin, P., & Buerger, M. (1989). Hot spots of predatory crime: Routine activities and the criminology of place. *Criminology, 27,* 27-55.

Simcha-Fagan, O., & Schwartz, J. (1986). Neighborhood and delinquency: An assessment of contextual effects. *Criminology, 24*(4), 667-703.

Taylor, R., Gottfredson, S., & Brower, S. (1984). Block crime and fear: Defensible space, local social ties, and territorial functioning. *Journal of Research in Crime and Delinquency, 21*(4), 303-331.

Weisburd, D., Maher, L., & Sherman, L. (1992). Contrasting crime general and crime specific theory: The case of hot spots of crime. In F. Adler & W. Laufer (Eds.), *Advances in criminological theory* (Vol. 4). New Brunswick, NJ: Transaction Publishers.

White, G. (1990). Neighborhood permeability and burglary rates. *Justice Quarterly, 7,* 57-67.

White, R. (1932). A relation of felonies to environmental factors in Indianapolis. *Social Forces, 10,* 498-509.

PART II

ANALYZING CRIME HOT SPOTS IN NEW YORK

In this section, several methods of identifying and analyzing geographic concentrations of criminal activity, or "hot spots," are demonstrated. Demarcating hot spots is one of the most important contributions that crime mapping makes in improving the efficiency and effectiveness of law enforcement. Knowing where the most dense areas of criminal activity occur may impact a broad range of police and government decision making, including officer deployment, precinct station location, and the geographic focus of both police and social service anticrime initiatives.

Precisely identifying hot spots, however, is conceptually and statistically complex. In Chapter 5, John E. Eck, Jeffrey Gersh, and Charlene Taylor use a method of research they call repeat address mapping, which identifies and maps individual addresses that account for a small number of places but are locations of a high percentage of crimes. In Chapter 6, Sanjoy Chakravorty and William V. Pelfrey demonstrate exploratory data analysis techniques using SpaceStat, an advanced spatial statistics software program. They pay particular attention to two measures of spatial autocorrelation, Moran's I and G_i^*, to identify and map census tract hot spots. In perhaps the most sophisticated use of crime mapping and spatial statistics, the kernel smoothing techniques used by Sara McLafferty, Doug Williamson, and Philip G. McGuire in Chapter 7 use a density algorithm to generate "weather maps" of criminal activity from point data. In Chapter 8, Robert H. Langworthy and Eric S. Jefferis examine whether schools being closed or in session alters burglary hot spots identified by STAC software.

The strength of this part is that it shows how various conceptualizations of hot spots suggest different methods of crime analysis. At one extreme, Eck, Gersh, and

Taylor focus attention on a unit of analysis as small as an individual building. Langworthy and Jefferis, however, identify hot spots that in some cases encompass more than a square mile. The techniques used by Chakravorty and Pelfrey can be applied to any collection of polygons. For the unit of analysis examined, each method is powerful.

One of the reasons that kernel smoothing is becoming an increasingly popular technique, however, is its versatility. The three techniques discussed previously tend to limit classification of areas to either hot or cold or assign a particular value to an entire polygon, regardless of the variation within the polygon. Kernel smoothing avoids this problem by assigning a crime density value to every point. Analysts interested in small areas may decide to examine only areas with the highest crime densities. Policymakers with broader mandates may choose to view entire cities or states to see overarching patterns.

The sophistication of hot spot identification methods is constantly increasing as potential flaws are identified and remedied. This set of chapters makes the point that no one technique can work for all purposes.

CHAPTER 5

Finding Crime Hot Spots Through Repeat Address Mapping

JOHN E. ECK
JEFFREY S. GERSH
CHARLENE TAYLOR

For most police applications, the mapping technique of choice is the plotting of crime sites on a base map. Computers have made this task less labor-intensive and more flexible than in the past, but these are still spot maps. The reasons for their continued utility are many: They are easy to make, they do not require mathematical calculations, and most audiences find them easy to interpret. In short, computer spot maps are useful because they are flexible and people understand them. We should not expect to replace them any time soon.

Even with these strengths, computer spot maps have several basic weaknesses. First, when there are many crime events, the number of spots plotted becomes hard to interpret. In the extreme, the cloud of dots obscures the base map, and clusters of spots blend into a single cloud of crime. This is particularly a problem when the analyst is plotting crimes from a long time period on a small-scale map. In addition, repeat crime locations and one-time crime places receive the same degree of attention. This may make distinguishing fleeting crime events from permanent crime problems difficult. Analysts can address this problem by making dot size proportional to the number of events, using bar charts, or using other techniques. These are useful approaches when places are few and far apart, but when the density of crime places is great these techniques increase map clutter and make interpreting the underlying pattern of events more difficult.

These problems frequently occur at the Washington/Baltimore High Intensity Drug Trafficking Area (HIDTA), which is where the techniques explained in this

AUTHORS' NOTE: All of the tables and figures to which this chapter refers can be found on the World Wide Web at http://www.urbanresearch.org

chapter were developed. In this chapter, we describe a simple technique, repeat address mapping (RAM), that we use to identify high-crime places and to evaluate the effectiveness of law enforcement interventions. The technique is grounded in criminological theory and research. Although in the early stages of development, we believe RAM has the potential to improve crime pattern clarity and increase the precision of crime prevention targeting. It also appears to have widespread applicability.

First, we describe the theory and research that underpins our use of hot spots. Next, we provide a series of hypotheses about relationships concerning hot spots and other crime sites. We then use RAM maps for a part of the Bronx to explain the simple procedures for identifying hot spots in crime event data. Finally, we apply RAM to a police district in Baltimore to demonstrate how it can be used to identify drug market patterns.

HOT SPOTS, THEORY, AND MAPPING

Some form of theory dictates the choice of a map's scale, the features shown, and the types of crimes plotted (Eck, 1997). The theory can be explicit, stemming from an academic discipline such as criminology, geography, economics, and urban planning, or it may be implicit, based on commonly held assumptions shared by the analyst and decision makers. The more explicit the theory, the more useful the map will be to decision makers. As one of us has shown in an earlier paper, if we hold the data constant and increase the explicit theoretical content of crime maps, our understanding improves and the maps become easier to interpret. This is also true of analytical techniques used to process the data plotted on maps (Eck, 1997).

We are concerned with theories describing the influence of places on crime. Crime is concentrated in relatively few places, even in neighborhoods in which crime is common. Because places have received relatively little attention in crime policy, however, it is important to define "place." A *place* is a very small area reserved for a narrow range of functions, often controlled by a single owner, and separated from the surrounding area. By small, we mean that a place is smaller than a neighborhood or community. Communities are composed of many places. Examples of places include stores, homes, apartment buildings, street corners and short segments, addresses, subway stations, and drug treatment facilities.

Routine activity theory (Cohen & Felson, 1979) and offender search theory (Brantingham & Brantingham, 1981) predict the concentration of crime at places. Routine activity theory gives places a central position in the explanation of crime events (Eck & Weisburd, 1995). Places are where offenders and targets meet. Unless they can meet at accessible locations that have weak controls, crime is unlikely. Offender search theory describes how offenders move among places of residence, work, school, recreation, shopping, and other activities and how their movement gives them information about potential targets. Offender search theory draws attention to the role of arterial routes used by offenders and nonoffenders alike. Together, these two theories describe why crime places tend to be along these arterial routes. Many of the places along these routes are commercial or rental properties, so they are accessible to the public. Commercial sites contain many targets. Some places along arterial routes impose few controls on the actions of the people using the locations. Finally, offenders notice places along arterial routes because they routinely use these streets. In short, offender search theory describes the geographic patterns of crime places, and routine activity theory describes why some places have more crime than others, even in the same area.

There is considerable evidence for the concentration of crime at relatively few places. Researchers found some of the original evidence for place concentration of crime in Boston (Pierce, Spaar, & Briggs, 1986) and Minneapolis (Sherman, Gartin, & Buerger, 1989). In England and Canada, a growing body of research reveals that in high-burglary neighborhoods most residences have no burglaries, but a few residences suffer repeated burglaries (Farrell, 1995). Most tavern-related violence occurs at a small number of bars (Sherman, Schmidt, & Velke, 1992). Ten percent of the fast-food restaurants in San Antonio, Texas, accounted for one third of the property crimes at such restaurants (Spelman, 1995). In Kansas City and Indianapolis, Sherman and Rogan (1995b) found gun crimes were focused at a few places. Drug dealing is concentrated in a few locations, even within areas with a high volume of drug dealing (Eck, 1995; Sherman & Rogan, 1995a).

Crime concentration at places is most apparent when compared to repeat offending and repeat victimization. Spelman estimated that 10% of the victims in the United States are involved in approximately 40% of the victimization, 10% of the offenders are involved in more than 50% of the crimes, and 10% of the places are sites for approximately 60% of the crimes (Spelman & Eck, 1989). Furthermore, concentration of crime at a few places is relatively stable over time (Spelman, 1995). These findings suggest that something about a few places facilitates crime, and something about most places prevents crime.

Theory and evidence suggest that we should think more about the mapping of crime places than the mapping of crime incidents. That is, we should interpret spot maps as describing crime place patterns. This is more than a semantic difference. It has implications for what we map, how we interpret maps, and how we act on findings suggested by maps. In particular, focusing on places implies that we should think about how to map repeat crime locations. This also draws attention to land use, traffic patterns, the design of public spaces, and the rules governing access and use of places. Furthermore, it suggests crime prevention tactics to address traffic flow, environmental design, and the management of places.

Crimes are transitory events. They occur for a brief time period, usually measured in seconds and minutes. The reasons for a crime occurring when and where it does can be random or systematic. Random occurrences hold little interest because these events are unlikely to repeat, cannot be predicted, and are hard to prevent. Systematic occurrences are of great interest. When crime repeatedly occurs at the same place, we refer to the place as a "hot spot." As we will discuss later, mapping hot spot places can be more meaningful than mapping transitory events.

PATTERNS OF HOT SPOTS
AND PATTERNS OF CRIME

Hot spots are places that have shown persistent tendencies to be sites of crime. It makes sense to concentrate police and other prevention resources on those places that make the greatest contribution to crime. Where crime is continuously distributed, hot spots can be thought of as the centers of clouds of crime. We elaborate on this last point in detail.

There are three hypotheses describing how hot spots may be linked to the less concentrated clouds of crime places that surround them. First, hot spots may attract offenders or facilitate offending or both, causing crime to spill into surrounding areas. In other words, a hot spot may be a center of contagion. Successful law enforcement or prevention intervention at hot spots may reduce crime at nearby locations. This hypothesis explains why we might find prevention diffusion (Clarke & Weisburd, 1994) rather than crime displacement. We call this the "central place" hypothesis of hot spots.

The second explanation is the "side effect" hypothesis of hot spots. Imagine a set of places, each with a weak attraction to offenders. Offenders would also notice nearby places with interesting crime targets. Thus, each place can be considered a center of attention to offenders, and each increases the chances of surrounding places becoming crime sites. Now imagine each place as a dot. Assume that each has a weak criminogenic effect on nearby places, and that this weak effect spreads outward in a circle or ellipse that declines with distance from the center. We now have a set of low-crime places surrounded by overlapping circles. Places that happen to be located where several circles overlap may have many more crimes than other places because many offenders pass by and notice them on their way to the other low-crime places. These would be the hot spots of crime. If this hypothesis is correct, then effective law enforcement or prevention tactics at these hot spots should reduce crime at these places, but there would be no diffusion of benefits. Furthermore, such actions would do little to address the conditions that gave rise to the crime pattern.

The third hypothesis suggests that hot spots and the surrounding cloud of crime places are not causally connected. Instead, area characteristics give rise to both hot spots and non-hot spots of crime. Some places are disproportionately vulnerable; these will become hot spots in crime-prone areas but not in crime-resistant areas. The less vulnerable places may become crime places on occasion but not regularly in either type of area. Some places may be virtually invulnerable to crime in both types of areas. We call this the "area effect" hypothesis. If this hypothesis is correct, concentrating law enforcement intervention on hot spots might reduce the overall crime in crime-prone areas because most crime is concentrated at hot spots. We would not expect, however, to see a diffusion of benefits from interventions at hot spots. Under some limited conditions, we might observe some spatial displacement of crime from successful interventions. This would occur if untapped crime opportunities exist at other nearby places that are similar to the former hot spots, and offenders seek out these opportunities. This displacement, however, should be restricted to crime-prone areas and is unlikely to cross into crime-resistant areas. Absent these two conditions (untapped opportunities and offenders searching for them), spatial displacement will be slight or nonexistent.

Any of the three hypotheses provides reasons for mapping hot spots. According to each, the distribution of hot spots on a map should suggest stable patterns of criminal offending. The interpretation of the maps should be different, however. If the central place hypothesis is correct, then a map of these hot spots reveals two important facts. It shows exact targets for enforcement and prevention, and it also shows the relationship among the hot spots. If the side effect hypothesis is correct, then the map shows only a skeletal pattern of crime. If the area effect hypothesis is correct, then hot spot patterns point to neighborhood conditions.

These hypotheses of crime hot spots may not apply to some calls-for-service hot spots. A call for service may be prompted by a wide range of phenomena of varying importance to law enforcement. If the address recorded by the police is the address of the caller, then repeat calls may indicate the sensitivity of callers and not the underlying seriousness of conditions. A map of such hot spots would show the distribution of sensitive people.

Some calls for service, however, do reflect serious crime events. Calls about gunshots, for example, are not just recordings of disturbances but document violent behavior. Clusters of gunshot calls might be common if single-gunshot events generate calls from several nearby places. Calls about drug-dealing activity are similar in this regard. Drug dealing is usually a protracted series of events unfolding over some period of time. The same caller may make repeated attempts to involve the police, thus generating a hot spot. If several neighbors do this, we would expect a cluster of hot spots. This cluster would have a single cause, however.

Records of calls for service can identify places that are sources of disturbances (rather than addresses of complainants). Hot spots revealed by these data should not be as clustered as hot spots based on callers' addresses. We would, however, expect to find calls for service regarding public problems to be more highly concentrated than crime reports because such problems influence many people, so a single disturbance might generate multiple calls about a problem place. Under these conditions, 10% of the worst calls-for-service places should account for a higher proportion of calls than crimes accounted for by the 10% worst crime places.

Finally, we consider police activities, particularly arrests. Arrest statistics reflect a confluence of an opportunity to make an arrest and a decision by officers to make arrests. Because police have discretion to overlook arrest opportunities, maps of arrests are better measures of the distribution of police activity than they are of crime. Nevertheless, for underreported crimes, such as drug dealing, gambling, and prostitution, arrest data are often used as a proxy for crime. We would expect concentrations of arrests at places once the places became known to the police as centers of criminal behavior. Therefore, for some crimes, such as drug dealing, arrests may be more concentrated than reported crimes. The clustering of arrest hot spots should be pronounced when police focus their efforts in small areas. Again, it is important to note that the concentration of arrests and the clustering of arrest hot spots may or may not reflect the distribution of criminal behavior. Independent verification, using other data sources, is required to make this assertion.

Whether we are discussing hot spots of reported crime, calls for service, or arrests, it is important to consider their geographical distribution. We have offered several alternative hypotheses. Any or all of them may be valid in some circumstances. We do not test these hypotheses in this chapter but simply propose them as plausible descriptions of relationships between hot spot patterns and other event patterns.

MEASURING CONCENTRATION

We can measure the concentration of crime (or calls for service or arrests) by examining the places with the most crime and estimating the proportion of crime that occurs there. Imagine a list of places with at least one crime event during a given time period. Most of these places will have only a single crime for the time period, some will have two, a lesser number will have three crimes, and so on until we find very few places with many crimes. Sort these places so that the place with the most crime is at the bottom of the list, the place with the second most crime is listed next, and so on until the top of the list shows places with only one crime.

Next, we start at the bottom of the list of crime places. Divide it into 10 sections, each with 10% of the places. (Ten is a matter of convenience and convention.) From the bottom, the first 10% contains the most crime-ridden 10% of the places. The second 10% contains the second most crime-ridden 10% of the places. Finally, the last 10% of places contain the fewest crimes.

What proportion of the crime took place at the worst 10% of the crime places? If crime is concentrated at a few places, then each of the bottom few groups will have more than 10% of the crime, and each of the top few groups will have less than 10% of the crime. If no place had more than a single crime, then the worst 10% of the places would have only 10% of the crime, just like the least crime-prone 10% of the places.

Starting at the bottom, we add the percentage of crime in successively less crime-ridden places. The resulting table indicates the proportion of all crime that occurred in the top 10% of the most crime-ridden places, followed by the proportion of crime in the top 20% of the most crime-ridden places. The top entry shows 100% of all crime occurring at 100% of the places.

Mapping the worst crime places gives a different perspective on crime patterns than mapping all crime events. To illustrate this point, we examine data from the Bronx using procedures we developed at the Washington/Baltimore HIDTA.

REPEAT CRIME ADDRESSES IN THE BRONX

The New York City Police Department and the Center for Applied Studies of the Environment supplied the data used in this example. We estimated the crime con-

TABLE 5.1 Concentration of Bronx Crimes[a]

# of Events	All Crimes		Robberies		Assaults		Burglaries		Grand Larceny		Auto Theft	
	Places	Crimes	Places	Crimes	Places	Crimes	Places	Crimes	Places	Crimes	Places	Crimes
1	1.0000	1.0000	1.0000	1.0000	1.0000	1.0000	1.0000	1.0000	1.0000	1.0000	1.0000	1.0000
2	0.2851	0.5602	0.1703	0.3513	0.1677	0.3441	0.2200	0.4253	0.1010	0.2424	0.1288	0.2878
3	0.1291	0.3683	0.0547	0.1704	0.0477	0.1550	0.1303	0.2115	0.0321	0.1263	0.0391	0.1412
4	0.0696	0.2584	0.0209	0.0913	0.0176	0.0837	0.0525	0.1126	0.0128	0.0774	0.0142	0.0802
5	0.0394	0.1840	0.0110	0.0601	0.0069	0.0500	0.0202	0.0578	0.0070	0.0579	0.0080	0.0597
6	0.0243	0.1377	0.0062	0.0415	0.0031	0.0349	0.0103	0.0368	0.0048	0.0487	0.0052	0.0484
7	0.0163	0.1079	0.0043	0.0324	0.0019	0.0295	0.0059	0.0256	0.0031	0.0401	0.0033	0.0389
8	0.0107	0.0839	0.0028	0.0244	0.0011	0.0253	0.0036	0.0188	0.0029	0.0387	0.0022	0.0327
9	0.0073	0.0673	0.0019	0.0190	0.0008	0.0229	0.0017	0.0123	0.0022	0.0338	0.0013	0.0272
10	0.0053	0.0562	0.0011	0.0130	0.0004	0.0203	0.0004	0.0072	0.0017	0.0301	0.0012	0.0263
11	0.0042	0.0496	0.0010	0.0121	0.0004	0.0203	0.0002	0.0064	0.0017	0.0301	0.0012	0.0263
12	0.0034	0.0437	0.0005	0.0079	0.0004	0.0203	0.0002	0.0064	0.0017	0.0301	0.0011	0.0252
13	0.0028	0.0394	0.0002	0.0056	0.0004	0.0203	0.0002	0.0064	0.0012	0.0253	0.0006	0.0205
14	0.0023	0.0355	0.0001	0.0044	0.0004	0.0203	0.0002	0.0064	0.0012	0.0253	0.0006	0.0205
15	0.0018	0.0310	0.0001	0.0044	0.0004	0.0203	0.0002	0.0064	0.0012	0.0253	0.0005	0.0191
16	0.0016	0.0291	0.0001	0.0044	0.0004	0.0203	0.0002	0.0064	0.0010	0.0222	0.0004	0.0176
17	0.0014	0.0274	0.0001	0.0044	0.0002	0.0178	0.0002	0.0064	0.0007	0.0189	0.0004	0.0176
18	0.0011	0.0245	0.0001	0.0044	0.0002	0.0178	0.0002	0.0064	0.0007	0.0189	0.0004	0.0176
19	0.0009	0.0218	0.0001	0.0044	0.0002	0.0178	0.0002	0.0064	0.0005	0.0153	0.0004	0.0176
20	0.0006	0.0190	0.0001	0.0044	0.0002	0.0178	0.0002	0.0064	0.0005	0.0153	0.0004	0.0176
21	0.0006	0.0181	0.0001	0.0044	0.0002	0.0178	0.0002	0.0064	0.0005	0.0153	0.0004	0.0176
22	0.0005	0.0172	0.0001	0.0044	0.0002	0.0178	0.0002	0.0064	0.0002	0.0110	0.0004	0.0176
23	0.0004	0.0163	0.0001	0.0044	0.0002	0.0178	0.0002	0.0064	0.0002	0.0110	0.0004	0.0176
>23	0.0003	0.0153	0.0001	0.0044	0.0002	0.0178	0.0002	0.0064	0.0002	0.0110	0.0002	0.0154
Total	28,848	46,891	8,213	10,504	5,236	6,644	9,095	12,343	4,137	4,909	8,293	10,145

a. Cumulative distributions from bottom up.

centration at places for robberies, assaults, burglaries, grand larcenies, auto thefts, and all reported crimes from October 1, 1995, through October 31, 1996.

Table 5.1 shows the concentration for all crimes. If we mapped only places with four or more crimes (<7% of the places), we can account for more than one fourth of the crime. By mapping places with three or more crimes (approximately 13% of the places), we would account for more than one third of the crimes. A single place in the Bronx had 392 crimes. Outliers such as this need to be investigated to determine if they are truly super hot spots. It is possible that such an outlier is the result of data collection and coding errors or some other anomaly. Table 5.1 also shows the concentrations of five specific crimes. Specific crimes are not as concentrated as all crime taken together. This means that some places have multiple crimes of different types.

TABLE 5.2 Concentration of Crime at Bronx Places

10% of Places Include . . .	All Crime	Robberies	Assaults	Burglaries	Grand Larcenies	Auto Thefts
	31.5%	30.9%	23.7%	13.6%	24.1%	24.1%
Minimum plotting density (MPD)	3	2	2	3	2	2
Places						
(a) Total	28,848	8,213	5,236	9,095	4,137	8,293
(b) ≥ MPD	3,724	1,399	878	1,185	418	1,068
(c) %	12.9	17.0	16.8	13.0	10.1	12.9
Events						
(d) Total	46,891	10,504	6,644	12,343	4,909	10,145
(e) ≥ MPD	17,270	3,690	2,286	2,611	1,190	2,920
(f) %	36.8	35.1	34.4	21.2	24.2	28.8
Efficiency (1 − [c/f])	.649	.515	.513	.384	.583	.552

To use this information for RAM, we typically create a summary table, as illustrated in Table 5.2. The first row shows the percentage of events found at the most active 10% of the places for each type of event. For example, 10% of the places with a burglary account for approximately 14% of all burglaries. It can be seen that the concentration of events is lowest for burglaries and highest for all crimes combined.

The remaining rows of Table 5.2 provide information we used to develop a map that displays only hot spots. The minimum plotting density (MPD) is the smallest number of events desired for plotting a place on a map. We selected MPDs by searching for a whole number of events per place that allowed us to plot approximately 10% of the places. These densities are shown in the second row of Table 5.2. In the following rows, we show the total number of crime places for each crime type (row a) and the numbers of such places with events equal to or greater than the MPD (row b). We also show the percentage of places plotted at this density (row c). Similar data are shown for events in rows d, e, and f.

The last row of Table 5.2 shows the efficiency of the MPD selected. It is calculated by subtracting from 1 the ratio of the proportion of places plotted to the proportion of the events plotted. The greater the efficiency, the fewer places that need to be plotted to account for most of the events. Burglaries had the smallest concentration and had the lowest mapping efficiency. All crimes had the highest concentration and were very efficiently mapped.

We arbitrarily selected one area within the Bronx to illustrate the results of mapping repeat addresses. Figure 5.1 is a map of all crimes in this area. With a mapping efficiency of zero, it is so cluttered that crime patterns are barely discernible. Figure 5.2 shows crime places with four or more crimes of any type. At this

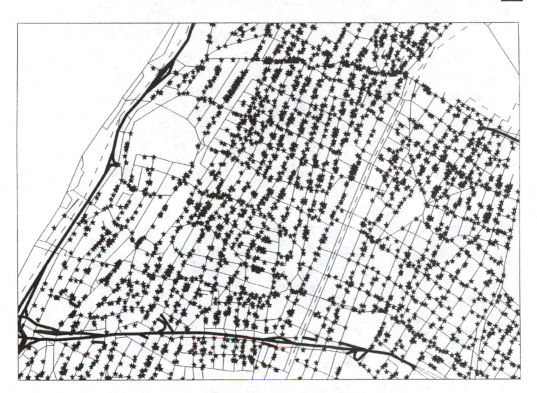

Figure 5.1. All Crime Events, October 1, 1995, to October 31, 1996

Figure 5.2. Addresses With Four or More Crime Events, October 1, 1995, to October 31, 1996

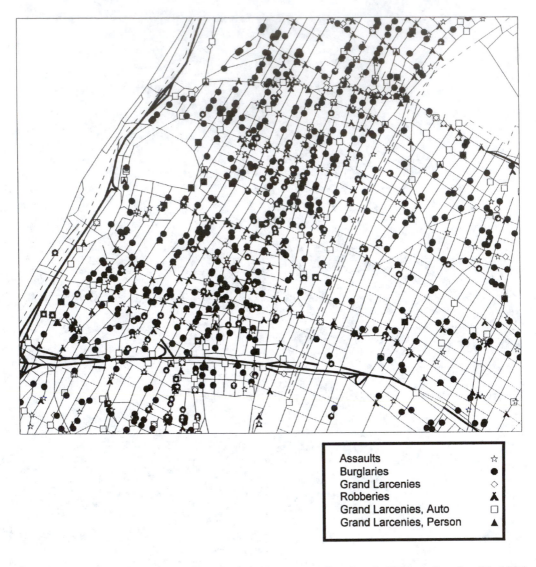

Assaults	☆
Burglaries	●
Grand Larcenies	◇
Robberies	⋏
Grand Larcenies, Auto	□
Grand Larcenies, Person	▲

Figure 5.3. Addresses With Two or More Crime Events, October 1, 1995, to October 31, 1996

MPD, all crimes together have a mapping efficiency of .73. Several clusters of places with many criminal events can plainly be seen.

Figures 5.3 and 5.4 show crime-specific repeat address maps. Figure 5.3 shows places with a MPD of two or more crimes of the same type. Robbery, assaults, grand larcenies, and auto theft each have mapping efficiencies of more than .50, and burglary has a mapping efficiency of .48. Note that hot spots cluster both for specific crime types (i.e., burglary spots near other burglary spots) and for several crimes (e.g., burglary, assault, auto theft, and robbery warm spots near and on each other). Figure 5.4 shows places with a MPD of three or more specific crimes. The mapping efficiency for robbery, assaults, grand larcenies, and auto theft has

Assaults	☆
Burglaries	●
Grand Larcenies	◇
Robberies	⋏
Grand Larcenies, Auto	□
Grand Larcenies, Person	▲

Figure 5.4. Addresses With Three or More Crime Events, October 1, 1995, to October 31, 1996

increased to more than .67, but burglary mapping efficiency has decreased to .38. Several intense clusters of spots are readily apparent in this map.

REPEAT ADDRESS MAPPING FOR BALTIMORE DRUG CALLS

At the Washington/Baltimore HIDTA, we use RAM for operations planning, targeting decisions, and evaluations. We use a mixture of drug call-for-service data and crime data. The drug calls—based on citizen complaints to 911 about drug dealing—are particularly valuable for identifying drug market locations.

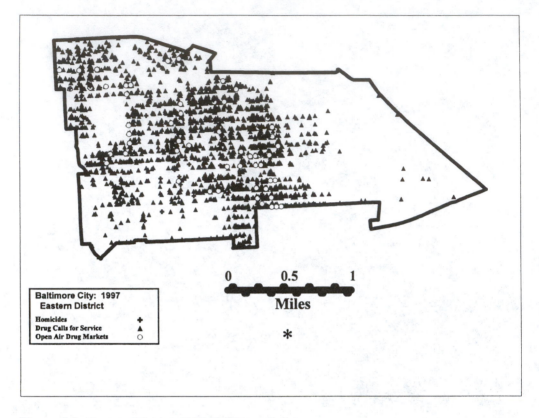

Figure 5.5. Eastern District, 1997 (All Drug Calls)

In Baltimore, in which we have done extensive mapping of drug markets, these calls are highly concentrated, but our first maps did not account for this. Before we began plotting hot spots using RAM, analysts produced several maps of drug calls and violent crime. These maps were helpful for describing the sections of Baltimore that had drug and violence problems, but there were so many crimes, calls, and arrests that large clouds of spots covered vast sections of the city. These maps were not precise enough to show where the HIDTA should focus its scarce drug enforcement and treatment resources.

To illustrate the efficiency of RAM, consider the problem of mapping more than 30,000 drug calls for the city of Baltimore in 1997. With this many calls, even large-scale maps of parts of the city were of little utility. Using the process described previously, we determined that if we plotted places with nine or more drug calls we could map 10% of the places[1] with drug calls and account for 66% of these calls. This resulted in a drug map with an efficiency of more than 85%. Figures 5.5 and 5.6 show how RAM at a minimum plotting density of nine (Figure 5.6) compares to mapping all drug calls (Figure 5.5) for one high drug-call police district in 1997. Also shown are drug-dealing locations identified by drug investigators and homicide locations. These sites correspond more closely to the repeat drug-call places than they do to the single drug calls. This example shows that there are patterns of crime obscured by crime incident mapping that are revealed by RAM.

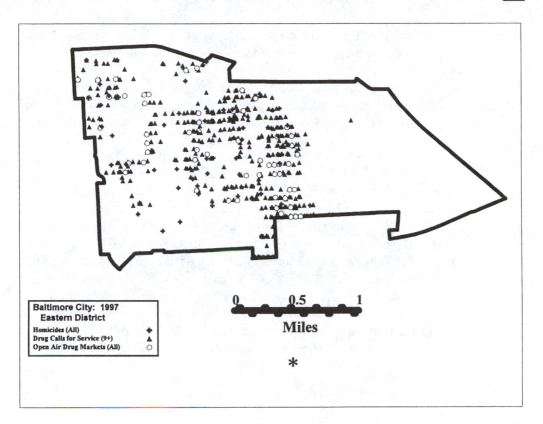

Figure 5.6. Eastern District, 1997 (Minimum Plotting Density of Nine)

CONCLUSIONS

In this chapter, we attempted to show the utility of mapping hot spot places rather than events. Mapping hot spot places focuses attention on persistent problem locations, and the distractions created when all events are mapped are avoided. This approach reduces map clutter, aids understanding, and reveals hidden patterns among hot spot places. This technique also has strong theoretical underpinnings supported by empirical research findings.

To explain why hot spots may cluster, we developed several hypotheses and described why the concentration of events at places, and clustering of hot spots, may be related to the type of data used (reported crimes, calls for service, or arrests). The illustrations from the Bronx and Baltimore demonstrate that hot spot mapping can be applied to different settings and a variety of crimes. We also introduced concepts and measures to help analysts construct these maps, describe what they are plotting, and compare maps.

Of particular importance is the concept of mapping efficiency. Crime mappers suffer from an abundance of data. The volume of incidents can obscure patterns as well as reveal them. Paying attention to mapping efficiency helps address this problem.

Mapping efficiency and concentration are closely related, but they are not synonymous. The analyst controls efficiency, in part, by selecting the MPD, but concentration puts limits on the maximum efficiency. If all crimes were at separate locations, then the maximum efficiency an analyst could achieve would be zero. If all crimes were at a single location, the minimum efficiency the analyst could achieve would be 1. Most circumstances fall between these extremes, so the analyst has some control over efficiency by selecting the MPD.

Mapping efficiency is not the same as mapping effectiveness. Effectiveness is how well a map aids its users. Although a map with zero efficiency will often be less effective than a more efficient map, even a very efficient map may not be particularly effective. Changes in scale, symbols, shading, color, and features depicted can all influence effectiveness. Because showing fewer places increases efficiency, RAM can also increase a map's effectiveness. Efficiency and effectiveness are related though not synonymous. The Baltimore drug-call maps illustrate this point.

The Washington/Baltimore HIDTA is currently using these techniques and exploring new ways to use maps to aid law enforcement, treatment, and prevention decision making. We continually search for analytic methods that are simple to use, easy to understand, and provide clear guidance. We have found that paying close attention to crime theory is the most pragmatic way of achieving this objective.

NOTE

1. In this example, the places are a mix of addresses, corners, and block faces because the police were unable to provide an address more specific than a hundred block (e.g., 2300 E. Rhymney) for many of the calls. Because the places with the most number of calls often had hundred block addresses, we assume that many of them are blocks or corners.

REFERENCES

Brantingham, P. L., & Brantingham, P. J. (1981). Notes on the geometry of crime. In P. J. Brantingham & P. L. Brantingham (Eds.), *Environmental criminology*. Beverly Hills, CA: Sage.

Clarke, R. V., & Weisburd, D. (1994). Diffusion of crime control benefits: Observations on the reverse of displacement. In Ronald V. Clarke (Ed.), *Crime prevention studies. Vol. 2.* Monsey, NY: Willow Tree Press.

Cohen, L. E., & Felson, M. (1979). Social change and crime rate trends: A routine activity approach. *American Sociological Review, 44,* 588-605.

Eck, J. (1995). A general model of the geography of illicit retail marketplaces. In J. Eck & D. Weisburd (Eds.), *Crime prevention studies: Vol. 4. Crime and place.* Monsey, NY: Criminal Justice Press.

Eck, J. (1997). What do those dots mean? Mapping theories with data? In T. McEwen & D. Weisburd (Eds.), *Crime mapping and crime prevention.* Monsey, NY: Criminal Justice Press.

Eck, J., & Weisburd, D. (1995). *Crime and place.* Monsey, NY: Criminal Justice Press.

Farrell, G. (1995). Preventing repeat victimization. In M. Tonry & D. P. Farrington (Eds.), *Crime and justice: Vol. 19. Building a safer society: Strategic approaches to crime prevention.* Chicago: University of Chicago Press.

Pierce, G. L., Spaar, S., & Briggs, L. R. (1986). *The character of police work: Strategic and tactical implications* [Photocopy]. Boston: Northeastern University, Center for Applied Social Research.

Sherman, L., & Rogan, D. P. (1995a). Deterrent effects of police raids on crack houses: A randomized, controlled experiment. *Justice Quarterly, 12,* 755-781.

Sherman, L., & Rogan, D. P. (1995b). Effects of gun seizure on gun violence: "Hot spots" patrol in Kansas City. *Justice Quarterly, 12,* 673-694.

Sherman, L., Schmidt, J. D., & Velke, R. J. (1992). *High crime taverns: A RECAP project in problem-oriented policing* (Final report to the National Institute of Justice). Washington, DC: Crime Control Institute.

Sherman, L. W., Gartin, P. R., & Buerger, M. E. (1989). Hot spots of predatory crime: Routine activities and the criminology of place. *Criminology, 27,* 27-55.

Spelman, W. (1995). Criminal careers of public places. In J. Eck & D. Weisburd (Eds.), *Crime prevention studies: Vol. 4. Crime and place.* Monsey, NY: Criminal Justice Press.

Spelman, W., & Eck, J. E. (1989). Sitting ducks, ravenous wolves, and helping hands: New approaches to urban policing. *Public Affairs Comment, 35,* 1-9.

CHAPTER 6

Exploratory Data Analysis of Crime Patterns

Preliminary Findings From the Bronx

SANJOY CHAKRAVORTY
WILLIAM V. PELFREY JR.

There is little doubt that the distribution of crime incidents is not spatially random; because the distribution of population and the types of built environments around which many types of crime are anchored are known to exhibit clear spatial patterns, it is expected that the distribution of certain types of crime will also follow identifiable spatial patterns. This chapter, like others in this book, concentrates on using spatial analytical methodologies to better understand the distribution of crime. The use of geographical tools in analyzing crime has had some precedent, such as the digital mapping of crime incidents, the creation of spatial profiles of serial criminals, and the use of spatial algorithms for the detection of crime clusters or "hot spots" (Hirschfield, 1994; Maltz, Gordon, & Friedman, 1991). We locate this chapter in this emergent area with a twofold focus. First, we argue for a clearer understanding of the spatial principles that underlie the use of spatial methodology (Chakravorty, 1995). Second, we argue for the use of the exploratory spatial data analysis (ESDA) approach suggested by Anselin and Getis (1992) in the statistical analysis of crime. The bulk of the chapter is devoted to the use of two ESDA techniques, the Moran scatterplot and the G_i^* statistic of Getis and Ord (1992). Both techniques will be applied to burglary data for 2 months in the Bronx using Luc Anselin's SpaceStat software.[1] The findings indicate that these new methodologies offer insights that are unavailable through the use of simple mapping or hot spot identification techniques (which have their advantages, as discussed later) and add analytical and statistical rigor.

AUTHORS' NOTE: All of the tables and figures to which this chapter refers can be found on the World Wide Web at http://www.urbanresearch.org

PRINCIPLES

The purpose of spatial analysis is to identify patterns in the data and, where relevant, model the underlying process generating the pattern. Anselin and Getis (1992) argue that this twofold approach may respectively be termed ESDA and confirmatory spatial data analysis (CSDA). They write,

> Under [ESDA] we classify inductive approaches to elicit insight about pattern and relations from the data, without *necessarily* [italics added] having a firm preconceived theoretical notion about which relations are to be expected. We could also call this "data-driven" analysis to stress the emphasis on "letting the data speak for themselves." The final module then is confirmatory analysis, where the point of departure is a theoretical notion or model ("model-driven" analysis). This would include most of the "traditional" techniques of spatial data analysis, such as hypothesis tests, estimation of spatial process models, simulation and prediction . . . and thus could encompass a wide range of urban, regional, and multiregional models. (p. 22)

This chapter focuses on the use of some ESDA tools with crime data. It begins with a general assumption that the crime incidents are distributed as points in a given area. We acknowledge that there may be incidents that may be treated as lines (e.g., chases) or as polygons (e.g., large arson sites), but most incidents (arrests, burglaries, homicides, etc.) may be treated as point data.[2] How do we elicit patterns from the data? First, we may seek patterns, such as clusters, in the distribution of the points themselves (i.e., by assuming that the points exist in abstract homogeneous space). Here, some of the enduring pioneering work has been done by plant ecologists and botanists (Boots & Getis, 1988). The usual method of testing the null hypothesis of complete spatial randomness (CSR) is by using quadrat analysis. This technique superimposes a regular grid on the study area and counts the number of points in each cell of the grid. The difference between the distribution of expected values in CSR and the values actually recorded reveals whether clustering exists in the given distribution.

A serious problem with this methodology is that it is oblivious to the values in adjoining cells. White (1983) termed this the "checkerboard problem" with reference to segregation research. For a given distribution, the same value of segregation is obtained regardless of how the cells are arranged (see Wong [1993] for an approach to solving this problem in the context of segregation measurement). Another significant problem with this approach is the assumption of environmental homogeneity. The use of a regular grid presupposes that the underlying area is homogeneous with respect to population and built environment variables. Every location in this assumed homogeneous space is assumed to be as likely to receive a point as every other location. We know that, ceteris paribus, crime incidents are more likely in locations in which population densities are higher. Hence, the assumption of population homogeneity tends to result in obvious conclusions being drawn—for example, crime is higher in central cities (which have higher population densities).

A simple solution is to use census geography as the base map or grid. The use of census blocks (or the street network) may be a solution, but in very densely settled areas this could result in a very fine grid and lead to some practical computing problems.

The use of census geography also mitigates a third, twofold problem with the analytical aspects of the quadrat approach. When modeling is necessary or indicated, whether or not the crime incidents are treated as dependent or independent variables, devices that yield statistically significant indexes or summaries are to be preferred to simple averages or counts. More important, the other model variables are often socioeconomic variables taken from the census or other surveys. In other words, the appropriate unit of analysis is a spatial unit for which other data must also be available if the CSDA or modeling aspect is to be carried out. The use of quadrat-based approaches yields noncomparable, nonstandardized indexes that are not attached to any standard spatial disaggregation, and hence CSDA is not possible using such approaches. The use of hot spot mapping, typically using a quadrat-based software such as STAC (Spatial and Temporal Analysis of Crime), is becoming quite popular in criminal justice. It is a useful approach for visual pattern identification on a day-to-day basis or to obtain a quick picture from a large quantity of data, but it is not suitable for more rigorous analysis or model building.

The solution to these three problems, at least for analytical (as opposed to descriptive) purposes, is to abandon the quadrat-based approach and make use of significantly more sophisticated tools that have been developed since the late 1980s. These tools must account for the spatial concepts of contiguity and proximity. They should be able to explicitly incorporate information on relative location. Also, these tools must be able to work with irregular grids or base maps, in which the grids (derived perhaps from census geography) are representative of the underlying population distribution. A reasonable compromise that offers a fair degree of disaggregation while leaving the computing problems manageable may be the use of census geography at the tract level.

THE TOOLS AND THEIR APPLICATIONS

We begin by plotting the crime points on an irregular grid or base map, counting the decrease in number of points in each cell of the base map, and then proceed with our exploratory procedures. The use of a geographic information system (GIS) makes this process simple. GIS software, such as Arc/Info, MapInfo, and Atlas, allows overlaying points on polygons without much difficulty. The following steps are needed to accomplish this task:

1. Generate a database of street addresses for crime incidents so that every incident is associated with at least the address at which the crime incident occurred. There may be additional data attached to each incident, such as the address of the perpetrator, date and time of day, arresting

officer's identification, and follow-up data, but at a minimum the address of the incident location is needed.

2. Use address-matching software to generate a point map or coverage of the incidents. Any of the previously mentioned GIS software may be used for this purpose.

3. Overlay the point map on the polygon base map (e.g., a census tract map or coverage of the study area). Use database management software to count the number of incidents in each parcel, and associate this count with the parcel identification number (e.g., the census tract ID).

We approach this exploratory study with a limited set of the Bronx crime data provided by the New York City Police Department (NYPD). We chose to examine burglaries in the study region to determine if the ESDA approach would yield any information beyond that provided by simple choropleth mapping. We selected burglaries because of the high frequency in the database (12,343 incidents of a total of 46,891 incidents) and because property crimes (as opposed to violent crimes) often have a significant spatial dimension. We elected not to use the entire burglary database but chose the 2 months with the maximum and minimum number of incidents. As expected, there was a seasonal variation. The selected months were August (with 867 incidents, the least number of recorded burglaries) and November (with 1,183 incidents, the maximum).

These addresses were disaggregated into two separate database files and generated as point coverages in Arc/Info. We overlaid the burglary data on a census tract map of Bronx County (FIPS Code 36005 with 356 tracts) extracted from the Wessex Pro Filer collection.[3] A simple database program was written to total the number of incidents for each census tract by month, and all resulting data and coverages were transformed from the original decimal degree (or latitude-longitude) format to a state plane projection in feet. At the conclusion of this process, we were left with a coverage for the Bronx at the census tract level, in which for every census tract we had two new fields containing the number of burglaries in the tract for the two selected months. Simple thematic maps suggested spatial clustering for both months, with the November data somewhat more dispersed in the south-central section of the study area (see Figures 6.1 and 6.2 on web site).

To ascertain whether clustering exists in this distribution, we used indicators derived in the literature on spatial autocorrelation (Cliff & Ord, 1973; Odland, 1987). Perhaps the most widely used of these measures is Moran's I, which is given by the following equation:

$$I = N/S_0 \; ij \; w_{ij} \times (x_i - \mu) \times (x_j - \mu)/i(x_i - \mu)^2$$

where

N is the number of observations (or parcels; census tracts in this case),
w_{ij} is the element in the spatial weights matrix corresponding to the observation pair i, j,

x_i is the number of points or incidents in parcel i,

x_j is the number of points or incidents in parcel j,

μ is the number of points per parcel (or average of points per parcel), and

S_0 is a scaling constant given by $ij\ w_{ij}$ or the sum of all weights.

The concept of the spatial weights matrix needs explanation. This is a method of organizing the data on spatial arrangements (i.e., of contiguity or proximity) of parcels. Formally, a spatial weights matrix W is composed of elements w_{ij}, where the ij index corresponds to each observation pair. The nonzero elements of this matrix reflect the level of spatial interaction between pairs of parcels. Anselin (1992, pp. 10-11) noted, "This may be expressed in different ways, such as simple contiguity (having a common border), distance contiguity (having centroids within a critical distance band), or in a function of inverse distance or squared inverse distance." The theoretical mean of Moran's I is $[-1/N - 1]$, which suggests that the expected value of I under the condition of spatial randomness is negative. It is also dependent on the number of parcels in the study area, and for a large number of parcels the value of I tends to zero. A positive value of I indicates positive spatial autocorrelation, which implies that high values are clustered together, as are low values. A negative value of I is difficult to interpret because it indicates that high values are contiguous or proximate to low values. For the purpose of inference, it is preferable to use standardized z values rather than the calculated values of I.[4]

We used five distance-contiguity tests on the August and November data. We used the SpaceStat software designed by Anselin (1992) to create the data matrix and spatial weight matrices for our study area. For all the ESDA tests, we used five different weight matrices, each based on intercentroid distance, at 0.25, 0.50, 1, 1.5, and 2 miles. Therefore, in the 1-mile spatial weight matrix, for every x_i, all x_j that were within 1 mile were nonzero elements (equal to 1 in the unstandardized matrix) in the weights matrix (WCON1). Similarly, four other weight matrices were created with 0.25, 0.50, 1.5, and 2 miles, respectively, as the cutoff points (i.e., WCON025, WCON050, WCON1.5, and WCON2). The Moran's I values resulting from these three weights matrices are shown in Table 6.1, and they clearly indicate that the distribution of burglaries in both months exhibited strong positive spatial auto-correlation (or clustering of high values with high values and low values with low values). Table 6.1 also contains data for a sixth cutoff distance of 0.125 miles; the low (but significant) z scores for this cutoff distance indicate that clustering effects become weak at such small distances for these given spatial conditions (dense urban settlements). Hence, we have not used the 0.125-mile cutoff data for any further analysis.

THE MORAN SCATTERPLOT

Moran's I provides an indication of whether similar values are spatially clustered—that is, high values are close to each other and low values are close to each other. Moran's I provides no indication of how each of the individual parcels that com-

TABLE 6.1 Moran's *I* Test for Spatial Autocorrelation (Normal Approximation)

Weights Matrix	Cutoff Distance (Miles)	Variable	I	Standard Deviation	z Value	Probability
WCON125	0.125	August	.6503	0.3324	1.965	.05
		November	.5613	0.3324	1.697	.09
WCON025	0.25	August	.3758	0.0661	5.727	.00
		November	.3510	0.0661	5.382	.00
WCON050	0.50	August	.2332	0.0305	7.728	.00
		November	.2655	0.0305	8.782	.00
WCON1	1	August	.2701	0.0166	12.663	.00
		November	.1874	0.0166	11.482	.00
WCON1.5	1.5	August	.1642	0.0108	15.475	.00
		November	.1497	0.0108	14.130	.00
WCON2	2	August	.1155	0.0081	14.543	.00
		November	.1122	0.0081	14.130	.00

NOTE: The variable August refers to the number of burglaries in each census tract in August. Similarly, the variable November refers to burglaries in November.

prise the study area has contributed to the global Moran statistic. In other words, the calculation of the global Moran statistic is a necessary first test in the ESDA process, but it provides no information on how individual parcels have contributed to the global statistic. A useful graphic device called the Moran scatterplot provides such local information, and it helps identify outliers (parcels with scores far higher or lower than the mean) and anomalous cases (in which the expected association of high-high and low-low values is violated).

In O'Loughlin and Anselin's (1996, p. 146) study of trade bloc formation, the authors provide an innovative example of the use of the Moran scatterplot, which "is a [plot] of the spatially lagged values of each observation $(Wx)_i$ against the observation x_i (with the x in the standardized form)." The lagged value $(Wx)_i$ is calculated as the weighted Moran of all neighbors *j* of tract *i* (in the case of the weights matrix WCON1, this means every parcel or tract whose centroid is within 1 mile of the centroid of *i*). When the standardized or *z* values of the lagged value are plotted against the corresponding observation, each resulting point is categorized into one of four quadrants. When spatial autocorrelation is not indicated, these points should form a random cloud around the origin. The lower-left quadrant includes points for those tracts whose crime rate is below the mean and whose neighbor's rates are also below the mean (a low-low autocorrelation). Similarly, the upper-right quadrant includes the high-high tracts—high crime tracts that are surrounded by high crime tracts. The outliers in these quadrants are interesting because they represent the extreme values of the high-crime and low-crime clusters. The upper-left quadrant includes those parcels with low crime values surrounded by high-crime parcels and

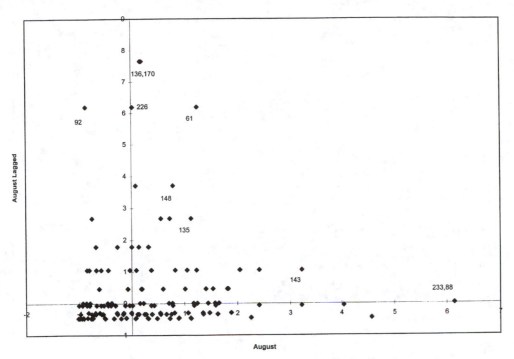

Figure 6.3. August Moran Scatterplot of Burglaries, 0.25-Mile Buffer

vice versa for the lower-right quadrant. The outliers in these quadrants are interesting because they represent parcels that are most dissimilar from their neighbors.

We created 10 Moran scatterplots for our data, 5 each based on the five contiguity files discussed previously for August and November. Four of these (November and August data at 0.5 and 1.5 miles) are shown in Figures 6.3 through 6.6. In these figures (and for the data not shown), it can be seen that the majority of points are in the lower-left quadrant. This indicates that for the majority of cases, as expected, low-crime tracts are surrounded by low-crime tracts. Also, as expected, there are many points in the high-high quadrant. In a clustered system, this type of distribution is typical—low values neighboring low values and high values neighboring high values. There are also several points in the low-high and high-low quadrants.

The extreme cases in these quadrants have been marked with their census tract numbers. Interestingly, the different iterations of the scatterplot exercise (for different months and for different contiguity matrices) reveal many different extreme value census tracts. Closer examination reveals that these are mostly neighboring or proximate tracts and helps identify zones of extreme values. For the August data, it is clear that Tracts 383 and 243 (both in the cluster of high-crime tracts west of the zoo and botanical gardens) consistently have lower crime values than those of their neighbors; this is especially clear when using contiguity matrices of 1 mile or longer. Determining why this is the case may affect police deployment or other policy decisions. Tract 383 also appears as an anomalous case for two of the five November scatterplots, again as a tract with low crime relative to its neighbors. Tract 421 (on the south border of the Mosholu golf course), however, appears as a

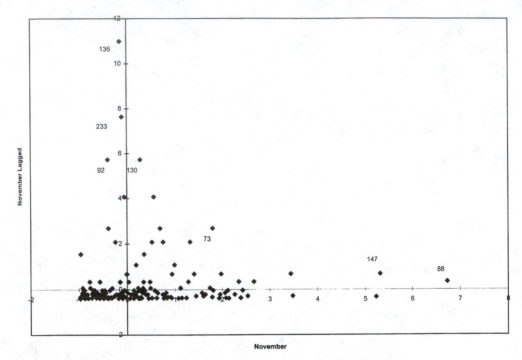

Figure 6.4. November Moran Scatterplot of Burglaries, 0.25-Mile Buffer

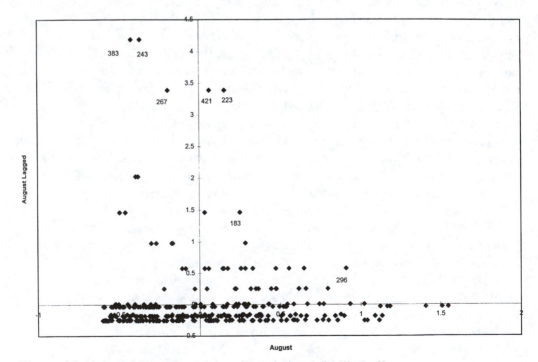

Figure 6.5. August Moran Scatterplot of Burglaries, 1.5-Mile Buffer

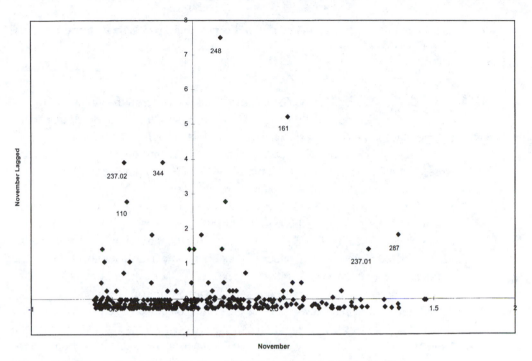

Figure 6.6. November Moran Scatterplot of Burglaries, 1.5-Mile Buffer

relatively high-crime tract in August with high-crime tracts surrounding it. Also, in two of the November iterations, Tract 225 (and its neighbor, Tract 226) appears as the center of a high-crime area.

THE G STATISTIC

A different approach to the measurement of spatial association was suggested by Getis and Ord (1992). Their family of $G(d)$ statistics is interesting for several reasons. First, these statistics can be used to identify areas of local instability. Second, these measures allow us to map what the authors call positive and negative spatial autocorrelation (respectively, the high-high and low-low values of the Moran scatterplot). The measure used here, the G_i^* index, allows us to distinguish between the autocorrelation of small values and the autocorrelation of large values. Formally, the G statistic for a chosen critical distance d is given by

$$G(d) = ij \ w_{ij}(d)x_i x_j / ij \ x_i x_j,$$

where x_i is the value observed at location i, and $w_{ij}(d)$ is derived from an unstandardized contiguity matrix derived, as before, from the critical distance d (which is the distance within which every j is considered a neighbor in the case of the numerator). In addition to this global measure, it is possible to derive a measure for every parcel i so that G_i is given by

$$G_i = j \ w_{ij}(d)x_j/j \ x_j.$$

A related measure is the G_i^* measure. The two differ in the number of observations that are included in the denominator. Anselin (1992, p. 23) noted that "(t)he G_i^* provides a measure of spatial clustering that includes the observation under consideration, while the G_i measure does not." According to O'Loughlin and Anselin (1996), the G_i^* measure is preferable for ESDA mapping to identify clusters and to visually examine for spatial nonstationarity.

The results of mapping the G_i^* measure are shown in Figures 6.7 through 6.10 (see web site). As mentioned previously, the 10 iterations refer to five critical distances each (at 0.25, 0.50, 1, 1.5, and 2 miles) for the August and November data. We plotted the high and low z values of the G_i^* statistic in a standardized form. The implication is that the low (negative) z value areas can be thought of as low-crime clusters, whereas the high z value areas are the high-crime clusters. Even a cursory examination of the maps reveals that as the critical distance is increased (especially for critical distances of 1.5 and 2 miles), the cluster patterns for both August and November begin to look very similar. The number of tracts that have significant z values also increases as the critical distance is increased, and the eastern edge of the zoo/botanical gardens appears to act as the border of the high- and low-crime zones.

This effect of greater inclusion with larger critical distances is expected. By increasing the critical distance, we are effectively defining larger neighborhoods and weakening the localized effects. This suggests that more effective tests of local instability should be conducted with lower critical distances for this set of spatial arrangements. Given that we earlier rejected the 0.125-mile cutoff as too low, we argue that the quarter-mile and half-mile cutoff distances are appropriate at this scale and density of settlement. It should be noted that with the critical distance at 1 mile or less, the patterns of clustering in August and November are somewhat different. With the 1-mile cutoff, there is a small cluster of high crime in the eastern half of the study area (in November), and the August high-crime cluster appears to be more clearly delineated (remember that August was the low-crime month).

TENTATIVE CONCLUSIONS

This exploratory exercise reveals the utility of the ESDA approach in at least two specific ways. First, using the G_i^* statistic, we are able to identify clusters (so-called hot spots) using assumptions and methods that are geographically and statistically robust. Second, we are able to identify tracts that are spatial outliers and that belong in clusters that are significantly different from the general study area. In all cases, these ESDA approaches offer substantially superior tests compared to other spatial and nonspatial tests because we are able to conduct standard statistical tests (such as for statistical significance) on the values derived.

In the specific example used here, the differences between August and November burglary patterns are less important than the similarities between them. That is, the spatial patterns of burglaries in November and August are generally very similar (the minor differences were pointed out earlier). Had we compared two different crime types, such as burglaries and drug sales or aggravated assaults, the general patterns may have been quite different. We encourage the use of these methodologies using different variables (by crime type, season/month, time of day, etc.) to examine whether different patterns result.

The next step in the analysis would be the use of CSDA approaches. The identification of spatial patterns using ESDA approaches on different variables (both independent and dependent) would help in the specification of models. The model thus specified is likely to be more robust, especially if one takes the effects of spatial dependence into account. Such models are often termed spatial autoregressive models and are increasingly being used in a wide variety of situations, including modeling fertility, migration, and urban population density (Arlinghaus, 1996). The eventual goal of analysis is to better inform policy and policing, and we submit that the use of the ESDA and CSDA approaches significantly improves crime analysis.

NOTES

1. Due to space limitations, only a fraction of the data analyzed and graphed are shown here.

2. In many instances, whether or not a crime incident is a point or a polygon may depend on the scale of mapping and analysis. In small-scale maps, even an event as large as a block fire may become a point, and only a larger event (e.g., a forest fire) may become a polygon. We will not refer to scale issues in general in the remainder of this chapter. The general assumption is that we will be dealing with urban data drawn at intermediate scales of approximately 1:10,000.

3. The overlay operation resulted in the loss of a few of the records from the original database. For August, 855 incidents of the 867 that were extracted were successfully overlaid; for November, the number of overlays was 1,168, whereas 1,183 records had been extracted.

4. The z value for Moran's I is given by $z = [I - E(I)]/SD(I)$, where $E(I)$ is the theoretical mean of I, and $SD(I)$ is the theoretical standard deviation.

REFERENCES

Anselin, A., & Getis, A. (1992). Spatial statistical analysis and geographic information systems. *Annals of Regional Science, 26,* 19-33.

Anselin, L. (1992). *SpaceStat tutorial: A workbook for using SpaceStat in the analysis of spatial data.* Morgantown: West Virginia University, (r)MD-BO_Regional Research Institute.

Arlinghaus, S. L. (Ed.). (1996). *Practical handbook of spatial statistics.* Boca Raton, FL: CRC Press.

Boots, B. N., & Getis, A. (1988). *Point pattern analysis.* Newbury Park, CA: Sage.

Chakravorty, S. (1995). Identifying crime clusters: The spatial principles. *Middle States Geographer, 28,* 53-58.

Cliff, A. D., & Ord, J. K. (1973). *Spacial autocorrelation.* London: Pion.

Getis, A., & Ord, J. K. (1992). The analysis of spatial association by use of distance statistics. *Geographical Analysis, 24,* 189-206.

Hirschfield, A. (1994). *Crime and the spatial concentration of disadvantage in northern Britain: An analysis using geographical information systems.* Liverpool, UK: University of Liverpool, Urban Research and Policy Evaluation Regional Research Laboratory.

Maltz, M. D., Gordon, A. C., & Friedman, W. (1991). *Mapping crime in its community setting: Event geography analysis.* New York: Springer-Verlag.

Odland, J. (1987). *Spatial autocorrelation.* Newbury Park, CA: Sage.

O'Loughlin, J., & Anselin, L. (1996). Geo-economic competition and trade bloc formation: United States, German and Japanese exports, 1968-1992. *Economic Geography, 72,* 131-160.

White, M. (1983). The measurement of spatial segregation. *American Journal of Sociology, 88,* 1008-1019.

Wong, D. W. S. (1993). Spatial indices of segregation. *Urban Studies, 30,* 559-772.

CHAPTER 7

Identifying Crime Hot Spots Using Kernel Smoothing

SARA McLAFFERTY
DOUG WILLIAMSON
PHILIP G. McGUIRE

For decades, crime analysts have used maps to identify *hot spots,* areas where crimes cluster in space and time. Hot spots are geographical areas that contain an unusually high concentration of crime events. In identifying hot spots, one can focus narrowly on crimes of a particular type or with specific characteristics or broadly on places where the overall risk of crime is high. Hot spot areas are of great importance for crime control and prevention. Experience in cities as diverse as Jersey City and Minneapolis shows that place-based strategies that target crime control efforts to hot spot areas result in a significant decrease in reported crime and calls for service (Kennedy, Braga, & Piehl, 1997).

In this chapter, we discuss a relatively new spatial statistical method, kernel estimation, which can be used to display and identify crime hot spot areas. Kernel estimation generates a smooth surface that represents variation in the density of crimes over space. Hot spots appear as irregularly shaped areas of high crime density, areas that can be analyzed in their own right to target crime prevention efforts and assess change over time in crime activity. This chapter describes our experiences in using kernel estimation to identify crime hot spots in Brooklyn, New York, and discusses technical and operational challenges in implementing the method.

METHODS FOR IDENTIFYING HOT SPOTS

The past decade has seen dramatic advances in the development of methods for identifying crime hot spots. Advances in geographic information systems (GIS)

AUTHORS' NOTE: All of the tables and figures to which this chapter refers can be found on the World Wide Web at http://www.urbanresearch.org

and spatial analysis make it possible to visualize and analyze real-time, geocoded crime information in ways unimaginable in previous decades. Two general classes of methods exist for identifying hot spots: area-based methods and point-based methods.

In area methods, crime data are aggregated into geographical areas, such as blocks, precincts, and census tracts. For each area, the analyst computes a measure of crime intensity, such as the total number of crimes and density in relation to land area, population, or opportunities. Location quotients can be used to describe the relative density of crimes by area (Brantingham & Brantingham, 1997). Using standard choropleth mapping methods, levels of crime intensity can be displayed to show geographical variation. Hot spots are areas, or groups of contiguous areas, with high crime intensity.

Area-based methods provide an effective means for identifying hot spots based on familiar geographical or administrative areas; they have several well-known limitations, however. Changes in the number and configuration of areas used can strongly affect the results: This is the modifiable area unit problem (Monmonier, 1991; Openshaw, 1984). Furthermore, area-based results are strongly affected by spatial uncertainty or error in crime locations. Even minor positional errors that result from mistakes in geocoding or incomplete address information can cause crimes to be misassigned among areas. Also, crimes that occur along area boundaries or at intersections may have no obvious assignment.

These problems are avoided using point-based methods because they work with point locations—the sites at which crimes occur—rather than aggregating locations to areas. One of the most widely used and innovative point-based methods is the Spatial and Temporal Analysis of Crime (STAC) system. STAC works by counting the numbers of crimes that occur in overlapping circles spread evenly across the study area (Block, 1995). *Hot circles* are circles that contain the largest numbers of crime incidents and *hot ellipses* identify the areas of densest crime activity. Many law enforcement agencies currently use STAC to summarize, visualize, and analyze the large quantities of spatial crime data that they handle on a continual basis (Block, 1997). Although STAC is the most well-known and widely used point-based method, analysts have examined other spatial clustering methods for crime analysis, including the Geographical Analysis Machine (Hirschfield, Yarwood, & Bowers, 1999) and Knox's test of space-time clustering (Canter, 1997).

Both the Geographical Analysis Machine and STAC use simple geometric shapes (circles and ellipses) for identifying hot spot areas. As a result, they have difficulty in pinpointing irregularly shaped hot spots. The spatial pattern of crime reflects the underlying uneven geographical distributions of streets, land use, population, housing, and facilities. Hot spot areas often bend and twist and are shaped by the local contexts that affect criminal behavior and crime opportunities (Eck, 1997). To identify hot spots more accurately requires spatial statistical methods that can capture these irregularly shaped areas. One general category of methods for accomplishing this is spatial smoothing.

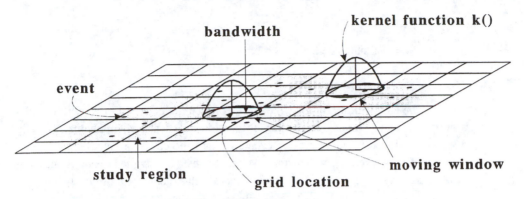

Figure 7.1. Visual Definition of Kernel Estimation

SPATIAL SMOOTHING

Spatial smoothing methods (SSMs) are methods for determining the density of point events (i.e., crimes) at different locations. Although crimes occur at discrete locations, the risk of crime exists almost everywhere. Thus, crime density can be viewed as a spatially continuous variable, with "peaks" representing areas of high crime (hot spots) and "valleys" areas of low crime. Spatial smoothing methods are used to generate such a continuous surface from point data. Simple SSMs such as quadrant mapping have existed for many years, but these methods have well-known limitations (Bailey & Gatrell, 1995). A superior approach is kernel estimation, a new and robust procedure for smoothing point data that has increasingly been applied in geographical epidemiology (Gatrell, Bailey, Diggle, & Rowlingson, 1996).

The goal of kernel estimation is to estimate how the density of events varies across a study area based on a point pattern. Bailey and Gatrell (1995, p. 84) note that "kernel estimation was originally developed to obtain a smooth estimate of a univariate or multivariate probability density from an observed sample of observations." In the spatial case, kernel smoothing creates a smooth map of density values in which the density at each location reflects the concentration of points in the surrounding area.

In kernel estimation, we begin by laying a fine grid across the study area. A circular window with a constant radius or *bandwidth* is moved across the study area, centered at each grid point (Figure 7.1). The density of events is computed within this circular window. Events within the window are weighted according to their distance from the center of the window, the point at which density is being estimated (Gatrell et al., 1996). Events located near the center have a greater weight than those distant from the center. In this way, kernel estimation reflects the underlying geographic locations of events within each window.

Let *s* refer to a grid point location. The density of crime events at grid point *s*, $\lambda(s)$, is estimated as shown in Figure 7.1 defined as follows.

$$\lambda(s) = \sum_{d_i < \tau} 1/t^2 \, k(d_i/\tau)$$

Where

$\lambda(s)$ = estimated density at grid point s
d_i = distance from point i to grid point s
τ = bandwidth

The bandwidth, t, defines the radius of a circle, centered on s, within which density is being estimated. The kernel function, $k()$, describes mathematically the weight assigned to points (crime events) within the circle in calculating density. Weight varies inversely with distance so that the weight assigned to any crime event decreases as its distance (d_i) from s increases. Thus, nearby events are given more weight in the density calculation than those farther away.

This means that density depends on both the number of crimes within a circle and their spatial configuration. Even if two grid points have the same numbers of crimes within their respective circles, if the spatial patterns of crimes differ then density will differ. A grid point with crimes clustered nearby will be assigned a much higher density than one with crimes more widely dispersed. In this respect, kernel smoothing differs from more traditional "binning" methods that simply count the number of events within regularly spaced circles, hexagons, or squares.

After computing kernel estimates of crime density for each regularly spaced grid point, one can generate a smooth map of density values. The results may be displayed as a standard contour map, a three-dimensional surface, or a continuously shaded raster map with gray or color tones representing density levels (LeBeau, 1995).

Figure 7.2 (on web site) presents a point map that shows the locations of robberies in the command of Brooklyn South for a 4-week period. During this period, 650 robbery incidents occurred in the command area. Because of the large number of incidents, it is difficult to interpret the point map. Although several concentrations of robberies are evident, differences in the numbers and intensity of events are unclear. In the densest areas, dots conceal other dots, giving a false impression of the true crime density. Although this problem can be addressed by using graduated circles—circles whose size is proportional to the number of incidents—when density is very high, even graduated circles can hide each other. By comparison, Figure 7.3 (see web site) shows a continuous map of crime density for the same data set that was created using kernel estimation. Distinct hot spots appear as shaded peaks on the map. Spatial variation in crime density across the study area is clearly visible on the smooth density map.

ADVANTAGES OF KERNEL ESTIMATION

The result from the kernel estimation method is a simple, aesthetically pleasing image from which users can identify hot spot areas based on contours of density (see Figure 7.3 on web site). Contour loops corresponding to high-density levels can be used to define the boundaries of hot spot areas, which can then be analyzed in their own right. A hot spot is an area in which crime density exceeds a critical cutoff value. Defined this way, the hot spots will often be irregular in shape. It is unlikely, unless the crime distribution is uniform, that the contours will be circles or ellipses as required in other crime clustering methods (Block, 1995). Under kernel smoothing, the hot spots encompass a uniquely defined area and are not limited to any jurisdiction or to any man-made boundary. The hot spots may cover several separate geographic entities, such as police precincts or sectors, representing the fact that clusters of crime often cut across political boundaries. Figure 7.4 (on web site) shows robbery hot spots (referred to on the map as "target areas") in Brooklyn South based on a cutoff density value of one robbery per two-block area. Sixteen hot spots appear on the map, the largest being Area 9, which extends north-south through the center of the region.

Once hot spot areas are defined, we can prepare charts and graphs that describe the characteristics of crimes located within each hot spot area, including the number of crimes, their locations, and the dates and times of their occurrence. Figure 7.5 (on web site) presents summary graphs of crime occurrence in hot spot Area 9 by shift, time of day, and week during the 4-week study period. This information can be useful in planning crime prevention strategies and in analyzing the impact of interventions on the numbers and types of crimes in the area. Also, analysts can zoom in to get a more detailed view of the locations of crimes within hot spots and to assess the links between crime occurrence and the locations of streets, buildings, parks, and other facilities (Figure 7.6 on web site).

Another strength of kernel estimation is its usefulness in analyzing change over time. Hot spots are not static. Rarely will the densities remain the same over time. Therefore, hot spots from multiple time periods can be overlaid and compared. This allows crime analysts to examine how hot spots change shape, size, and location over time. Again, this is invaluable not only for making deployment decisions but also for understanding the movements of crime within an area.

To evaluate whether crime density has shifted over time, the raster images of density at different points in time can be compared or used as input into correlation analysis or time series analysis. The correlation analysis can work in one of two ways. Two consecutive time periods can be compared (e.g., one month to the next), or one time period can be compared to a similar one (e.g., a month in a year could be compared to the same month in a previous year). Either way, the user would expect to see high values in an area from one period corresponding to high values in the same area for the other period. In addition, maps that show the change in crime density over time can be prepared. For each grid point in the image, we compute the difference in density values from one time period to another and create a "difference map" of the density values. These difference maps can be used to gauge the impacts of law enforcement interventions on local crime intensity and to depict the displacement, if any, of criminal activity from one location to another after interventions take place (Rossmo, 1995).

CHALLENGES

Although kernel estimation holds great potential for visualizing and analyzing crime patterns, there are several challenges in implementing the method in a law enforcement setting, including the choice of a radius, or bandwidth, for the region of influence; the selection of a cutoff value for delineating hot spots; issues related to comparing densities over time; and the boundary problem.

Selecting an appropriate bandwidth is a critical step in kernel estimation. The bandwidth determines the amount of smoothing of the point pattern. The bandwidth defines the radius of the circle centered on each grid cell, containing the points that contribute to the density calculation. In general, a large bandwidth will result in a large amount of smoothing and low-density values, producing a map that is generalized in appearance. In contrast, a small bandwidth will result in less smoothing, producing a map that depicts local variations in point densities. Using a very small bandwidth, the map approximates the original point pattern and is spiky in appearance.

Several rules of thumb have been suggested for estimating bandwidth. ESRI (Redlands, CA), the maker of ArcView, the only GIS software to incorporate kernel estimation, uses a measure based on the areal extent of the point pattern as the default bandwidth. Specifically, the bandwidth is determined as the minimum dimension (X or Y) of the extent of the point theme divided by 30, or min (X, Y)/30. Bailey and Gatrell (1995) suggest a bandwidth defined by 0.68 times the number of points raised to the -0.2 power scaled to the areal extent of the study area, or $0.68(n)^{-0.2}$. This can be adjusted depending on the size of the study area by multiplying by the square root of the study area size.

The problem with both these procedures for estimating bandwidth is that neither one takes into account the spatial distribution of the points. Bailey and Gatrell's (1995) estimate is based on average point density, but this is limited at best. Large sample sizes result in small bandwidths, whereas small sample sizes result in large bandwidths, but no consideration is given to the relative spacing of the points. The ArcView default is also arbitrary. Dividing by the number 30 appears to have no statistical basis. A more practical approach to selecting a bandwidth would take into consideration the relative distribution of the points across the study area. One way to achieve this is to base the bandwidth on average distances among points (Williamson, McLafferty, Goldsmith, McGuire, & Mollenkopf, 1998). Alternatively, one can use different bandwidths in different parts of the study area, an approach known as *adaptive kernel estimation* (Bailey & Gatrell, 1995). Small bandwidths are used in areas of high density to show detailed local variation in crime occurrence, whereas larger bandwidths smooth the point pattern in areas of low density.

In using kernel estimation to define hot spot areas, another important issue is to specify the "cutoff" value for hot spots. That is, what density value constitutes a hot spot? In a visual sense, imagine the three-dimensional surface of densities, with peaks representing high crime and valleys low crime. To distinguish hot spots, the user would have to slice the surface with an imaginary plane. There are an infinite number of planes that can cut the surface (these planes are analogous to the contours described earlier). The problem, then, is which plane (contour) should be used to define the hot spots. There is no statistical method for addressing this problem. Because the density values at each point are not independent, standard statistical tests cannot be used. Several options are available to the user, however. First, the

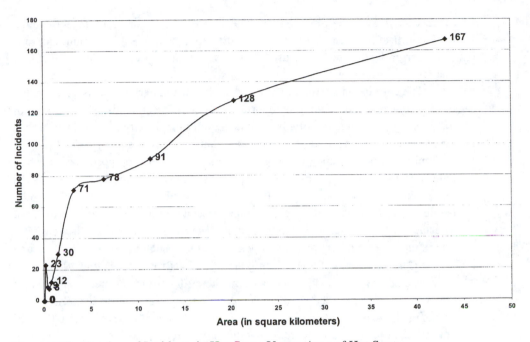

Figure 7.7. Number of Incidents in Hot Spots Versus Area of Hot Spot

definition can be made from a tactical standpoint. If, for example, the average patrol beat is a quarter of a square mile (0.5 × 0.5 miles) and, on average, there are 10 incidents per beat, then a logical density cutoff would be 40 (10/0.25 = 40). Any value higher than 40 would indicate above average criminal activity.

Another, more complicated approach takes into account the sizes of the hot spots. In this approach, the user is trying to find the smallest size hot spots that account for the largest number of incidents. By plotting the area contained within hot spots (contour loops) against the number of incidents in the hot spots for different cutoff values, the user can determine at which value the number of incidents dramatically changes (Figure 7.7). This inflection point then becomes an appropriate cutoff value to use in identifying hot spots. From Figure 7.7, a logical cutoff value would be 70 because, after this point, increasing the hot spot area does not result in a great increase in the number of crime incidents located in the hot spots. Both these approaches can produce meaningful results; they are not based on formal tests of statistical significance, however.

As stated previously, mapping and analyzing change over time is relatively easy to do with kernel estimation, but certain issues require attention. Using correlation analysis to assess the association between densities at two points in time is a straightforward procedure, but significance tests may be misleading. The t test used in testing statistical significance of correlation coefficients is dependent on the degrees of freedom, or $N - 1$. In the case of kernel estimation, N will be the number of grid cells in the image, which depends on the cell size. Consider a study area 10 × 10 km. If the grid cell size is 10 m, which is not unreasonable, the resulting kernel grid will be 1,000 × 1,000, for a total (N) of 1 million grid cells. The degrees of freedom in this case would be 999,999 and would suggest a high level of statistical significance, even for a very small correlation coefficient. To counteract this, a coarser grid cell size can be used, but information may be lost due to a lack of meaningful resolution.

The correlation coefficient provides a global summary of the association between crime densities, but more important for law enforcement is an assessment of local changes in crime density. Is the change in crime density in an area from one time period to the next statistically significant, or does it simply reflect normal random variation in crime over time? Addressing this question poses several challenges. Density values at various locations are spatially autocorrelated and thus not independent. Many standard significance tests require observations to be independent. Furthermore, without a long time series of spatial crime data, it is difficult to establish the normal variation in crime density over time for small areas. Researchers are currently exploring the use of methods such as control charting and Monte Carlo simulation for addressing these issues (Brown & Dalton, 1998).

A final challenge in using kernel estimation for defining crime hot spots is the boundary problem. Rarely will a study area be a regular geometric shape with data points in all areas. In calculating densities near the edge of the study area, the kernel estimator may operate in areas in which it should not, outside the study region. For example, the circular region of influence used in estimating density may extend into areas such as water bodies in which no crime exists. There are two possible solutions to this problem, both of which may be used in conjunction with one another. The easiest solution is to create a mask of "no data" so that whenever the operator reaches one of these locations, a value of no data is assigned. The other solution, which is more difficult, is to have a boundary or edge correction feature (Bailey & Gatrell, 1995). This adjusts the density values estimated for grid points near the boundary based on the proportion of the region of influence that falls within the study area. Regardless, care must be taken in interpreting density values near the boundary of the study area.

CONCLUSION

Crime analysts often face the daunting challenge of sifting through vast quantities of georeferenced crime information. Kernel estimation is a tool that can assist this process. The method harnesses the display and computational capabilities of today's computing technology to process crime information and represent crime patterns in time and space. Hot spots are clearly evident as areas of high crime intensity, areas that reflect the uneven social and environmental gradients that influence criminal activity. Maps created by kernel estimation also show hot spots within hot spots and thus offer a finer-grained display of the spatial distribution of crime than do existing methods.

Despite these advantages, using kernel estimation for crime mapping in a law enforcement setting presents many challenges. We have discussed in detail the various technical challenges to implementation; other issues, however, also require attention. Little is known about how policymakers perceive and analyze spatially smoothed crime maps and how they use such maps for decision making. Are smoothed maps more accurate and easier to interpret than maps created by more traditional methods such as pin maps or hot spot ellipse maps? Understanding how people interact with complex spatial statistical methods such as kernel smoothing in a law enforcement setting is an important topic for future research.

REFERENCES

Bailey, T., & Gatrell, A. (1995). *Interactive spatial data analysis.* New York: John Wiley.

Block, C. R. (1995). STAC hot-spot areas: A statistical tool for law enforcement decisions. In C. Block, M. Daboub, & S. Fregly (Eds.), *Crime analysis through computer mapping* (pp. 15-32). Washington, DC: Police Executive Research Forum.

Block, C. R. (1997). The Geo-Archive: An information foundation for community policing. In D. Weisburd & T. McEwen (Eds.), *Crime mapping and crime prevention* (pp. 27-82). Monsey, NY: Criminal Justice Press.

Brantingham, P., & Brantingham, P. (1997). Mapping crime for analytic purposes: Location quotients, counts and rates. In D. Weisburd & T. McEwen (Eds.), *Crime mapping and crime prevention* (pp. 263-288). Monsey, NY: Criminal Justice Press.

Brown, D., & Dalton, J. (1998, February). *Regional crime analysis program.* Paper presented at the Crime Mapping meeting, National Institute of Justice, Washington, DC.

Canter, P. (1997). Geographic information systems and crime analysis. In D. Weisburd & T. McEwen (Eds.), *Crime mapping and crime prevention* (pp. 157-192). Monsey, NY: Criminal Justice Press.

Eck, J. (1997). What do those dots mean? Mapping theories with data. In D. Weisburd & T. McEwen (Eds.), *Crime mapping and crime prevention* (pp. 379-406). Monsey, NY: Criminal Justice Press.

Gatrell, A., Bailey, T., Diggle, P., & Rowlingson, B. (1996). Spatial point pattern analysis and its application in geographical epidemiology. *Transactions* (Institute of British Geographers), *21,* 256-274.

Hirschfield, A., Yarwood, D., & Bowers, K. (1999). Crime pattern analysis, spatial targeting and GIS: The development of new approaches for use in evaluating community safety initiatives. *http://ds.dial.pipex.com/liv.strategy.*

Kennedy, D., Braga, A., & Piehl, A. (1997). In D. Weisburd & T. McEwen (Eds.), *Crime mapping and crime prevention* (pp. 219-262). Monsey, NY: Criminal Justice Press.

LeBeau, J. (1995). The temporal ecology of calls for police service. In C. Block, M. Daboub, & S. Fregly (Eds.), *Crime analysis through computer mapping* (pp. 111-128). Washington, DC: Police Executive Research Forum.

Monmonier, M. (1991). *How to lie with maps.* Chicago: University of Chicago Press.

Openshaw, S. (1984). The modifiable areal unit problem. In *Concepts and techniques in modern geography* (Vol. 38). Norwich, CT: GeoBooks.

Rossmo, K. (1995). Strategic crime patterning: Problem-oriented policing and displacement. In C. Block, M. Daboub, & S. Fregly (Eds.), *Crime analysis through computer mapping* (pp. 1-14). Washington, DC: Police Executive Research Forum.

Williamson, D., McLafferty, S., Goldsmith, V., McGuire, P., & Mollenkopf, J. (1998). Smoothing crime incident data: New methods for determining the bandwidth in kernel estimation. 1998 ESRI User Conference Proceedings, http://www.esri.com/library/userconf/proc98/PROCEED.HTM.

CHAPTER 8

The Utility of Standard Deviation Ellipses for Evaluating Hot Spots

ROBERT H. LANGWORTHY
ERIC S. JEFFERIS

Only recently have criminologists begun widespread use of spatial analysis techniques to understand crime data. This stems in large measure from a shift in emphasis from efforts to understand criminals to an effort to understand crime.[1] The drift toward a spatial focus is compelling because factors converge in space to produce crime. If we begin to understand the spatial characteristics and dynamics of crime, then we may be able to draw insights into the causes of crime.

Efforts at spatial analysis of crime, with few exceptions, have focused on the production of crime maps in various formats. Much of this work was a by-product of the National Institute of Justice-sponsored Drug Market Analysis Program (DMAP), which urged spatial analysis during the late 1980s and early 1990s to detect and monitor drug markets (see Institute for Law and Justice [1994] for an overview of the DMAP program). Although mapping is a reasonable first step in the spatial analysis of crime, it is important that the next step, inferential analysis of spatial crime data, be taken. This chapter explores the utility of one device for analyzing spatial data—standard deviational ellipses (SDEs).[2]

The purpose of this chapter is to examine the uses of SDEs in understanding program and project effects in crime analysis. Many criminologists have used SDEs to inform their studies, but these have been largely restricted to identifying "hot spots" (Block, 1993; Hirschfield, Bowers, & Brown, 1995) and describing aspects of spatial distributions (Langworthy & LeBeau, 1992; LeBeau, 1987). None have

AUTHORS' NOTE: The points of view expressed in this chapter are those of the authors and do not necessarily represent the view of the U.S. Department of Justice or the National Institute of Justice. All of the tables and figures to which this chapter refers can be found on the World Wide Web at http://www.urbanresearch.org

used them as inferential tools. Levine, Kim, and Nitz (1995), in an informative study of traffic accidents, uses centrographic measures as effective inferential tools, and their work shapes this chapter.

A SDE is a graphic representation of the co-joint variation of observations about major and minor axes in two-dimensional space. The major axis is the line of best fit rotated so that the correlation $r_{x,y} = 0$. The minor axis is the line perpendicular to the major axis through the mean center. Variation is the standard deviation about the major and minor axes. This graphic has many advantages compared to other depictions of spatial data. It describes the distribution in two dimensions rather than one, as does the standard radius, and it does not make the same level of assumptions about the two-dimensional distribution as do other statistics. Also, the ratio of the major axis variation to the minor axis variation produces a statistic, the coefficient of circularity (CC),[3] that describes the degree of linearity in the two-dimensional distribution.

These strengths are countered by two problems. First, the SDE is appropriate for continuously distributed phenomenon and is misleading if the distribution is multimodal. Second, although the CC is an interesting descriptive statistic, tests for statistical significance to compare CCs have not been developed. This chapter explores these two problems using data from the Bronx provided by the New York City Police Department.

This research analyzes an intervention to determine if a change in one variable affects the distribution of another variable. Because we were not in a position to make changes in the Bronx, we settled for contriving a change—whether school was in session or not. We wanted to determine if school being in session was associated with changes in the spatial distribution of burglary. The thesis is that the small percentage of school-age children involved in criminal activity might be reduced while school is in session. If this is true, we might well see a varying distribution of burglaries depending on whether school is in or out of session.[4] Although numerous factors other than school being in session may influence crime patterns, the following analysis can be used as a methodological example.

With this in mind, we selected burglaries occurring between noon and 6 p.m. during the period between April 1 and August 31, 1996, and divided them into four groups: Group 1, noon to 3 p.m., April 1 to June 15; Group 2, 3 to 6 p.m., April 1 to June 15; Group 3, noon to 3 p.m., June 16 to August 31; and Group 4, 3 to 6 p.m., June 16 to August 31. The resulting groups included the locational information for the following number of burglaries: Group 1, $n = 500$;[5] Group 2, $n = 383$; Group 3, $n = 427$; and Group 4, $n = 322$. Figure 8.1 overlays the spatial distribution of burglaries and SDEs for the total sample and for each of the groups on maps of Bronx precincts.

The analysis unfolds in two stages. First, we explore the global properties of the SDEs for the four groups comparing the "school in session cluster" (Group 1) to three "school out of session" clusters (Groups 2-4). This analysis is followed by another that focuses attention on variation within groups when clusters are examined. This analysis is designed to focus attention on within-group clusters that are defined by the Spatial and Temporal Analysis of Crime (STAC) system and by hierarchical cluster analysis.

8.1a. April 1 - Aug. 31 Noon - 6 p.m.

8.1b. April 1 - June 15 Noon - 3 p.m.

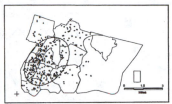
8.1c. April 1 - June 15 3 p.m. - 6 p.m.

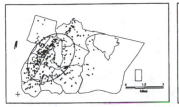
8.1d. June 16 - Aug. 31 Noon - 3 p.m.

8.1e. June 16 - Aug. 31 3 p.m. - 6 p.m.

Figure 8.1. Bronx Burglaries

We used several different software packages in the course of this research, including Systat, MapInfo, and PowerPoint. Systat "drew" ellipses that were then superimposed on MapInfo maps of the Bronx and imported into PowerPoint. Statistical analysis relied on Centro,[6] Systat, SPSS, and STAC. Systat and STAC were used to isolate clusters, whereas Centro produced centrographic measures of the distributions studied.

THE GLOBAL ANALYSIS

In the course of defining SDEs, many inferential statistics are produced. These statistics allow us to test hypotheses about means, variances (dispersion), and coefficients of circularity (the shape of the distribution). In program evaluation research, we ask the following: Has the center of the distribution moved? Has the distribution become more or less diffuse? and Has the shape of the distribution changed? In summary, we have powerful inferential tools to address the question, Has the program changed the spatial distribution of the targeted problem?

The global analysis attempts to determine if the distribution of burglaries changes when school is not in session compared to when school is in session. We compared the distribution of Group 1 burglaries to Groups 2 through 4 burglaries by examining the associated mean centers and shapes of SDEs. Table 8.1 presents statistics that describe the distribution of burglaries for the four groups.

Table 8.1 arrays a variety of statistics that describe the spatial distributions of burglaries in Groups 1 through 4. The mean center is the colocation of the mean latitude (X) and longitude (Y). The angle of rotation represents the degrees of rotation necessary such that X and Y are uncorrelated. The standard deviations of transformed X and Y are the standard deviation about X, the major axis, and Y, the minor axis, after rotation. The coefficient of circularity is the ratio of the standard deviation about X to the standard deviation about Y. Finally, the area of the ellipse is computed as $\pi \times s_x \times s_y$.

The null hypothesis that we are testing is that the spatial distribution of burglaries is the same regardless of whether school is in or out of session. To test this hypothesis, we compare the Group 1 mean centers, variances, and coefficients of circularity with those of Groups 2 through 4.

MEAN CENTERS

Tests for differences in group mean centers are performed using t tests that compare the Group 1 mean latitude and longitude to the other groups' mean latitudes and longitudes. Review of Table 8.1 highlights three differences: The mean latitude and longitude of Group 3 are different than those of Group 1, and the mean longitude of Group 4 is different than that of Group 1. This suggests that the mean center of the spatial distribution of Group 3 burglaries is slightly north and east of the distribution of burglaries when school is in session. Similarly, the center of the Group 4 spatial distribution of burglaries is slightly south of the Group 1 center. Furthermore, the differences are not after-school differences but differences associated with school being out of session.

DIFFUSE DISTRIBUTIONS

Tests for equality of variance allow us to explore the diffusion of the distributions. Comparing Group 1 standard deviations of transformed X and Y with Groups 2 through 4 standard deviations reveals two statistically significant differences. Group 4 is statistically more diffuse than Group 1 along the major axis (X), and Group 3 is more diffuse than Group 1 along the minor axis (Y). There are no statistically significant differences between groups in both dimensions, suggesting that the detected differences may not be substantial. As in the previous case, the detected differences are for the summer period when school is not in session.

SHAPE OF THE DISTRIBUTION

The CC describes the degree of roundness of a distribution. CCs approaching 1 indicate a circular distribution of points, whereas those approaching 0 suggest a linear distribution. CCs can be compared by testing for the equality of proportions. When the Group 1 CC is compared to those of Groups 2 through 4, no statistical differences are detected. Therefore, we conclude that the shapes of the distributions of burglaries are not different when school is in or out of session.

The foregoing contrived tests explore the possibility that school being in session affects the pattern of burglary. The logic of the tests is that if school shapes

TABLE 8.1 Standard Deviational Ellipse Statistics: Burglaries in the Bronx Between Noon and 6 p.m. During the Period Between April 1, 1996, and August 31, 1996

Group	Number of Observations	Mean Latitude (X)	Mean Longitude (Y)	Angle of Rotation	Standard Deviation of Transformed Y (×100)	Standard Deviation of Transformed X (×100)	Coefficient of Circularity	Area of Ellipse (×10,000)
April 1–June 15								
Group 1 (noon–3 p.m.)	500	−73.892	40.848	39.98	1.841	2.561	.719	14.804
Group 2 (3–6 p.m.)	383	−73.892	40.847	39.27	1.951	2.746	.710	16.822
June 16–August 31								
Group 3 (noon–3 p.m.)	427	−73.888*	40.853*	36.15	2.001	2.815*	.711	17.687
Group 4 (3–6 p.m.)	322	−73.891	40.845*	34.38	2.097*	2.785	.753	18.338

*Statistically different than group 1 at α = .05.

burglary patterns, this should be shown in varied spatial patterns of burglary. We tested this possibility by determining whether the centers of the distributions are different, whether distribution are more or less diffuse, and whether the shapes of the distributions differed.

We found some indication that summer distributions have different centers and are somewhat more diffuse than spring distributions, but the shapes of the distributions were the same. Also, we found that there were no statistically significant differences between school in session and after-school distributions. The overall similarity of the distributions that was apparent in Figure 8.1 is confirmed statistically in Table 8.1.

ANALYSIS OF CLUSTERS

One of the principal problems associated with centrographic measures is the distribution requirements. Like assumptions for parametric statistics, centrographic measures assume a continuous distribution of observations. Multimodal distributions in particular make interpretation of centrographic measures problematic. A bimodal distribution of points will produce meaningless mean centers, inflate variances, and depress coefficients of circularity.

It is often the case in social geography that phenomena are not continuously distributed. For example, it is not possible to have residential burglaries where there are no residences. Therefore, there are lapses in space where there are no residences, so it is not possible for the spatial distribution of burglaries to be continuous. In an effort to mitigate this problem, we explored two clustering routines: hot spot detection and hierarchical cluster analysis. The aim of this study was to isolate clusters of continuously distributed points and describe the resultant distributions as we did in the foregoing analysis. The tables presented in the following sections describe numerous clusters for each of the groups discussed previously. Because the purpose of this analysis is to demonstrate the utility of these statistics (rather than a substantive concern with the possibility that school might shape the pattern of burglary offending), however, we focus our discussion on Group 1 clusters.

STAC Hot Spot Clusters

STAC is an integrated statistical "toolbox" designed by the Illinois Criminal Justice Information Authority to support crime analysis (Block, 1993; Levine, 1996). The toolbox contains modules to conduct both spatial (SPACE module) and temporal analyses (TIME module). This study used the SPACE module to identify hot spots of burglary. Files containing members of each hot spot cluster were output to Systat and to Centro for further analysis.

Table 8.2 presents the statistics for hot spots of all four groups. STAC isolated two hot spots for Group 1 and three each for Groups 2 through 4. There are several

TABLE 8.2 Standard Deviational Ellipse Statistics: Burglary Hot Spots in the Bronx Between Noon and 6 p.m. During the Period Between April 1, 1996, and August 31, 1996

Hot Spot	Number of Observations	Mean Latitude (X)	Mean Longitude (Y)	Angle of Rotation	Standard Deviation of Transformed Y (×100)	Standard Deviation of Transformed X (×100)	Coefficient of Circularity	Area of Ellipse (×10,000)
Group 1 (noon-3 p.m., April 1-June 15)								
1	39	−73.901*	40.859*	21.32	0.278	0.350	.793*	0.305
2	46	−73.912*	40.846*	170.07	0.377	0.393	.961*	0.465
Group 2 (3-6 p.m., April 1-June 15)								
1	33	−73.907	40.851	32.91	0.241	0.438	.549	0.331
2	29	−73.914	40.837	123.25	0.314	0.882	.356	0.870
3	18	−73.878	40.827	9.31	0.154	0.186	.828	0.090
Group 3 (noon-3 p.m., June 16-August 31)								
1	41	−73.900	40.861	179.96	0.242	0.472	.512	0.359
2	27	−73.907	40.850	125.86	0.254	0.265	.958	0.211
3	12	−73.887	40.871	21.01	0.077	0.219	.353	0.053
Group 4 (3-6 p.m., June 16-August 31)								
1	25	−73.904	40.864	71.33	0.249	0.349	.714	0.273
2	21	−73.912	40.839	144.92	0.243	0.346	.702	0.264
3	13	−73.906	40.851	67.52	0.147	0.247	.594	0.114

NOTE: Statistical test for equality of means, variances, and coefficients of circularity are restricted to Group 1 hot spots.

*Statistically different pairs at α = .05.

points of interest in Table 8.2. First, we were able to produce the same range of statistics for these clusters as we did for the larger samples and therefore have the same range of inferential statistics available to us. Focusing on the Group 1 hot spots, it appears that the mean latitudes and longitudes and CCs of the hot spots are different. This suggests that the centers and the shapes of the distributions of the two hot spots of burglary are different. Also, it is apparent that this clustering procedure focuses on a small percentage of each of the group members (25% of Group 1, 21% of Group 2, 19% of Group 3, and 18% of Group 4). This clustering was expected because STAC is designed to focus attention on dense areas of activity.

Figure 8.2 displays the hot spot SDEs for Group 1 burglaries. The figure presents the total Group 1 distribution of burglaries (Figure 8.2a) and the hot spot ellipses (Figures 8.2b and 8.2c). The statistics presented in Table 8.2 are confirmed in Figure 8.2. It is apparent that the two hot spots are centered in different locations and contain very few Group 1 observations. What is not as apparent is that the shapes of the distributions are different and that the hot spots are equally diffuse—this information is most clearly gleaned from Table 8.2.

Hierarchical Clusters

Spatial clusters of burglaries were isolated using Systat's hierarchical clustering procedure and then output to Centro for analysis. Table 8.3 presents the statistics for clusters of all four groups. The clustering procedure produced five clusters for Group 1 and four for Groups 2 through 4.

As mentioned previously, we produced the same statistics used for the larger samples. Again focusing on Group 1, it appears that all the mean latitudes and longitudes of the Group 1 clusters are different from each other.[7] Also, there are statistical differences in cluster diffuseness and in the shapes of the distributions. Comparing the largest and smallest transformed X and Y variances (for X, numbers 2 and 5, respectively; for Y, numbers 4 and 3, respectively), we find that there are statistically significant differences.[8] This suggests that number 2 is more diffuse along the major axis than number 5, and that number 4 is more diffuse along the minor axis than number 3. Comparing largest and smallest CCs (cluster numbers 5 and 2, respectively), the shapes of the distributions vary and number 5 is more linear than number 2.

Unlike the STAC hot spots, the hierarchical clusters assign nearly all burglaries to a cluster. Ninety-seven percent of Group 1 burglaries are assigned to clusters, as are 96% of Group 2 burglaries, 99% of Group 3 burglaries, and 95% of Group 4 burglaries. Thus, in contrast to STAC, which focuses on areas of dense activity, the hierarchical clusters array the entire distribution.

Figure 8.3 displays the hierarchical cluster SDEs for Group 1 burglaries. Figure 8.3a is the distribution of Group 1 burglaries (the same as Figures 8.1b and 8.2a). This figure highlights the differences in centers, and it confirms that some distributions are more diffuse than others and that some shapes of distributions are different than others. Figure 8.3f provides additional information about this particu-

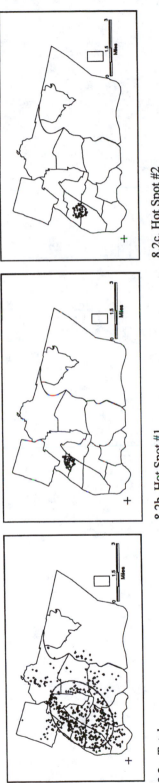

8.2a. Total

8.2b. Hot Spot #1

8.2c. Hot Spot #2

Figure 8.2. Bronx Burglary Hot Spots (April 1 to June 15, Noon to 3 p.m.)

TABLE 8.3 Standard Deviational Ellipse Statistics: Burglary Clusters in the Bronx Between Noon and 6 p.m. During the Period Between April 1, 1996, and August 31, 1996

Cluster	Number of Observations	Mean Latitude (X)	Mean Longitude (Y)	Angle of Rotation	Standard Deviation of Transformed Y (×100)	Standard Deviation of Transformed X (×100)	Coefficient of Circularity	Area of Ellipse (×10,000)
Group 1 (noon-3 p.m., April 1-June 15)								
1	137	−73.917*	40.834*	85.70	0.627	1.341	.468	2.640
2	147	−73.898*	40.862*	98.57	0.766**	1.089	.703**	2.619
3	83	−73.892*	40.827*	32.06	0.611	0.949**	.644	1.821
4	67	−73.862*	40.843*	95.68	0.713	1.425**	.500	3.190
5	49	−73.868*	40.884*	35.04	0.481**	1.267	.380**	1.914
Group 2 (3-6 p.m., April 1-June 15)								
1	96	−73.878	40.839	123.80	1.041	1.222	.852	3.994
2	34	−73.900	40.873	128.48	0.384	0.960	.400	1.158
3	183	−73.911	40.836	81.45	0.877	1.572	.558	4.329
4	54	−73.859	40.881	8.07	1.085	1.649	.658	5.618

Group 3 (noon-3 p.m., June 16-August 31)

1	69	−73.855	40.880	88.24	1.146	1.579	.726	5.682
2	74	−73.912	40.823	176.33	0.865	1.350	.640	3.667
3	222	−73.898	40.859	52.01	0.912	1.558	.585	4.462
4	57	−73.859	40.830	3.68	0.805	1.668	.482	4.216

Group 4 (3-6 p.m., June 16-August 31)

1	41	−73.866	40.833	17.80	0.713	1.151	.620	2.577
2	149	−73.906	40.851	58.93	0.849	1.439	.590	3.836
3	46	−73.867	40.880	52.55	1.007	1.489	.676	4.708
4	71	−73.905	40.816	17.71	0.654	1.457	.449	2.992

NOTE: Statistical test for equality of means, variances, and coefficients of circularity are restricted to Group 1 hot spots.

*All means are different from one another at $\alpha = .05$.

**Tests were limited to comparison of minimum and maximum values at $\alpha = .05$.

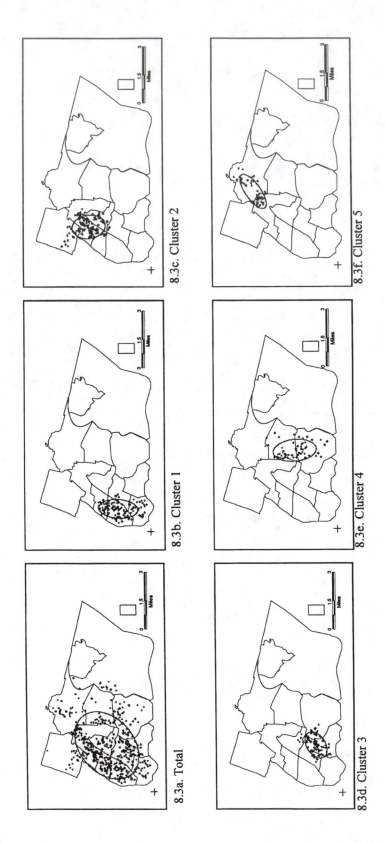

8.3a. Total

8.3b. Cluster 1

8.3c. Cluster 2

8.3d. Cluster 3

8.3e. Cluster 4

8.3f. Cluster 5

Figure 8.3. Bronx Burglary Clusters (April 1 to June 15, Noon to 3 p.m.)

lar cluster. It is quite probable that this cluster would be better portrayed as two clusters because this appears to be a bimodal distribution.

Table 8.4 presents the statistics for Figure 8.3f (Cluster 5) and its disaggregate parts, Clusters 5a and 5b. Splitting this cluster produces different results. First, splitting the cluster produces different mean centers and highlights the meaninglessness of the aggregate mean when the distribution is bimodal. Second, reviewing the angles of rotation suggests that the subclusters are oriented differently.[9] Third, the subgroups are less diffuse than the aggregate, and the shape of one of the subgroups (Cluster 5b) is statistically different from that of the aggregate cluster.[10]

Figure 8.4 permits graphic comparison of the bimodal cluster and its component parts and confirms the statistical analysis presented in Table 8.4. More important, the figure highlights a situation analogous to Simpson's paradox, wherein correlation of X and Y produces misleading results because X and Y are not drawn from the same population. In the extreme, a positive correlation masks negative correlations that are characteristic of the subgroups.[11]

CONCLUSIONS

This chapter focused on demonstrating some of the potential for inferential analysis of spatial crime data. We hope that in the future there will be articulated hypotheses about distributions of crime, and that these hypotheses will be subjected to rigorous statistical testing. There are, however, impediments to the routine application of inferential statistics to spatial data.

First, software that permits seamless integration of hypothesis testing and esoteric mapping graphics is not widely available. Indeed, in this project we were constantly exporting the proceeds of one analysis and importing them into another program. Mapping packages tend not to be very helpful for statistically comparing spatial distribution (IDRISI may be an exception), and statistical packages tend not to provide graphics output that can be readily mapped. The continued development of "tool kits" such as STAC will encourage more widespread inferential analysis of spatial crime data (see Chapter 13).

Second, we remain frustrated by our inability to develop a statistical test that would permit comparisons of angles of rotation.[12] Angles of rotation express the compass orientation of ellipses. Comparing angles would permit program evaluators and analysts to determine if different circumstances, such as treatment, time of day, day of week, and season, produce different spatial orientations. We had hoped that a procedure analogous to comparison of slopes would work, but this approach has proved fruitless to date. We hope that, in future spatial analysis tool kits, tests will be incorporated that permit statistical comparison of angles of rotation.

Finally, we hope that the discipline will be creative in extending the use of inferential statistics in the spatial analysis of crime. We believe, for example, that exploring the persistence of hot spots by comparing mean centers could be an effective technique. If the same mean center appeared at different times or in different

TABLE 8.4 Standard Deviational Ellipse Statistics: Burglary Clusters in the Bronx Between Noon and 3 p.m. During the Period Between April 1, 1996, and June 15, 1996

Cluster	Number of Observations	Mean Latitude (X)	Mean Longitude (Y)	Angle of Rotation	Standard Deviation of Transformed Y (× 100)	Standard Deviation of Transformed X (× 100)	Coefficient of Circularity	Area of Ellipse (× 10,000)
5	49	−73.868	40.884	35.04	0.481	1.267	.380	1.914
5a	28	−73.877*	40.878*	142.85	0.287*	0.473*	.608	0.426
5b	21	−73.857*	40.891*	71.44	0.407	0.655*	.621*	0.837

*Statistically different than Cluster 5 at α = .05.

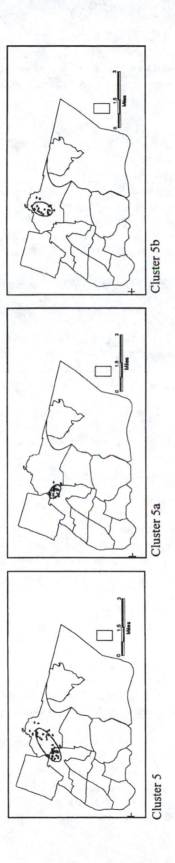

Cluster 5

Cluster 5a

Cluster 5b

Figure 8.4. Disaggregated Burglary Cluster 5 (April 1 to June 15, Noon to 3 p.m.)

circumstances, it suggests a persistent center of criminal activity. This kind of analysis could help isolate important factors that shape crime distributions and may indeed provide insights into interventions that could then be tested for impact.

NOTES

1. This focus on crime is a reasonable product of routine activities theory (Cohen & Felson, 1979), the emergence of environmental criminology (Brantingham & Brantingham, 1981), and interest in problem-oriented crime prevention (Clarke, 1992).

2. For general discussions of centrographic measures, see Hultquist, Brown, and Holmes (1971), Stephenson (1980), Lefever (1926), LeBeau (1987), Kellerman (n.d.), and Soot (1975).

3. See Hultquist et al. (1971) for a more complete discussion of the coefficient of circularity.

4. We would have preferred to focus on residential burglary, but the data did not allow this possibility.

5. Centro restricts the number of cases to 500 or fewer. This group actually included 503 cases from which 500 were randomly selected.

6. Centro is a statistical package that computes centrographic measures. Originally written in FORTRAN for an IBM 360, James LeBeau ported it over for DOS-based personal computers in the mid-1980s.

7. One-way analysis of variance with Scheffe post hoc tests was used to determine which means, if any, were statistically different from others.

8. See Glass and Hopkins (1984) for a discussion of the Hartley F_{max} test for the homogeneity of variances.

9. See discussion concerning statistical tests for the angle of rotation. Although the observed difference between angles seems pronounced, we do not know of a statistical test that permits statistical comparison.

10. The z score for the difference between subgroup 5a and the total cluster is -1.93, which is statistically different at \alp = .1.

11. For a detailed discussion of Simpson's paradox, see Rossman (1996).

12. We are not the only ones to lament the lack of a test of the angle of rotation (Levine et al., 1995, p. 671).

REFERENCES

Block, C. (1993). STAC hot spot areas: A statistical tool for law enforcement decisions. In C. Block & P. Daboud (Eds.), *Workshop in crime analysis through computer mapping: 1993*. Chicago: Illinois Criminal Justice Information Authority.

Brantingham, P., & Brantingham, P. (Eds.). (1981). *Environmental criminology*. Prospect Heights, IL: Waveland.

Clarke, R. (Ed.). (1992). *Situational crime prevention: Successful case studies*. Albany, NY: Harrow & Heston.

Cohen, L., & Felson, M. (1979). Social change and crime rate trends: A routine activity approach. *American Sociological Review, 44,* 588-608.

Glass, G., & Hopkins, K. (1984). *Statistical methods in education and psychology* (2nd ed.). Englewood Cliffs, NJ: Prentice Hall.

Hirschfield, A., Bowers, K., & Brown, P. (1995). Exploring relations between crime and disadvantage on Merseyside. *European Journal on Criminal Policy and Research, 3*(3), 93-112.

Hultquist, J., Brown, L., & Holmes, J. (1971). *Centro: A program for centrographic measures* (Discussion paper No. 21). Columbus: Ohio State University, Department of Geography.

Institute for Law and Justice. (1994). *The Drug Market Analysis Project: Defining markets and effective law enforcement practices.* A draft report prepared for the National Institute of Justice by the Institute for Law and Justice, Alexandria, VA.

Kanji, G. (1993). *100 statistical tests.* Newbury Park, CA: Sage.

Kellerman, A. (n.d.). Centrographic measures in geography. In *Concepts and Techniques in Modern Geography* (CATMOG No. 32). Norwich, UK: Geo Abstracts.

Langworthy, R., & LeBeau, J. (1992). Spatial evolution of a sting clientele. *Journal of Criminal Justice, 20*(2), 135-145.

LeBeau, J. (1987). The methods and measures of centrography and the spatial dynamic of rape. *Journal of Quantitative Criminology, 3*(2), 125-141.

Lefever, D. (1926). Measuring geographic concentration by means of the standard deviational ellipse. *American Journal of Sociology, 32,* 88-94.

Levine, N. (1996). Spatial statistics and GIS: Software tools to quantify spatial patterns. *Journal of the American Planning Association, 62*(3), 381-391.

Levine, N., Kim, K., & Nitz, L. (1995). Spatial analysis of Honolulu motor vehicle crashes: I. Spatial analysis patterns. *Accident Analysis and Prevention, 27*(5), 663-674.

Norusis, M. (1993). *SPSS: SPSS for Windows base system user's guide, Release 6.0.* Chicago: SPSS.

Rossman, A. (1996). *Workshop statistics: Discovery with data.* New York: Springer-Verlag.

Soot, S. (1975). *Methods and measures of centrography: A critical survey of geographic applications* (Paper No. 8). Urbana-Champaign: University of Illinois, Department of Geography.

Stephenson, L. (1980). Centrographic analysis of crime. In D. Georges-Abeyie & K. Harries (Eds.), *Crime, a spatial perspective.* New York: Columbia University Press.

APPENDIX

Statistical Tests

- Test for equality of means (two means)—use t-test independent samples (Norusis, 1993, p. 254).

- Test for equality of means (more than two means)—use one-way analysis of variance with post hoc multiple comparisons (Norusis, 1993, Chapters 14 and 15).

- Test for equality of variance (two variances)—put the largest variance in the numerator and the smallest in the denominator (this is an arbitrary assignment as long as the test is nondirectional). Test $F = {}_{.025}F_{n1,n2}$ (Glass & Hopkins, 1984, pp. 262-265):

$$F = s^2_1/s^2_2.$$

- Test for equality of variance (more than one variance)—use Hartley's F_{max} test (Glass & Hopkins, 1984, pp. 265-266):

$$F_{max} = s^2_{largest}/ s^2_{smallest}.$$

- Test for equality of proportions (test for equality of coefficients of circularity) (Kanji, 1993, p. 25):

$$z = (p_1 - p_2)/\{P(1 - P)(1/n_1 + 1/n_2)\}^{1/2}$$

where $P = (p_1n_1 + p_2n_2)/(n_1 + n_2)$.

PART III

CRIME AND FACILITIES

As Charles Swartz pointed out in Chapter 4, analysts have long known that crime is not evenly distributed throughout cities, states, or nations. Why crime occurs more in some places than in others is a hotly debated topic. The four chapters in this part seek to go beyond identifying hot spots by offering various explanations for spatial variation in crime. Chapters 10 through 12 focus on the impact of various types of facilities—transit stops, schools, and public housing projects—on the crime patterns.

In Chapter 9, Thomas Kamber, John H. Mollenkopf, and Timothy A. Ross link crime and census data. After demonstrating two methods of identifying crime hot spots, the authors show how newly developed spatial regression techniques help explain the causes of residential burglary patterns. The authors find that the two best predictors of the number of burglaries in a census tract are the number of housing units in the tract and the number of burglaries in neighboring tracts. Demographic variables, such as income and race, were much less reliable predictors.

Jeffrey Fagan and Garth Davies discuss the relationship between crime and public housing projects in Chapter 10. Contrary to popular stereotypes, the authors report that many factors, including median age, income, and degree of criminal violence, vary between public housing projects. The authors find that although crime rates within public housing projects are not uniformly high, the areas immediately surrounding the projects tend to be especially dangerous. Although disturbing, the authors point out that more information is needed to substantiate a causal relationship between crime and public housing.

In Chapter 11, Carolyn Rebecca Block and Richard Block examine the influence of rapid transit stops on street robbery patterns. The presence of elevated railway stops in Chicago and subway stations in New York appears to increase the likelihood of street robberies in surrounding areas. As Fagan and Davies demonstrate for housing projects, Block and Block show that the facility in question may increase crime rates more in nearby zones than in the stations or housing projects themselves.

Dennis W. Roncek, in Chapter 12, reports on his statistical analysis of the relationship between robbery and various types of schools. He finds that blocks containing schools or blocks adjacent to blocks containing schools have more robberies than those that do not, but the impact varies substantially depending on whether the school is public or private and elementary or secondary. Roncek also finds that although schools are statistically related to robberies, the association is not strong once other factors are taken into account.

Each of these chapters contributes to our understanding of the causes of crime. The strongest impression they make collectively, however, is the degree of complexity involved in identifying causes of crime. What makes crime so difficult to combat, perhaps, is the number of factors that contribute to its occurrence.

CHAPTER 9

Crime, Space, and Place

An Analysis of Crime Patterns in Brooklyn

THOMAS KAMBER
JOHN H. MOLLENKOPF
TIMOTHY A. ROSS

Technological advances present new opportunities for analysts to explain the spatial distribution of crime events. This chapter explores several techniques that allow for a better understanding of where crime incidents occur and what factors are associated with particular crimes. Specifically, we examine block aggregation, local indicators of spatial autocorrelation (LISA), and spatial regression to show how they can be used to identify crime clusters and to test theoretical explanations for the causes of crime. In addition to crime data provided by the New York City Police Department (NYPD), we also incorporate data sets created by the United States Census Bureau.

DATA SETS

NYPD Crime Data

The Brooklyn data set used in this chapter consists of 58,744 felonies, including assault (16.6% of the incidents), burglary (25.8%), grand larceny auto (21.6%), grand larceny (11.4%), rape (1.3%), and robbery (23.2%), reported during 1997. The data are derived from the NYPD's on-line complaint system and were originally used in the much-heralded COMPSTAT process (Bratton, 1998; see Chapter 2). The data set provides much information specific to each crime incident, including

AUTHORS' NOTE: All of the tables and figures to which this chapter refers can be found on the World Wide Web at http://www.urbanresearch.org

address, date and time, shift, and if a gun was involved. This allows analysts to identify temporal hot spots: Grand larceny and burglary occur less frequently on weekends (perhaps because people are home to protect their possessions), whereas as many as 25% more assaults and 30% more rapes take place on Saturday than on any other single day of the week. In summary, the crime incident data set used for this project is one of the most accurate and precise databases constructed by a big-city police department.

1990 Census Data

Despite controversy concerning the undercount of low-income and especially minority areas in the 1990 census, the data from the decennial census are significantly more thorough than any other source available. At the tract level, the census reports many critical characteristics, including precise breakdowns of age, gender, race, ethnicity, income, and family structure. In addition, the census also contains housing data concerning occupancy status, resident status (owned or rented), median building age, and housing value.

The primary weakness in using 1990 census data for this project involves the mismatch between times of collection. In a mobile and immigrant-rich city such as New York, matching data collected at times separated by 9 years introduces an element of error. This situation, however, may not be as problematic as some might expect. According to the Census Bureau's Current Population Survey, Brooklyn's population total remained virtually unchanged from 1990 to 1997. Although considerable turnover may occur during 9 years, neighborhood characteristics tend to remain stable. Changes in the housing stock take place at a relatively slow rate, and the housing stock significantly influences the characteristics of a neighborhood. High-rent, high-density areas with many studio and one-bedroom apartments in 1990, for example, are likely to continue to house many young urban professionals in 1997, although the high rate of mobility among this group may mean that few of the 1990 inhabitants still live in the neighborhood. The process of neighborhood change usually takes place incrementally, and both expansion and contraction of existing communities tend to occur on the margins as residents of the same ethnicity (especially immigrants) and class tend to cluster together.[1] In terms of presenting analysis techniques, the accuracy of the data is of lesser importance.

CRIME ANALYSIS TECHNIQUES USING COMPUTER MAPPING

Data Aggregation

Problems With Point-Level Data

Many police departments, including the NYPD, now geocode crime incident locations. This allows crime analysts to determine precisely where a particular crime occurred and, by using the information tools supplied with most geographic information systems (GIS), learn precise details about specific crimes. There are, however, several drawbacks to relying on point-level data alone. Crimes at the same location may cover one another, disguising the extent of crime at a particular address. Using graduated dots may help alleviate this problem, but graduated dots may overlap smaller dots, again leading to misinterpretation. These difficulties are exacerbated by the subjective nature of identifying clusters based on point-level data alone. Examining large areas or long time periods that encompass a high number of crime incidents magnifies these problems.

Aggregating to Census Geographies

Many GIS packages, such as MapInfo and ArcView, allow users to easily aggregate the number of points in a polygon. Typically, police departments aggregate their crime data to the precinct level. The data can then be used to examine trends and in some cases evaluate performance (see Chapter 2). Using other units of aggregation and incorporating demographic data from the census, however, produces more revealing maps that identify hot spots and provide the foundation for further analysis. The following examples show how aggregating crime data by census geographies, such as tracts and blocks, can extract kernels of knowledge out of the mass of information collected by law enforcement.

Brooklyn contains more than 2 million people divided into 789 census tracts. The average tract contains approximately 3,000 people, although some tracts are home to more than 10,000 people and others contain none at all. A point map of the 11,824 residential burglaries reported in Brooklyn in 1997 suggests that residential burglary is a widely dispersed crime not concentrated in any particular neighborhood. Indeed, the overlay of residential burglary points on the map obscures most other features.

Once the points are aggregated to the tract level, however, a different pattern appears. A thematic map showing the deciles of residential burglaries by census tract (Figure 9.1) indicates that this crime tends to concentrate in the central part of Brooklyn, east of Prospect Park. The periphery of the borough, parts of which contain commercial and industrial areas, has fewer residential burglaries. Parts of the periphery, however, contain individual tracts with many burglaries, as revealed by the darker areas in parts of Coney Island on the borough's southern rim.

The great advantage of using tracts, of course, is the ability to link data from the decennial census. Figure 9.2 shows a map similar to that in Figure 9.1, except that it uses residential burglaries per 1,000 residents instead of a simple count of crimes.[2] Figure 9.2 shows that although the central part of Brooklyn has a high number of incidents, on a per person basis residential burglary is much less concentrated. Indeed, a map of Brooklyn's population appears very similar to the map of burglary incidents (Figure 9.1). Linking the census data with the crime data indicates that central Brooklyn experiences more residential burglaries in part because it contains more targets than other sections of the borough. Rates, however, should be used carefully. Areas with low populations but high amounts of foot traffic, such as commercial strips, industrial zones, and parks, usually have inflated rates for

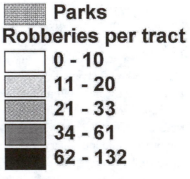

Figure 9.1. Residential Burglaries by Census Tract, Brooklyn, 1997.
SOURCE: New York City Police Department. (Cartography: Timothy Ross).

Parks
Robberies per tract

	0 - 2.405
	2.405 - 4.016
	4.016 - 5.285
	5.285 - 6.944
	6.944 - 29.851

Figure 9.2. Residential Burglaries per 1000 Residents, Brooklyn, 1997.
SOURCE: New York City Police Department. (Cartography: Timothy Ross).

many crimes. In addition, there are many other factors that might account for the number of crimes and crime rates, as Swartz's review indicates (see Chapter 4). Aggregating to the tract level, however, reveals important information. Crime analysts can identify tracts with a high number of crimes or crime rates and then create profiles of these tracts using the wide range of descriptive variables available at the tract level.[3] We discuss this issue in-depth later.

Tract-level information may show interesting patterns that are useful to crime analysts, but the tract itself has little relevance to beat cops or their supervisors. Tracts do not follow police precinct or sector boundaries, and they are often too large to aid in deployment decisions. Aggregating data to census blocks solves this problem: Block maps, with few exceptions, are identical to street maps.

Block maps are simple to use and understand, and they allow for the precise delineation of crime hot spots. Figure 9.2 shows residential burglaries aggregated to the block level. The large hot spot east of Prospect Park identified at the tract level (Figure 9.1) appears to be considerably different on the block map. Instead of identifying the entire area as crime ridden, the block map reveals that some blocks experienced as many as 24 burglaries, whereas 12 adjacent blocks in the same area experienced only 15 burglaries combined. This is especially revealing for a crime such as residential burglary, which has few mistaken incident locations compared to grand larceny auto and other crimes in which a victim or witness may not precisely recall where a crime took place.

The precise definition of hot spots made possible by using block maps is partially offset by four drawbacks. First, block size varies. In some cases, one census block incorporates an entire development that has internal streets that do not appear on city maps. Large blocks may have high numbers of crime incidents but are not especially hot compared to their less expansive counterparts. Another drawback is the small but noteworthy chance that block-level maps will not identify a crime-infested area. Relatively few incidents lead to a block being identified as a hot spot. In Figure 9.2, for example, a block experiencing seven residential burglaries was categorized in the top three deciles. If adjacent block faces (two sides of the same street but in different blocks) have five incidents each, and the rest of each block has no incidents, neither block appears as a hot spot even though parts of each block clearly have a problem.[4] In our experience, this is less of a drawback for maps plotting a year's worth of data. For short time periods such as a month, the probability of missing a hot spot increases as the number of incidents required to reach hot spot status declines.

Indeed, a third weakness of the block technique is that it usually does not lend itself to analysis using short time periods because it is difficult to differentiate between statistical noise (a block coincidentally having a high number of crimes during a month) and a genuine hot spot. In addition, the opportunities for more in-depth analysis are limited because the Census Bureau releases only a small amount of information at the block level. Finally, unless printed on a plotter capable of poster-sized maps, the usefulness of block maps is limited to relatively small area sizes.

These potential drawbacks are not lethal flaws, but they indicate that analysts should be certain they are using aggregation techniques appropriately. The methods discussed previously provide crime analysts at the local and citywide level with a quick and inexpensive way to identify hot spots. City planning departments usually have tract- and block-level maps, which are also available from commercial vendors. Most GIS software packages contain aggregation tools, and little programming is necessary. These advantages do not apply to the techniques discussed later, which require specialized software and at least some statistical training and may have greater utility for criminologists and researchers.

Using Local Indicators of Spatial Autocorrelation to Identify Crime Hot Spots

Most social science data contain some spatial characteristics. Until the recent advent of inexpensive technology for mapping and data analysis, most researchers ignored the spatial aspects of their data. Anselin and Hudak (1992), for example, argue that spatial autocorrelation and other spatial effects occur frequently but are often left out of empirical analysis. This section shows how spatial autocorrelation can be used to identify crime hot spots. Readers interested in this subject should also see Chapter 6.

Spatial autocorrelation exists when the value of a variable is associated with the values in neighboring geographic areas. Consider an example in crime analysis. Dunn (1980) points out that many studies focus on the relationship between socioeconomic status, family structure, ethnicity, and crime. Such studies often conclude that low-socioeconomic-status areas have more crime, and high-status areas have less crime. It may be, however, that criminal activity is spatially correlated: When crime in one area is high, crime in neighboring areas is also high independent of the socioeconomic characteristics of the neighboring area. Theoretically, low-status areas might be located closer to high-crime industrial sites and suffer from spillover effects. The predicted crime rates for the neighboring areas would be correlated with that of their neighbors. The errors would not be independent, and the analysis would suffer from spatial autocorrelation. Not only does most empirical work usually fail to take this possibility into account but also popular commercial statistical and GIS software packages are only beginning to incorporate basic tests for spatial effects (Anselin, 1995a; Anselin & Getis, 1992; see Chapter 13).

At least two LISAs test for the presence of spatial autocorrelation—Geary's c and Moran's I. Anselin, a recognized expert in this field, recommends using Moran's I (for the formula, see Odland, 1987, p. 10).[5] Moran's I can be calculated both globally and locally. The global Moran indicates whether all values have some degree of spatial autocorrelation. The local Moran indicates whether the values observed at a particular location are associated with those observed at neighboring locations. The distinction between the two versions is that the global statistic measures the autocorrelation in the entire data set, whereas the local Moran measures autocorrelation for a specific subunit. It is possible, for example, that crime may be randomly dispersed except in certain areas. For the whole data set, the global Moran may be small, but the local Moran may be high for certain polygons.

In crime analysis, Moran's *I* can measure the level at which crime is associated with neighboring places rather than randomly distributed. In other words, it measures clusters. Positive values of Moran's *I* indicate that the number of crimes that take place in a polygon (e.g., a police precinct and a census block) is positively correlated with the number of crimes in neighboring polygons. Negative values indicate that the number of crimes in a polygon is negatively correlated with the number of crimes in neighboring polygons. A value of zero indicates no relationship between location and crime patterns. Positive values, then, may indicate a high-crime area surrounded by other high-crime areas or a low-crime area surrounded by other low-crime areas (a cluster pattern). High negative values indicate a high-crime area surrounded by low-crime areas or a low-crime area surrounded by a high-crime area (a checkerboard pattern).

We calculated the global Moran's *I* for burglary, grand larceny auto, and robbery data in Brooklyn by police sector. To compute Moran's *I*, we used SpaceStat 1.80, a software package developed by Luc Anselin (Anselin, 1995b). (For information concerning SpaceStat, see Chapter 13.) For details on calculating Moran's *I* using SpaceStat, see Chapter 6. The global Moran value for all types of burglary is .31, for grand larceny auto .13, and for robbery .52. These values suggest that grand larceny auto tends to be dispersed, whereas robbery has a concentrated spatial distribution.

We then focused on residential burglary. After calculating local Moran *I*'s for each tract, we mapped the Moran values for the number of residential burglaries and the rate of residential burglaries per 1,000 housing units. We also segmented the data by season to determine if concentrations of residential burglary varied by time of year. We computed Moran values for spring, summer, fall, and winter. The full-year Moran maps for the number of residential burglaries indicate a mean score of .44. This suggests moderate spatial clustering, a finding borne out by Figure 9.3 that shows central Brooklyn east of Prospect Park in darker colors. The mean Moran value after adjusting for the number of housing units (.0043) suggests that the rate of residential burglary is not clustered. In other words, knowing the residential burglary rate of one tract indicates nothing about neighboring tracts. Figure 9.4 (on web site), which shows that the majority of tracts have Moran values between −.0011 and .0007, supports this conclusion. The seasonal Moran values show remarkable stability. Mean Moran values ranged from .27 to .35, and the maps show a marked similarity. This suggests that regardless of seasonal variations in crime, the degree of clustering remains constant. At the block level, the values for Moran's *I* become more extreme. Nonetheless, the technique shows crime hot spot and cold spot concentrations identified by other cluster-identifying methods.

Using Moran's *I* values or other local indicators of spatial autocorrelation identifies crime hot spots in a statistically sophisticated way and can be used for a wide variety of data. There are several drawbacks to using this technique. The concept of spatial autocorrelation is not easily understood, especially by those with little or no statistical training. Even for those with mathematical skills, the negative scores are easy to misconstrue. In addition, Moran's *I* is affected by natural and man-made boundaries. Parks, cemeteries, and other places without residences, for

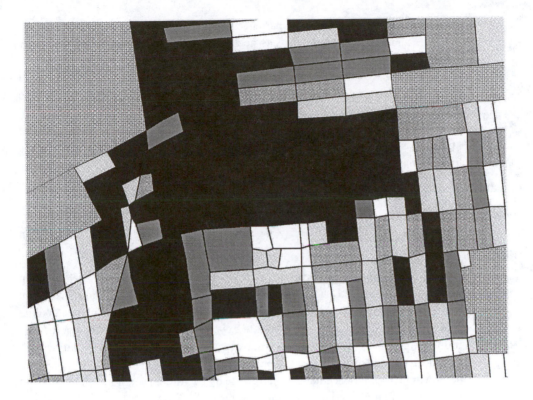

Figure 9.3. Residential Burglaries by Census Block, Brooklyn, 1997.
SOURCE: New York City Police Department. (Cartography: Timothy Ross).

example, have no residential burglaries and almost always have negative LISA scores. Prima facie, crime analysts know that no residential burglaries can occur in nonresidential areas, so the Moran value is not useful. From a criminological perspective, parks and other nonresidential areas might be better treated as missing data or nonpolygons, but doing so alters the geography on which the statistic depends. Moran's *I* and other LISA statistics can also be highly sensitive to the unit of analysis. In theory, LISA values at the precinct, tract, and block level may not be correlated, although we did not experience this phenomenon in practice. Finally, the database and software manipulations needed to calculate Moran's *I* are currently technically complex.

Although robust, Moran's *I* is not a statistic designed to explain the causes of crime. For such an undertaking, analysts may use regression analysis. Employing regression analysis on spatial data, however, introduces the possibility of spatial autocorrelation and many other difficulties. Although not yet fully mature, social and especially regional scientists have taken steps to develop spatial regression techniques.

Using Spatial Regression

We used SpaceStat's spatial regression function to examine the relationship between neighborhood characteristics as identified by the decennial census and crime patterns in Brooklyn. One of SpaceStat's advantages is the ability to calculate spatial lag variables, which are computed by taking the weighted average of surrounding polygons. Thus, a census tract with three neighboring tracts that had 10, 15, and 20 assaults would have a spatial lag of 15 [(10 + 15 + 20)/3]. Although not demonstrated here, SpaceStat can also create higher-order (neighbors of neighbors) weighted spatial lag variables (Sprague, 1998).

Spatial regression works poorly with crime rates because when even one crime occurs in areas with zero population, the crime rate for the area is infinity. In nonspatial regression, this problem is often addressed by eliminating tracts below a threshold population. Applying this technique to spatial regression, however, destroys the geography on which the technique is based. In our example, we use the number of residential burglaries per tract as the dependent variable and use the number of housing units as one of the independent variables.

We selected many variables that previous studies identified as significantly linked with crime (see Chapters 4 and 12). In addition, we created spatial lag variables for each of the variables in the analysis. Using all these variables in the regression equation, however, resulted in severe multicollinearity (the condition index exceeded 30). In addition, spatial regression analysis with these variables indicates a serious problem with heteroskedasticity, as measured by the LM Wald test. This is a common problem when using polygons that vary in size and shape. We narrowed our variable list to those we believed were theoretically interesting and suffered least from high intercorrelations.[6]

After considerable trial and error, and using various types of spatial regression offered in SpaceStat, we produced the following results (Table 9.1):

Dependent variable: Number of residential burglaries in tract

Observations: 789

R-squared: .5541

TABLE 9.1 Spatial Regression Output

Variable	Coefficient	Standard Deviation	z Value	Probability
Constant	6.6638	.5124	13.00	.000
Spatial lag for burglaries	8.6902	.5767	15.07	.000
Housing units	0.0080	.0007	11.94	.000
Single adults	−0.0120	.0062	−1.94	.052
Non-Hispanic black	0.0000	.0005	0.05	.960
Spatial lag for non-Hispanic blacks	1.629	.9026	1.80	.071
Single parents	0.0010	.0031	3.19	.001
Spatial lag for single parents	−2.86	.8719	−3.28	.001

The *R*-squared value of .55 indicates that these variables explain a large amount of the variation in crime. As indicated by the z values, the most important variables in explaining residential burglaries are the number of burglaries in surrounding tracts and the number of housing units. The racial variables used, the number of non-Hispanic blacks, and the spatial lag for non-Hispanic blacks show that neither variable is significant at .01 and that, even if they were, the variables play a very small role in determining the level of neighborhood victimization. The number of single adults also showed little connection to crime and was insignificant at the .01 level.

The number of single parents in a tract, as expected, showed a moderate association with higher levels of residential burglary, and this finding is significant at the stringent standard of .005. This finding supports a theory that asserts that areas with more single parents have a greater number of unguarded apartments and fewer "eyes on the street" when those single parents leave their apartments for work. The analysis indicates, however, that the effect of high numbers of single parents does not spill over into surrounding tracts. The negative z value for the spatial lag of the single parents variable suggests that tracts located next to tracts with high numbers of single parents actually have moderately lower rates of residential burglary. This might be explained by the availability of "soft targets" in nearby (high single parent) areas that deflect the attention of burglars.

Although we believe that these results may have some validity, they are shown here primarily for purposes of demonstration. We add this caveat in part because of the mismatch between the times of data collection and the numerous other factors that influence criminal activity, but also because there are many problems with spatial regression that have not been solved. Spatial regression, like standard ordinary least squares regression, can predict a negative number of crime incidents in some polygons and a positive number of incidents in others in which crime incidents may not be possible (e.g., residential burglaries in parks). In general, spatial regression does not work well with discontinuous distributions, nor is there a way to incorporate time series data. Heteroskedasticity is frequently encountered when using differently shaped polygons. Finally, using spatial lags can be problematic unless a "geosocial" island is being studied. The northeast perimeter of Brooklyn, for example, is bounded by Queens, but none of the Brooklyn perimeter tracts incorporate data from Queens into the spatial lag variables. This is not just a geographic problem: Islands may have bridges, subways, or other connections that are not incorporated into the analysis.

Despite these drawbacks, the potential for using spatial regression as a tool for crime research is impressive and worth further exploration. Combining census and crime data into a spatial regression might allow researchers to narrow the long list of characteristics associated with crime identified by Swartz (see Chapter 4) to the most significant causal factors. It would also allow more rigorous testing of theories that would provide guidance for a broad range of public safety policies. Furthermore, other types of databases, such as liquor stores and bars, can be incorporated into the analysis.

SUMMARY AND CONCLUSION

As a package, applying these techniques allows us to glean a tremendous amount of information from raw crime data. We started by examining temporal clustering, and then we used aggregation techniques to identify individual polygons with high crime rates. This spatial clustering was augmented by LISA statistics to show areas of relative clustering—that is, where high-crime polygons were located next to other high-crime polygons. Finally, we used spatial regression techniques to identify variables linked to the root causes of criminal behavior.

Two contradictory challenges stand out for future research. First, crime analysts and statisticians need to continue to refine and strengthen the methodological techniques in crime analysis. Crime is a multifaceted and complex phenomenon, and although the techniques discussed in this book are very powerful, more elaborate methodologies that can solve many of the problems identified here and elsewhere need development. A second challenge involves mainstreaming crime mapping technology. As calculations inside computers become more complicated, their presentation to police officers and administrators needs to be further simplified. Although crime research has made many advances, crime mapping will be an even more effective tool when top officials, beat officers, and eventually civilians can use it easily and effectively.

NOTES

1. Housing discrimination and bank lending practices may also affect where certain groups live, but the overall result still holds (Massey & Denton, 1994).

2. In all the examples using aggregation, overlaying crime points is helpful at small units of geography.

3. To preserve confidentiality, the Census Bureau releases the most detailed information at the highest levels of geography and the least detailed information at the lowest levels. Tracts combine a relatively small size with abundant information and are likely the most useful unit for creating neighborhood profiles.

4. One way to circumvent this problem is to create a map that includes counts of crimes in a buffer zone surrounding each street segment. Street segments can be displayed with different thicknesses or colors depending on the number of crimes.

5. T. Ross attended a class taught by Luc Anselin at the Interuniversity Consortium on Political and Social Research in the summer of 1997.

6. With additional time, a factor analysis might have aided the analysis. For demonstration purposes, however, the example is useful.

REFERENCES

Anselin, L. (1995a). *SpaceStat Version 1.80 user's guide.* Morgantown: West Virginia University, Regional Research Institute.

Anselin, L. (1995b). *SpaceStat, a software program for the analysis of spatial data, Version 1.80.* Morgantown: West Virginia University, Regional Research Institute.

Anselin, L., & Getis, A. (1992). Spatial statistical analysis and geographic information systems. *Annals of Regional Science, 26,* 19-33.

Anselin, L., & Hudak, S. (1992). Spatial econometrics in practice: A review of software options. *Regional Science and Urban Economics, 22,* 509-536.

Bratton, W. (1998). *Turnaround: How America's top cop reversed the crime epidemic.* New York: Random House.

Dunn, C. (1980). Crime area research. In D. Georges-Abeyie & H. Jones (Eds.), *Crime: A spatial perspective.* New York: Columbia University Press.

Lewis-Beck, S. (1987). *Applied regression: An introduction* (University Paper No. 22, 10th printing). Newbury Park, CA: Sage.

Massey, D., & Denton, N. (1994). *American apartheid: Segregation and the making of the underclass.* Cambridge, MA: Harvard University Press.

Odland, J. (1987). *Spatial autocorrelation.* Newbury Park, CA: Sage.

Sprague, J. (1998, May 15). *Murder patterns in St. Louis.* Paper presented at the City University of New York Graduate School, New York.

CHAPTER 10

Crime in Public Housing

Two-Way Diffusion Effects in Surrounding Neighborhoods

JEFFREY FAGAN
GARTH DAVIES

One of the more enduring traditions in American criminology has been the study of the relationship between crime and ecological or contextual effects, broadly referred to as the "criminology of place." During its approximately 100 years of evolution, the criminology of place has come to be dominated by a specific concern for crime and violence in inner-city "slums" and "ghettoes" (Anderson, 1978, 1990; Park, Burgess, & McKenzie, 1925; Rainwater, 1970; Shaw & McKay, 1943; Suttles, 1968; Thrasher, 1927; Whyte, 1943). Studies in this vein have tended to examine street life in neighborhoods of concentrated poverty and high population density, in which housing conditions were substandard though privately owned.

Populated at first by European immigrants, and later by in-migrants from rural areas of the American South, the neighborhoods came to be defined by the nature of their housing, the concentration of poor people in the neighborhoods, and the elevated rates of health and social problems, including crime and deviance. Consequently, housing in community or neighborhood studies now represents a vector of risk and protective factors within a multifactorial theory of place (Bursik & Grasmick, 1993). Informal social controls (and "semiformal" social control in the form of tenant councils) in public housing, for example, are part of the social organization of place that influences individual developmental trajectories and the social contexts that regulate everyday interactions to motivate or restrain potentially

AUTHORS' NOTE: The authors are grateful to the New York City Housing Authority for providing detailed data on the public housing sites in the Bronx and to the New York City Police Department for providing the crime complaint data. All of the tables and figures to which this chapter refers can be found on the World Wide Web at http://www.urbanresearch.org.

violent interactions. Public housing projects also present places in which individual risk is concentrated and in which risks accrue beyond simply the sum of individual risks to create ecological risks. Gangs are one example of the exponentiation of individual risk.

In recent years, violence and public housing have been intimately linked in the larger political and popular culture of the United States. Built in the 1950s and 1960s to assist the poor and working poor to escape slum conditions, most housing projects are clusters of high-rise towers that were placed in neighborhoods already in the midst of significant social structural change. In contrast to its predecessors, public housing design recently has begun to include low-slung garden apartments, but these were also built in neighborhoods that traditionally were slums with high concentrations of many of the correlates of violence. Often, these were neighborhoods in which crime rates already were climbing and in which rapid population change and economic decline had changed the fortunes of neighborhood residents. In fact, because of the predominantly negative perceptions that accompany public housing in general, Hirsch (1983) argues persuasively that projects are normally confined to areas that are unable to resist them. By their very nature, areas of severe economic decline and social instability lack the political resources and social capital required to successfully challenge or resist public housing development.

Almost since its advent approximately 50 years ago, public housing has been conflated in the public imagination with crime in public housing projects, and the projects came to symbolize the dangers of inner-city urban life. In recent years, in both high- and low-rise projects, tragic episodes of violence have reinforced the notion that public housing is a milieu with base rates of victimization and offending far greater than those of other locales (Lemann, 1991). The focus of drug control policies on public housing tenants also has served to confirm the connections between public housing and violence. In the absence of systematic epidemiological analysis of violence in public housing, these stereotypical beliefs have prevailed and anecdotal evidence has driven policy debates on social and design policies for public housing.

With few exceptions (Holzman, Kudrick, & Voytek, 1996; Roncek, Bell, & Francik, 1981), there has been almost no research on crime and violence in public housing, and there is no reliable evidence that base rates are greater in public housing than in comparably structured neighborhoods with primarily private housing. Moreover, no theory has been developed that would explain why public housing would elevate risks of violence and other crimes. Many of the putative risk factors in public housing are prominent in criminological theories of place generally and, in more recent analyses, of person-place interactions. For example, the social structural and compositional factors proposed as covariates of crime and violence in housing projects are not unique to public housing but rather are critical elements in an extensive literature on communities and crime (Reiss, 1986; Sampson, 1987; Taylor & Covington, 1988). The sociological literature on social comparisons and concentration effects also encompasses many of the adverse features of high-risk neighborhoods that are evident in public housing (Crane, 1991; Elliott et al., 1996). The official eligibility criteria and social selection processes in public housing also contribute to a concentration of individuals with social deficits and below-average human capital.

Additional issues concerning public housing as a crime milieu are raised by the few existing studies on crime in public housing. First, public housing sites do not constitute uniform constructs. Contrary to the perception of public housing as monolithic entities bereft of individuation, there is both spatial and temporal differentiation in crime rates across public housing. Using data supplied by the New York City Housing Authority, Williams and Kornblum (1990) identified housing projects with widely varying crime rates. Second, public housing projects are not temporally stagnant but rather have crime careers not unlike communities generally (Quicker, 1992; Schuerman & Kobrin, 1986). The developmental processes of change in both violence and its correlates at the aggregate level in housing projects, and potential differences in trajectories of change across public housing projects, suggest that there are developmental trajectories of housing projects that influence their crime rates over time. For example, only one of the four housing projects in the Williams and Kornblum (1990) study was found to have consistently high crime rates during a 10-year period.

Third, problems in calculating population denominators may result in crime rates in public housing that are lower compared to those of the surrounding area.[1] Although total complaints and arrests for violence may make public housing appear more dangerous than the surrounding areas, the actual point estimates are likely to be far lower than those based on official occupancy. Moreover, although increases in the surrounding areas may influence violence rates within public housing, it is not known whether there are housing projects with stable low-violence rates in the midst of increasing rates in the nearby neighborhoods. These "edge" problems are difficult to measure, and there has been no research on the issues of proximity and contagion within and around public housing. In this chapter, a case study of one densely populated borough of New York City, we attempt to address some of the issues raised by previous research and expand the base of empirical knowledge regarding the association between public housing and crime.

BACKGROUND

Research on crime in public housing has been extremely rare in the criminological, housing, and urban affairs literatures. Newman's (1972) work on defensible space focused on design features of housing generally and their relationship to crime rates. His work fostered an "environmental determinism" in research on crime and public housing that eclipsed social research and behavioral explanations for variation in crime rates. With the exception of the Department of Housing and Urban Development's Urban Anti-Crime Initiative (1985), nearly all research on crime in public housing for approximately 20 years focused on design. For example, a series of studies by Brill and associates (1975, 1977a, 1977b) extended Newman's work, marking the only citations on crime in public housing for nearly a decade.

Newman's influence is still felt today, and his concepts are still influential: Holzman et al. (1996) analyzed data from 1,547 residents in public housing authorities throughout the nation and showed that the size of development appears to be more closely associated with major crime problems than does the type of building.

Research on the social components of crime in public housing has been quite rare. Sullivan's (1989) study of three Brooklyn neighborhoods included one that was a public housing project in which the homicide of a policeman in a stairwell led to intensified enforcement in public housing in that vicinity. Sullivan, however, focused on crime trajectories of individuals, and the comparison across vastly different housing contexts weakened any conclusions about the effects of public housing on crime. By the late 1980s, sharp increases in drug-related violence and the crack cocaine epidemic revived interest in the social dimensions of crime in public housing.

A revival of ecological research during this period led to the inclusion by a few scholars (Skogan, 1990) of public housing as part of the urban landscape of increased crime and violence. The popular and ethnographic literature also has included recent assessments of life in public housing and its effects on individual development and interpersonal violence. Lemann (1991) showed the critical role of public housing as a context of reception for in-migrants in the 1950s and 1960s in Chicago. Kotlowitz's (1992) moving portrait of life in the Robert Taylor Homes, also in Chicago, showed the effects on violence risks for adolescents from the confluence of economic deprivation, concentration effects, and social problems, including gangs and drug markets. Like Williams and Kornblum (1990), Kotlowitz's work also illustrated the importance of informal mechanisms of social control.

Several dimensions of "place" offer perspectives to explain elevated rates of violence in public housing and also between-project variation in these rates. First, public housing is a context in which there are spatial and social concentrations of poor people. "Concentration effects" have been evident in studies on antisocial behavior (Crane, 1991; Elliott et al., 1996; Tienda, 1991). Aggregation effects are compounded by the larger ecological contexts in which projects are sited; indeed, public housing developments often take on and amplify the characteristics of the surrounding neighborhoods. Clark (1965), for example, noted the high rates of low socioeconomic status, "no father present," and welfare households in housing projects in Harlem in northern Manhattan. The existence of public housing developments may also prevent very poor areas from improving their structural position. Studies show that census tracts occupied by public housing more often fail to recover from concentrated poverty compared to other areas that once were very poor, and they retain consistently high scores on indicators of "underclass" behavior (Coulton, Korbin, Su, & Chow, 1995; Panday & Coulton, 1992).

Second, there is variation in the mechanisms of social control among structurally disadvantaged neighborhoods, leading to variation in crime rates (Sampson & Wilson, 1995). We can assume that similar variation exists in public housing. Williams and Kornblum (1992), for example, used comparative ethnographic methods to assess factors that explain differences in crime rates among public housing projects after controlling for the structural characteristics of the projects. They cited various mechanisms of informal social control among residents, and the semiformal control functions of the tenant councils, to explain differences in high- and low-crime housing projects. The inattention to interactions between housing projects and their surrounding neighborhoods, however, weakened their analysis, leaving unanswered questions of spatial autocorrelation and other larger contextual effects (Taylor, 1997; Taylor & Covington, 1988).

Third, the physical structure of some public housing developments compromises the establishment of "guardianship" in these microneighborhoods. Guardianship is one of the functions of community that are correlated with reduced crime rates (Cohen & Felson, 1979). Compromises to guardianship may occur in two ways. The vertical design of high-rise developments often creates many spaces with low visibility and high crime opportunity. Also, the location of some housing units in otherwise bleak areas with commercial traffic further threatens social cohesion and provides access to the open spaces of housing projects for people of limited liability to those neighborhoods. Thus, there is little social "traffic" to counter the creation of illicit markets, unsupervised street-corner scenes in which people congregate, and other problematic physical spaces. Risk is a nonrecursive process: Although the surrounding neighborhoods pose risks to the projects they surround, the risks of weak guardianship and concentration effects within projects pose risks to the surrounding areas. In this research, we translate this into a two-way diffusion process.

In summary, various perspectives on community and place predict variability in rates of violence and other antisocial behavior in public housing units. Like neighborhoods, public housing developments exist in an ecology of linked neighborhoods and social areas. Accordingly, we assess the relationship between public housing and violence from the perspective of neighborhoods, focusing on three structural dimensions: population dynamics (density and social position), physical characteristics of the projects, and the nested relationship of projects in the surrounding areas.

THIS STUDY

This study examines the spatial distribution of interpersonal violence in public housing projects and the immediate surrounding areas in Bronx County, one of the five boroughs of New York City.[2] The issues identified earlier suggest several important areas for research that this project will address. First, this study computes estimates of violence rates in public housing and compares them to the surrounding areas. This will allow for a detailed description of the variation in violent crime rates across public housing projects. Second, we assess the characteristics of housing projects that explain variation in their violence rates. Third, this research analyzes the role that public housing may play in explaining rates of violence in the immediate and larger ecological areas. This includes examining the potentially nonrecursive relationship between violent crime rates in public housing and their geographic contexts. Finally, the study concludes with recommendations regarding future research in this area.

METHODS

Data

Data were provided by the New York City Police Department, the Center for Applied Studies of the Environment, and the Center for Urban Research (Graduate School and University Center). The data set includes the type and location of all reported crimes in Bronx County in October 1995. Crime complaints were geocoded to facilitate aggregation analysis within meaningful spatial units. Social structural variables at the census tract- and block group-level measures were provided, including population, income, and human capital variables. Data on the structural characteristics and composition of the public housing projects used in this study were derived from two sources provided by the New York City Housing Authority (NYCHA): Project Data (1996) and Tenant Data (1996).

The Projects

According to NYCHA, there are 100 public housing projects in the Bronx. Of these, 7 are privately managed, 2 are sold cooperatives, and 3 are under construction. Because information on these 11 projects is not included in Tenant Data, these projects have not been included in the analysis. Moreover, the following pairs of housing projects have been amalgamated and are presented as single units in the Tenant Data: Mill Brook and Mill Brook Extension, Throgs Neck and Throgs Neck Addition, and Harrison I and Harrison II. Finally, information on four housing projects, Dr. Betances II through V, is missing from the Tenant Data. Thus, this study is actually based on 82 public housing projects in the Bronx.

Results

Although the geographic information system (GIS) represents a powerful tool in its own right, in some instances it is more appropriately considered as an important element in a larger analytic framework. Because of the large number of crimes in the Bronx, simple overlay maps appear very chaotic and are not easily interpretable. Information that is best extracted through GIS, however, can be combined with other statistical techniques to address more complicated research issues. This is the approach taken here. To begin, we calculated the number of violent criminal events in each public housing project and in each census tract in the Bronx. Using 1990 population data, crime rates per 1,000 members of the population in each tract were computed for four types of violent crime: rape, robbery, assault, and murder. A fifth category, lethal violence, is a composite measure composed of assault and murder (Wilkinson & Fagan, 1996).

DESCRIPTIVE STATISTICS

Consistent with previous research, Table 10.1 indicates significant diversity in both the social characteristics and the violent crimes rates across public housing projects. Figure 10.1 (on web site) shows the homicide rates for tracts with and without public housing developments; Figure 10.2 (on web site) shows rates of aggravated assaults. The public housing boundaries are outlined on the map. The developments range from very small and lightly populated sites to staggeringly large projects. Population density seems to increase with project size: The smaller projects have low population density, whereas the larger ones are stereotypically dense "vertical ghettos" (Newman, 1972; Popkin, Gwiasda, Rosenbaum, Olson, & Johnson, 1998). Some projects are predominantly populated with senior citizens, whereas others are inhabited primarily by family with children under the age of 21. Furthermore, there are major differences in family structure across housing projects with respect to the presence or absence of two parents. There are also notable distinctions in the racial composition of housing projects. The economic conditions for public housing residents, as measured by such data as the percentage of families on welfare and mean family income and per capita income, are similarly quite varied.

Previous research (Land, McCall, & Cohen, 1990) predicts that strong multicollinearity should exist between these variables. Significant multicollinearity, however, was not evidenced in the correlation table (not shown). Data reduction through factor analysis was attempted, but the resultant factors were not readily interpretable or significant. The disparate results (i.e., lack of multicollinearity) demonstrated by these data may be attributable to varying levels of analysis. In many ecological studies, including that of Land et al., analyses are constructed at the level of the city and are intercity in nature. Conversely, this study is an intracity analysis that uses more refined and smaller ecological units. For this reason, the results presented here are in greater accordance with those of Taylor and Covington (1989) than with those of Land et al.

Crime rates varied extensively between public housing developments. Table 10.1 shows that although some public housing projects are clearly very dangerous places to live, there are others in which the risk of victimization appears to be much less. If past research on public housing specifically and neighborhood effects more generally is correct, these results are not unexpected. Rather, we might reasonably expect that differences in project composition would translate into differential rates of violent crime. What is perhaps of greater interest is the actual role that population characteristics play in accounting for these differences.

EXPLAINING VIOLENT CRIME RATES IN PUBLIC HOUSING

Few studies systematically test hypotheses to explain between-site variation in crime rates in public housing developments. Most focus on characteristics of the

TABLE 10.1 Bronx Housing Projects Descriptive Statistics

Variable	Average	Minimum	Minimum Project	Maximum	Maximum Project
Population	1,307	85	Jennings Street	5,867	Castle Hill
Density	240	53	Randall and Balcom Avenues	545	West Tremont Rehab. II
% Under age 21	42	0	Six projects	64	South Bronx Site 402
% Over age 62	18	0	Stratford Avenue Rehab.	92	Glebe and Westchester
% White	4	0	16 projects	60	Middletown Plaza
% Black	47	16	Middletown Plaza	71	Sack-Wern
% Puerto Rican	39	21	Middletown Plaza	72	Stratford Avenue Rehab.
% Single-parent families with children under age 18	42	0	10 projects	78	Franklin Avenue II
% Families on welfare	32	1	Glebe and Westchester	68	Morris Heights Rehab.
% Single-parent families on welfare	24	0	9 projects	58	Morris Heights Rehab.
Per capita income ($)	5,064	2,581	Morris Heights	9,041	Middletown Plaza
Average gross family income ($)	11,965	6,950	Claremont R	22,824	Jennings Street Rehab.
Crime rates					
Rape	0.92	0.00	38 projects	11.76	College Avenue and W. 165th Street
Robbery	7.62	0.00	Claremont Rehab. V	31.67	Davidson
Assault	7.61	0.00	11 projects	54.26	Eagle Avenue and W. 163rd Street
Murder	0.26	0.00	55 projects	5.85	
Lethal violence	7.87	0.00	10 projects	54.26	Eagle Avenue and W. 163rd Street

developments themselves. Unfortunately, variables describing the social structural characteristics of public housing sites were generally weak predictors of violent crime rates. Table 10.2 shows results of ordinary least squares (OLS) regression models for crime in public housing. Because of differences in racial composition and racial homogeneity in the public housing sites, we estimated three models for each crime type, varying the racial composition in each model. No variable was consistently significant across all the models. Also, the R-squared for each model was in every case low to moderate.

TABLE 10.2 Ordinary Least Squares Analysis of Violent Crime in Public Housing

Variable	Rape			Robbery			Assault			Murder		
	t_1	t_2	t_3	t_1	t_2	t_3	t_1	t_2	t_3	t_1	t_2	t_3
Population	0.47	0.05	0.43	−0.02	−0.61	−0.22	−0.21	−0.36	−0.33	0.00	−0.11	−0.25
Density	0.57	0.26	0.34	0.03	−0.34	−0.36	−0.30	−0.39	−0.47	0.79	0.73	0.50
% Under age 21	−0.64	−0.06	−0.45		2.86*	2.48*	−0.92	−0.68	−0.67	−0.42	−0.27	−0.03
% Over age 62	−0.87	−0.77	−1.32	0.96	1.42	0.85		−2.78*	−2.98*		−0.98	−0.91
% Single-parent families	1.17	0.81	0.80		−3.67*	−3.58*	0.43	0.35	0.23	−0.18	−0.19	−0.43
% Welfare families	−2.04*	−2.20*	−2.00*	0.07	−0.11	0.09	−1.93	−1.98*	−1.92	−0.41	−0.41	−0.35
Mean family income	−2.33*	−3.13*	−3.06*	−0.48	−1.10	−1.26		−4.47*	−4.51*		−1.14	−1.61
% White	−2.18*			−1.57			−.19			−.66		
% Black		2.11*			2.68*			0.66			0.30	
% Puerto Rican			−0.86			−1.70			−0.75			−1.16
Model R^2	.23	.23	.18	.24	.29	.24	.32	.32	.33	.09	.08	.10

NOTE: t_1, t value for Model 1 using percentage white as the racial compositional variable; t_2, t value for Model 1 using percentage black as the racial compositional variable; t_3, t value for Model 1 using percentage Puerto Rican as the racial compositional variable.
*$p < .05$.

Two factors, however, suggest that although compositional characteristics of public housing sites are not directly related to their rates of violent crime, these characteristics may be part of a more complex ecological process involving dynamic social interactions and exchanges between public housing sites and their surrounding neighborhoods. First, omitted variables do not allow for more complex or sophisticated model specification. For example, measures such as residential mobility, social interactions between neighbors, processes of informal social control, and income inequality were unavailable. These variables, however, are important predictors of between-neighborhood differences in crime rates (Coulton & Panday, 1992; Sampson & Wilson, 1995). Accordingly, these models are likely to be underspecified with respect to salient predictors about variations in community crime rates.

Second, because public housing is not randomly distributed within cities (Bursik & Grasmick, 1993), the concentration of poverty in public housing may well reflect characteristics of the surrounding areas. Accordingly, the relative inefficiency of compositional predictors limited to public housing sites may be attributable to the fact that public housing is embedded within a larger ecological context that may intensify the effects of deprivation on social control and social interactions. Where public housing sites are located may either attenuate or aggravate the social control processes underlying crime rates. Thus, crime and criminality in public housing sites may reflect more complex social and spatial interactions in the areas that surround them.

These interactions include dynamic relationships between neighborhoods involving the movement of people and services across administrative boundaries. For example, basic services, such as supermarkets, dry cleaners, and video rental stores, exist in areas surrounding public housing and may be located in mixed-use residential areas. Public housing sites, however, may also be located in areas in which they are more likely to be next to off-track betting offices, closed businesses and other signs of disorder, liquor stores, and other potential problematic street-corner locations. These areas are often characterized by mixed populations, some of which have a greater stake in the community than others. Mixed populations may compromise social control, given their limited social integration in those commercial areas. Such variation should reasonably be expected to influence area crime rates. Accordingly, factors pertaining to the areas in which public housing is located, either directly or interactively, may be of greater importance in determining violent crime rates in public housing than compositional factors. In the following section, we discuss this specific issue.

VIOLENT CRIME, PUBLIC HOUSING, AND SURROUNDING AREAS

Table 10.3 presents preliminary evidence of both the strong criminogenic influence of public housing projects and the diffusion of violence out from the projects. The table reports the proportion of violent incidents (by type) that occurred solely within public housing. To examine diffusion effects, we constructed "perimeter zones" surrounding public housing. The first zone is the area within 100 yards of the public housing project, whereas the second is the area between 100 and 200 yards distance from the project. These represent distances of approximately one to three blocks in the more densely populated areas of the Bronx. For the second and third lines of Table 10.3, these two perimeter zones become the unit of analysis, whereas lines four and five illustrate the composite proportions of violence accounted for by public housing in conjunction with the perimeter zones.

For all five crime types, the proportion of total offenses in the Bronx is even greater in areas within 100 yards of the projects than in the projects themselves. Although remaining high, the proportion of violent crimes drops slightly in the areas 100 to 200 yards from the projects. This may suggest that the area of compromised social control may be restricted to the commercial zones surrounding public housing or, alternatively, to the residential areas that border public housing developments.

Although the results in Table 10.3 are disturbing, they do not address the direction of effects, either spatially or socially. Several factors complicate this concern. First, the social meanings of these perimeter zones vary. A zone of 100 yards

TABLE 10.3 Violent Crime in Public Housing and Immediate Surrounding Areas

Variable	Crime				
	Rape	Robbery	Assault	Murder	Lethal Violence
% in public housing	10.4	7.7	10.6	14.9	10.7
% Within 100 yards of public housing	12.4	13.9	14.3	16.8	14.3
% 100 to 200 yards of public housing	9.5	10.4	11.0	9.3	11.9
% in and within 100 yards of public housing	22.9	21.6	24.9	31.7	25.0
% in and within 200 yards of public housing	32.4	32.0	35.9	41.0	36.9

may be meaningful in one neighborhood but not in another. Variation in the zoning and land-use patterns in the surrounding areas also may be meaningful, as are qualitative differences in the nature of commercial zones. Second, the wellspring of the higher crime rates could be the expanding influence of public housing, the attraction of outsiders to areas of compromised social control, or a combination of the two. Nevertheless, the consistency of the patterns of higher crime rates in the surrounding areas is striking, especially the locations of crime in the immediate (100 yard) zone surrounding public housing developments. That these areas are difficult to characterize empirically has less to do with structural considerations and more to do with the ongoing social relationships in the area. Specifically, if these are areas of compromised social control, they are more likely to be infiltrated by people disposed to unlawful behavior (Stark, 1987).

VIOLENT CRIME, PUBLIC HOUSING, AND CENSUS TRACTS

To estimate the direction of these effects, we consider analytic efforts to incorporate contextual features of the surrounding areas into the model to assess how far these effects extend, the direction of the effects, and which types of crime may be diffusing inward or outward from public housing. We focus on substantively important diffusion effects and begin with neutral assumptions about the direction of any diffusion. On the one hand, violent crime rates evidenced in public housing may emanate or spread out from the projects to the surrounding areas. This would suggest that motivated offenders travel outward from public housing projects to the surrounding areas in which crime opportunities may be greater or social controls weaker or both. On the other hand, violent crime may move inward to public housing sites, which are often located in "bad" areas and in which the compositional characteristics may compromise controls on crime.

We use two-stage least squares regression to estimate the magnitude and direction of crime influences between public housing sites and the surrounding areas. Contrary to ordinary least squares regression, two-stage least squares regression is an analytic method that allows for correlated error terms between the dependent and independent variables. In terms relevant to this research, the OLS requirement of independent error terms does not allow for nonrecursive models in which there is a potentially reciprocal relationship between the dependent and independent variables. Because it is very probable that the rates of violence in public housing projects and census tracts affect one another, we instead must use two-stage least squares analysis.

In the left half of Table 10.4, the rates of each of the five violent crime types within public housing sites are regressed separately against corresponding rates for the surrounding census tract. For example, the rate of robbery in public housing projects acts as the independent variable, and the rate of robbery in the census tracts is the dependent variable. In the models presented in the right half of the table, the roles are reversed, with census tract rates predicting public housing rates. The results suggest that violence in public housing diffuses outward from the projects and increases the rates of violence in the census tract generally. The five models predicting census tract violence rates from public housing rates are all significant. For assaults and for the composite of lethal violence, however, there appear to be significant inward diffusion effects. Because homicide is included in the lethal violence indicator but is significant in its own model, we assume that the inward diffusion effect is limited to assaults. Assault is a heterogeneous crime, however, involving both life-threatening assaults and everyday fights. Thus, for the more serious and bellwether crimes of homicide and robbery, the diffusion effects appear to be exclusively in the direction of the outlying areas.

CONCLUSIONS

For this urban county, variation between public housing sites appears to be only weakly related to their compositional or structural characteristics. The limited support for these factors as predictors of violence rates in public housing sets the stage for more sophisticated conceptual analysis and theoretical development. These developments include the possibility of dynamic exchanges (social and spatial interactions) between projects and their surrounding areas both on violent crime and on the conditions that foster it. Models of this process suggest that violent crime diffuses outward from public housing sites to their surrounding areas. There is stronger, albeit preliminary, evidence that the areas in and immediately adjacent to public housing are particularly dangerous places with regard to the threat of violent victimization.

Accordingly, public housing sites may be viewed as an epicenter of dynamic exchanges across places that are facilitated by the "discontrol" in the areas adjacent to the sites. Although the zones around public housing are clearly areas of compro-

TABLE 10.4 Two-Stage Least Squares Analysis of Public Housing and Census Tract Crime Rates

Crime	Model 1: Census Tract Rate[a] From Public Housing Crime Rates		Model II: Public Housing Rate[b] From Census Tract Crime Rates	
	t	p	t	p
Rape	3.21*	.002	1.00	.322
Robbery	8.81*	.000	1.80	.077
Assault	8.50*	.000	4.12*	.000
Murder	2.75*	.007	1.84	.072
Lethal violence	8.65	.000	4.26	.000

a. Instrumental variable: Public housing density.
b. Instrumental variable: Census tract density.
*$p < .05$.

mised social control, we do not know exactly what it is about these areas that produces these conditions. Theory is needed that includes both the structural characteristics of each area and the dynamic social exchanges that occur within these areas. This form of ecological research presents conceptual and methodological challenges. First, how does one model analytically the zones surrounding public housing? Second, how does one measure social control in these areas? Furthermore, both of these questions raise issues related to the appropriate unit of analysis. This study also poses conceptual difficulties as we try to think about and analyze public housing in the more general context of community research. Are these areas nothing more than Thrasher's interstitial zones or, drawing on the community literature, are they areas in which no one takes responsibility and social control is highly dependent on economic activities rather than social cohesion?

There is also an important element of practical utility in this research, with implications for community development, crime prevention, and tactical policing. Specifically, it suggests that the planners in both criminal justice and public housing must consider the relationships between the boundaries of the sites, the areas that surround them, and the interactions and dynamic social and crime exchanges that occur in these contiguous border areas.

NOTES

1. "Official" crime rates often use occupancy data, but the actual populations of public housing units are likely to be far higher because individuals often "double up" with relatives and in extended families.

2. The Bronx was, for many years, viewed as the prototype of urban problems, with a decaying physical infrastructure, declining access to municipal services, and increasing economic deprivation and social isolation (Wallace, 1991).

REFERENCES

Anderson, E. (1978). *A place on the corner.* Chicago: University of Chicago Press.

Anderson, E. (1990). *Streetwise: Race, class and change in an urban community.* Chicago: University of Chicago Press.

Brill, S., & Associates. (1975). *Victimization, fear of crime, and altered behavior: A profile of the crime problem in four housing projects in Boston.* Washington, DC: U.S. Department of Housing and Urban Development.

Brill, S., & Associates. (1977a). *Victimization, fear of crime, and altered behavior: A profile of the crime problem in four housing projects in Capper Dwellings, Washington, DC.* Washington, DC: U.S. Department of Housing and Urban Development.

Brill, S., & Associates. (1977b). *Victimization, fear of crime, and altered behavior: A profile of the crime problem in four housing projects in Murphy Homes, Baltimore, Maryland.* Washington, DC: U.S. Department of Housing and Urban Development.

Bursik, R. J., Jr., & Grasmick, H. (1993). *Neighborhoods and delinquency.* New York: Lexington Books.

Clark, K. (1965). *Dark ghetto.* New York: Harper & Row.

Cohen, L., & Felson, M. (1979). Social change and crime rate trends: A theory of routine activities. *American Sociological Review, 44,* 588-613.

Coulton, C., & Panday, S. (1992). Geographic concentration of poverty and risk to children in urban neighborhoods. *American Behavioral Scientist, 35*(3), 228-257.

Coulton, C. J., Korbin, J. E., Su, M., & Chow, J. (1995). Community level factors and child maltreatment rates. *Child Development, 66,* 1262-1278.

Crane, J. (1991). The epidemic theory of ghettos and neighborhood effects on dropping out and teenage childbearing. *American Journal of Sociology, 96,* 1226-1259.

Elliott, D. S., Wilson, W. J., Huizinga, D., Sampson, R. J., Elliott, A., & Rankin, B. (1996). The effects of neighborhood disadvantage on adolescent development. *Journal of Research in Crime and Delinquency, 33,* 389-426.

Hirsch, A. R. (1983). *Making the second ghetto: Race and housing in Chicago, 1940-1960.* Cambridge, UK: Cambridge University Press.

Holzman, H. R., Kudrick, T. R., & Voytek, K. P. (1996). Revisiting the relationship between crime and architectural design: An analysis of data from HUD's 1994 Survey of Public Housing Residents. *Cityscape: A Journal of Policy Development and Research, 2,* 107-126.

Kotlowitz, A. (1992). *There are no children here.* New York: Anchor.

Land, K. C., McCall, P. L., & Cohen, L. E. (1990). Structural covariates of homicide rates: Are there any invariances across time and social space? *American Journal of Sociology, 95*(4), 922-963.

Lemann, N. (1991). *The promised land: The great black migration and how it changed America.* New York: Knopf.

Newman, O. (1972). *Defensible space: Crime prevention through urban design.* New York: Macmillan.

Panday, S., & Coulton, C. (1992). *Unraveling neighborhood change using a two-wave panel analysis: A case study of Cleveland in the 1980s.* Cleveland, OH: Case Western Reserve University, Center for Urban Poverty and Social Change.

Park, R. E., Burgess, E., & McKenzie, E. (1925). *The city.* Chicago: University of Chicago Press.

Popkin, S. J., Gwiasda, V. E., Rosenbaum, D. P., Olson, L. M., & Johnson, W. A. (1998). *The hidden war: The battle to control crime in public housing in Chicago.* New Brunswick, NJ: Rutgers University Press.

Quicker, J. (with Galeai, Y. N., & Batani-Khalfani, A.). (1992). Bootstrap or noose? Drugs, gangs, and violence in South Central Los Angeles. In J. Fagan (Ed.), *The ecology of crime and drug use in inner cities.* New York: Social Science Research Council.

Rainwater, L. (1970). *Behind ghetto walls: Black family life in a federal slum.* Chicago: Aldine.

Reiss, A. J., Jr. (1986). Why are communities important in studying crime? In A. J. Reiss Jr. & M. Tonry (Eds.), *Communities and crime* (pp. 1-33). Chicago: University of Chicago Press.

Roncek, D. W., Bell, R., & Francik, J. M. A. (1981). Housing projects and crime. *Social Problems, 29,* 151-166.

Sampson, R. J. (1987). Urban black violence: The effect of male joblessness and family disruption. *American Journal of Sociology, 93,* 348-382.

Sampson, R. J., & Wilson, W. J. (1995). Race, crime, and urban inequality. In J. Hagan & R. Peterson (Eds.), *Crime and inequality.* Stanford, CA: Stanford University Press.

Schuerman, L., & Kobrin, S. (1986). Community careers in crime. In A. J. Reiss Jr. & M. Tonry (Eds.), *Communities and crime* (pp. 67-100). Chicago: University of Chicago Press.

Shaw, C., & McKay, H. (1943). *Juvenile delinquency and urban areas.* Chicago: University of Chicago Press.

Skogan, W. G. (1990). *Disorder and decline: Crime and the spiral of decay in American neighborhoods.* New York: Free Press.

Stark, R. (1987). Deviant places: A theory of the ecology of crime. *Criminology, 27,* 893-910.

Sullivan, M. (1989). *Getting paid: Youth crime and unemployment in three urban neighborhoods.* New York: Cornell University Press.

Suttles, G. (1968). *The social order of the slum.* Chicago: University of Chicago Press.

Taylor, R. (1997). Crime and small places: What we know, what we can prevent, and what else we need to know. In *Crime and place: Plenary papers of the 1997 Conference on Criminal Justice Research and Evaluation.* Washington, DC: U.S. Department of Justice, Office of Justice Programs.

Taylor, R., & Covington, J. (1988). Neighborhood changes in ecology and violence. *Criminology, 26,* 553-590.

Tienda, M. (1991). Poor people and poor places: Deciphering neighborhood effects on poverty outcomes. In J. Huber (Ed.), *Macro-micro linkages in sociology* (pp. 244-262). Newbury Park, CA: Sage.

Thrasher, F. (1927). *A study of 1,313 gangs in Chicago.* Chicago: University of Chicago Press.

Wallace, R. (1991). Expanding coupled shock fronts of urban decay and criminal behavior: How U.S. cities are becoming "hollowed out." *Journal of Quantitative Criminology, 7,* 333-356.

Whyte, W. F. (1943). *Street corner society.* Chicago: University of Chicago Press.

Wilkinson, D. L., & Fagan, J. (1996). Understanding the role of firearms in violence "scripts": The dynamics of gun events among adolescent males. *Law and Contemporary Problems, 59,* 55-90,

Williams, T., & Kornblum, W. (1990). *Public housing projects as successful environments for adolescent development.* Unpublished manuscript, City University of New York Graduate Center, Center for Social Research, New York.

CHAPTER 11

The Bronx and Chicago

Street Robbery in the Environs of Rapid Transit Stations

RICHARD BLOCK
CAROLYN REBECCA BLOCK

Danger permeates the popular image of urban public spaces, but the degree of risk is not uniform across an entire city. Violence is rarely randomly distributed but rather is usually more likely to occur in some places and less in others. From a potential victim's point of view, the risk of being assaulted or robbed varies according to the nature of the specific place and the characteristics of the local area around that place (Block & Block, 1995). Of course, other factors are important in determining risk, such as the behavior of potential victims and offenders, time of day, and other characteristics of any particular situation, but the place and the surrounding space bring all these factors together.

The nature of danger varies by the kind of place and the space around it. Typical offenders, victims, and victim-offender interactions may differ for taverns, laundromats, high schools, or transit stops, and the same type of place will vary in riskiness according to the characteristics of the surrounding environmental space. Place and space provide the backdrop for a situation, and combinations of place and space produce situational and environmental factors that generate, attract, or control violence and other crime.

AUTHORS' NOTE: The Chicago analysis was completed with the cooperation of the Chicago Police Department but reflects only the views of the authors. Geocoding for the Chicago data was funded by the McArthur Foundation, and the analysis was partially supported by Loyola University through the Loyola Community Safety Project. The New York City Police Department's Crime Analysis and Program Planning Division supplied the Bronx data. All of the figures to which this chapter refers can be found on the World Wide Web at http://www.urbanresearch.org

RAPID TRANSIT STATIONS AS DANGEROUS PLACES

Rapid transit stations and bus stops are often viewed as dangerous places. Crime in and around rapid transit stations is the product of characteristics of transit stations and characteristics of the surrounding area (Block & Davis, 1996). Characteristics of the area affect the relative danger at a transit station, and the presence of a transit station often affects the relative danger in the immediate area. Like automated teller machine kiosks and laundromats, transit stops provide cover for potential offenders. They are transitional breaks in transportation, where standing around is not suspicious activity. By definition, transit stops are easy to enter and exit. Potential targets usually live some distance from the transit stop, are not always familiar with the surrounding area, and are unlikely to have previously met potential offenders.

The coincidence of targets and offenders and the availability of easy escape can result in high levels of predatory crime. Because rapid transit system managers understand that crime and fear of crime are bad for business, they pay close attention to the design of stations and hire personnel to limit criminal behavior (Chaiken, Lawless, & Stevenson, 1974; La Vigne, 1997; Webb & Laycock, 1992). They often focus on the station alone, however, and ignore the risk of street crime in the surrounding area. With a few exceptions, researchers have done the same (Levine, Wachs, & Shirazi, 1986; Loukaitou-Sideris & Banerjee, 1994; Plano, 1991). In this chapter, we consider the effects of rapid transit stops on the spaces that surround them. We begin by describing patterns of street robbery occurring near elevated railroad stations (ELs) on Chicago's Northeast Side. We then replicate that analysis with street robbery around rapid transit stations in the Bronx, examining the spatial relationships between transit stations, street robbery locations, and specific neighborhoods.

DATA SOURCES AND ANALYSIS METHODS

The analysis of northeast Chicago is based on a GeoArchive created by the Loyola Community Safety Project. A GeoArchive contains address-level data from both law enforcement and community sources that is linked to a computer mapping facility and set up so that it can be updated, maintained, mapped, analyzed, and used by those who are developing and carrying out crime-reduction strategies in the community (Block, 1998). The GeoArchive data used in this chapter include actual and attempted street robberies known to the Chicago Police Department that occurred in 1993 and 1994. The data do not include commercial robberies, home invasions, and, most important, robberies occurring on public transportation or inside transit stations. Although a street robbery may have occurred near a rapid transit station, there is no indication in the data as to whether the victim was en route to or from a station.

The Chicago analysis examines the risk of street robbery in the area surrounding the 10 EL stations in the two most northeastern police districts.[1] The study area is approximately 25 square kilometers and had 242,000 residents in 1990. The population has been stable or increasing during the past four decades. Chicago's Northeast Side is diverse ethnically, racially, and economically, with approximately half the population consisting of non-Latino whites in 1990 and the remainder equally divided among Latinos, non-Latino Asians, and non-Latino African Americans.

The analysis of the Bronx is based on data supplied by the New York City Police Department. In this research, we analyze those robberies identified as occurring on the street from October 1995 through October 1996. Although census data and limited land-use data were available for the analysis, no GeoArchive was created. A good spatial analysis of crime patterns might begin with a "blind" analysis of such limited information, but it could never end here. As with all GeoArchive analyses, it must be anchored in the field with information and feedback from police and community residents who know and understand the area. Although our blind analysis pinpoints the places and spaces at which the density of street robberies is greatest, we know almost nothing about them except their spatial relationship to rapid transit stations.

Both the Chicago GeoArchive and the analysis of the Bronx were implemented in MapInfo and use two spatial analysis software tools for describing patterns of events on a map: Spatial and Temporal Analysis of Crime (STAC) and Vertical Mapper. STAC is a point pattern analysis program developed by the Illinois Criminal Justice Information Authority to identify crime hot spots (Block, 1994). STAC searches for the most densely clustered points on the map and represents each cluster it finds by the best-fitting standard deviational ellipse—a hot spot.[2] The number, size, and density of hot spots are determined by the pattern of points on the map, by the search radius selected by the user, and by the search area boundary. Generally, larger search radii result in more incidents included in hot spots, but these areas are less useful for tactical analysis. Vertical Mapper, an extension of MapInfo, is used to analyze the overall pattern of street robbery in the Bronx. A square grid was overlain on the street robbery point pattern, and the number of incidents occurring in each grid square was counted. A thematic map was generated by interpolating the data using inverse distance weighting and shading. This technique generates a map for street robbery incidents that is similar to shaded elevations in a terrain map.

STREET ROBBERY PATTERNS NEAR RAPID TRANSIT STATIONS ON CHICAGO'S NORTHEAST SIDE

Many residents of Chicago's Northeast Side travel outside the area to work or play, and the area is well served by public transportation. The northernmost EL stop, Howard Street, is a major terminus at which three rapid transit lines and many

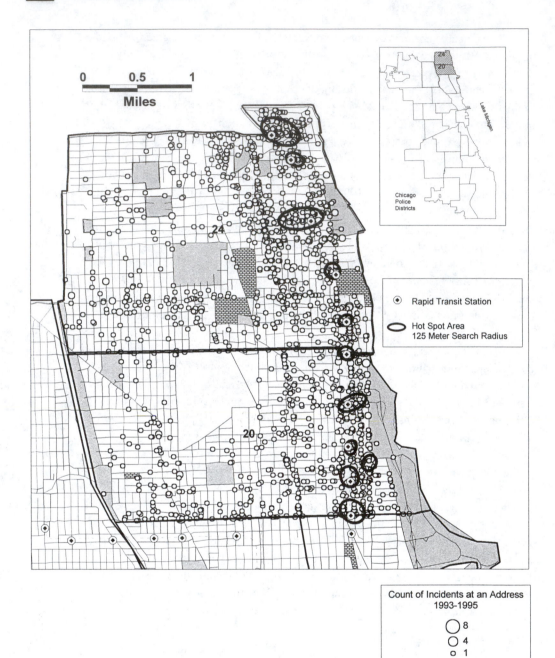

Figure 11.1. Chicago Far North Street Robbery Hot Spot Areas and Count at an Address, 1993-1995

SOURCE: Chicago Police Department

suburban and city bus routes converge. The remaining nine stations, all on a single line, connect neighborhood residents and those living farther west to the rest of the city via local buses. All the EL stations in the area are open 24 hours per day.

Between 1993 and 1994, 1,793 street robberies occurred at 1,563 different places in the area (Figure 11.1). Gray circles in Figure 11.1 represent locations at which incidents occurred. The greater the size of a circle, the greater the number of robberies occurring at that location. The shaded areas are parks, schools, cemeteries, and other institutions. Street robberies are concentrated along the rapid transit line, especially near stations, and along Clark Street, which runs west of and approximately parallel to the EL line. Thirty-six percent of the 1,793 incidents occurred within two block lengths (396 m or 1,300 ft) of a transit station.[3] Fifty-seven percent occurred within four blocks (792 m or 2,600 ft) of a transit station.[4]

The densest concentrations of street robbery incidents are shown by the 11 hot spots in Figure 11.1.[5] Every rapid transit station in the area is in a hot spot, and 10 of 11 hot spots include a rapid transit station. Of the 1,793 robberies, 373 occurred within the 0.76 square kilometers encompassed by the 11 hot spot areas. In contrast to the density of robberies within hot spots (524 street robberies per square kilometer), there were 56.6 street robberies per square kilometer in the area outside any hot spot ellipse. Overall, 22.1% of the street robberies occurred in 2.9% of the area, and the density of street robberies within hot spots was 9.3 times that outside hot spots.[6]

Near rapid transit stations on Chicago's Northeast Side, potential targets and offenders, service businesses (both legal and illegal), and a lack of guardians coincide to create a potentially profitable oasis for street robbers. Residential rapid transit stations not only attract many targets and offenders to public and semipublic spaces but also attract the legal and illegal businesses that serve them. Near these stations are bars, convenience stores, laundromats, and currency exchanges.[7] All these businesses are open late and make mostly cash transactions. Both legitimate and illegal businesses may attract and create additional risk, and they may shelter potential offenders. Several transit stations appear to have drug-dealing areas nearby.[8] The spaces surrounding rapid transit stations are convenient and relatively safe for both buyers and sellers of illegal drugs, particularly at the area north of the Howard terminus at the city's edge.

THE BRONX RAPID TRANSIT SYSTEM

The New York City and Chicago rapid transit systems present similar problems to their patrons: They are public spaces in which strangers must come into contact, everyone has easy access, and both potential targets and offenders assemble. The New York City system, however, is much larger and much more heavily patronized, with the number of stations in the Bronx alone nearly equal to the number in the entire Chicago system. Chicago's Northeast Side area is much smaller than the Bronx. Despite these differences, the relationship between street robbery and propinquity to a rapid transit station is remarkably similar.

From October 1995 to October 1996, approximately half (4,092) of all reported robberies in the Bronx occurred on the street at 2,661 different addresses.[9] As on Chicago's Northeast Side, the densest concentrations occurred near rapid transit stations. A STAC search across the entire area (250-m search radius) found that all seven hot spots are located in the southwest (Figure 11.2).[10] Each contains at least one subway station, and one contains five stations. Approximately 251 street

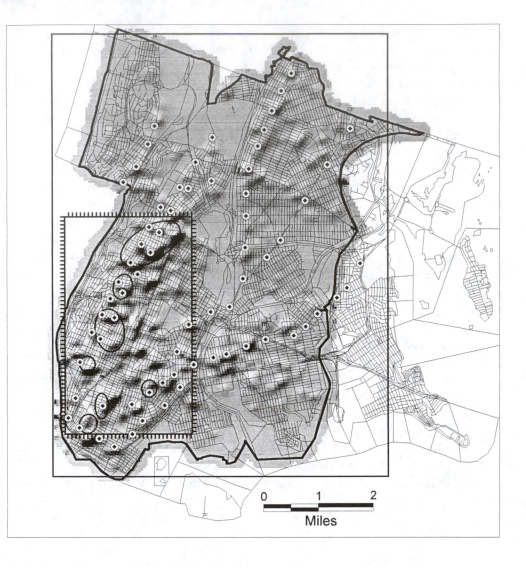

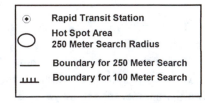

Figure 11.2. Bronx Street Robberies: Overall Pattern and Hot Spot Areas, October 1995-October 1996
SOURCE: New York City Police Department

robberies occurred per square kilometer within the hot spots, but only approximately 21 per square kilometer occurred in the area outside any hot spot ellipse. In the "hottest" hot spot, centered at "the Hub" of 3rd Avenue and 149th Street and including the 3rd Avenue subway station, there were 386 incidents per square kilometer.

The shading in Figure 11.2 reflects the overall pattern of street robbery, calculated with Vertical Mapper. The Bronx was divided into grid squares measuring 125 m on each side. The number of street robberies in each square was counted and used to create a map analogous to elevation on a topographic map. In this map, no street robberies occurred in the uniformly gray areas. Peaked areas, those that are bright on one side and dark on the other, had high levels of street robbery. Not all subway stations are in peaked areas. Even those stations that are not in hot spots, however, tend to be in areas with many street robberies.

Probably no resident of the Bronx would be surprised to learn that all hot spots of street robbery are in the southwest, shown by the geared rectangle in Figure 11.2. Of the 4,092 street robberies that occurred in the Bronx, 2,452 occurred within this boundary. Figure 11.3 magnifies the area. A more detailed STAC search (125-m radius) found 13 hot spots (shown by geared ellipses). Shadings are based on counts in a 75-m square grid interpolated by Vertical Mapper using the same search area as a boundary. Although not every hot spot contains a subway station, 10 of 13 either contain a station or are immediately adjacent to one. Within the geared rectangle but outside any hot spot, 91 street robberies occurred per square kilometer. Inside the hot spots, there were 558 street robberies per square kilometer. The hot spot areas cover only 2.8% of the 23.5 square kilometers in the rectangle, but they account for 15% of the street robberies.

With additional magnification, shading becomes less useful as an analysis tool. Places rather than areas become more important for police planning. In practice, we have found it more effective at this scale to indicate the actual address of occurrence and gauge the size of the symbol to represent the number of incidents. Even at high levels of magnification, however, STAC hot spots are a useful tool for tactical analysis. Figure 11.4 enlarges the northern part of Figure 11.3, with the same hot spots, and shows a section of the west-central Bronx with six subway stations. The size of each dot in Figure 11.4 represents the number of incidents at an address. All six subway stations are located where the larger and smaller hot spots coincide. Most stations have a concentration of street robberies in the immediate vicinity, with a declining number at a greater distance.[11]

Two hot spots in Figure 11.4, however, do not contain a subway station. The largest of these, Fordham Road from the Grand Concourse to Park Avenue, is the entry to Fordham University and includes a commuter train station and several bus lines. Thus, it is an area with very high-intensity use that represents an access corridor between public and private uses. Although not a subway station, it does represent a break in transportation and a place that gathers potential offenders and potential targets.

INTENSITY OF PLACE USE AND DISTANCE FROM A TRANSIT STATION

In his discussion of the intensity of place use in Oakland, Shlomo Angel (1968) anticipated the relationship between distance from a rapid transit station and num-

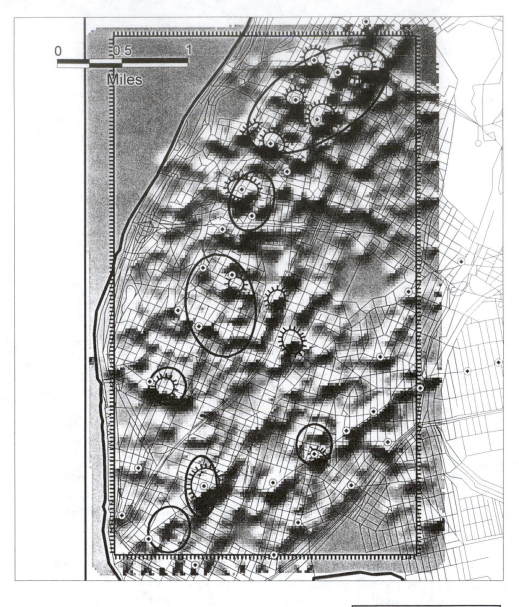

Figure 11.3. Southwest Bronx Street Robberies: Overall Pattern and Hot Spot Areas, October 1995-October 1996

SOURCE: New York City Police Department

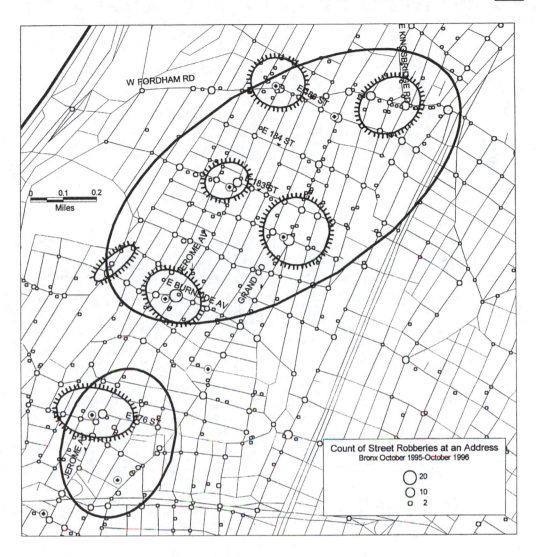

Figure 11.4. Near Fordham University and South: Street Robbery Count and Hot Spot Areas, October 1995-October 1996

SOURCE: New York City Police Department

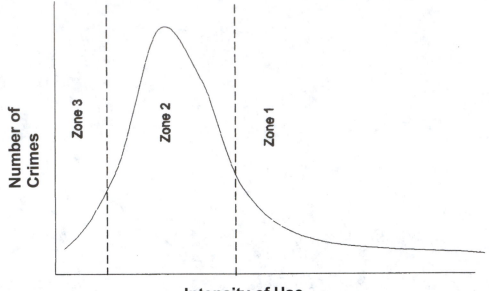

Figure 11.5. Crimes as a Function of Land-Use Intensity
SOURCE: From Angel, 1968, p. 16

ber of street robberies in both the Bronx and Chicago's Northeast Side. Angel's analysis of robbery near bus stops and major intersections is contemporaneous with Jane Jacobs's *The Death and Life of Great American Cities* (1961). Jacobs's recognition that streets with many pedestrians are safe areas predates the concept of natural surveillance that underlies Crime Prevention Through Environmental Design (CPTED). Angel's theoretical model is closely related to that of both Jacobs and CPTED (Figure 11.5).

Susan Wilcox (1973) provides the following cogent summary of Angel's (1968) work:

> Beginning with the assumption that crimes on the street are influenced both by the presence of witnesses, which deter crimes, and the presence of victims, which make them possible, this study postulated that different types of land use would affect the probability that a witness would show up in effective ranges during the time it takes to perpetrate the offense. . . . If the intensity of land use is very low this theory suggests that the level of crime will be low. The scarcity of potential victims reduces the availability of opportunity. [This is Zone 1 in Figure 11.5]
>
> As the intensity of use increases, the number of potential victims available increases sufficiently to attract the attention of potential offenders, but people are not sufficiently numerous to provide witnesses. This situation is called the "critical intensity zone," [Zone 2] and is the situation in which most street crimes are theorized to take place. When the intensity of use is very high [Zone 3] the level of activity is high enough to create a number of witnesses adequate to deter the potential offender. (pp. 86-87)

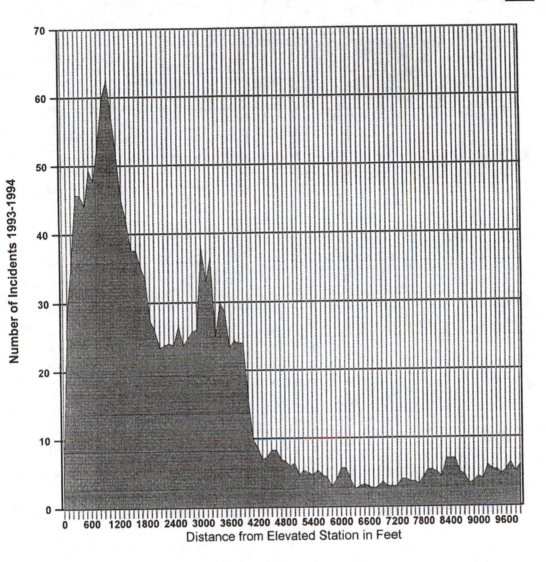

Figure 11.6. Northeast Side (Districts 20 and 24): Distance From Elevated Station by Number of Incidents, 1993-1994

Our analysis, with intensity of use of place measured by distance from an elevated or subway station, confirms Angel's (1968) hypothesis.[12] Of the 1,793 street robberies occurring at 1,563 places on Chicago's Northeast Side in 1993 and 1994, 39% occurred within 1,000 ft of a rapid transit station. Street robberies were not more frequent close to the station, however, but peaked in the "critical intensity zone" between 1 and 2 block lengths away from the station (a Chicago block is 650 ft or 200 m) (Figure 11.6). A secondary peak occurred at approximately 5 blocks distance, mostly along the Clark Street commercial strip that parallels the transit line (Block & Block, 1995). After this secondary peak, distance to a rapid transit station and number of street robberies were unrelated.

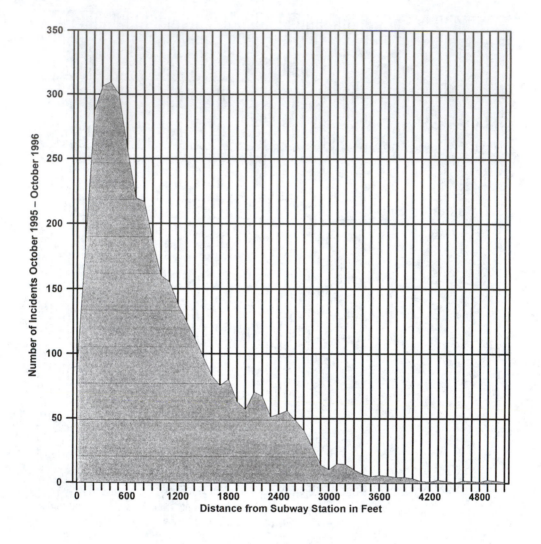

Figure 11.7. The Bronx: Distance From Rapid Transit Station by Number of Street Robberies, October 1995-October 1996

        Angel's (1968) model also predicts the relationship between distance from a subway station and number of street robberies in the Bronx (Figure 11.7). Bronx street robberies are even more concentrated than those on Chicago's Northeast Side. Of the 4,010 geocoded street robberies from October 1995 to October 1996, 63% occurred within 1,000 ft of a rapid transit station. As in Chicago, the critical intensity zone is not immediately adjacent to the station. It is 400 to 500 ft away, reflecting perhaps the shorter distance between blocks in New York City compared to Chicago. Fifty percent of all street robberies occur within 737 ft of a station. In both cities, the number of robberies peaks where the density of targets is still high but civilian and police surveillance are declining. Although peak distances are somewhat nearer stations in the Bronx than in Chicago, the shape of the curve describing distance from a rapid transit station of street robberies is nearly identical once Clark Street's concentration of incidents is excluded.[13]

These findings contradict those of Clarke, Belanger, and Eastman's (1996) study of the New York subway system, "Where Angel Fears to Tread." This analysis found no support for Angel's (1968) hypothesized relationship between intensity of use and risk of robbery. Clarke et al. analyzed only subway stations, however, and not their environs. As we pointed out previously, it is vital to consider both the place and the space surrounding it. In addition, Clarke and colleagues used patronage counts as a measure of intensity of use, whereas Angel suggested that distance is closer to his concept of use intensity. Distance measures the transition from a place with defined ownership and security responsibilities (the rapid transit station) through a public space with no specific ownership. Therefore, distance better reflects the everyday danger that a rapid transit rider or pedestrian may encounter.

SUMMARY AND CONCLUSIONS

The overall pattern of the Bronx is similar to that of Chicago's Northeast Side. The neighborhood characteristics that generate a high level of street robberies must be similar in the two areas. The backcloth, the stations and shops and services that serve their transit riders, may attract predatory offenders. The blocks surrounding EL stations in Chicago are sometimes a convenient market location for both drug buyers and sellers. These areas also have cash transaction businesses frequently patronized by transit travelers. For example, a small strip mall near the Howard Station contains a liquor store, a laundromat, a video shop, a pawn shop, and an adult book store. Similar business may surround the transit stations of the Bronx.

In both the Bronx and Chicago, rapid transit extends the potential offender's cognitive map to an area that is far from home. Normally, people concentrate their activities in places that they know, and these tend to be located in areas in which they live and work or in the areas on the route between the two. Criminals do this too. They tend to commit crimes a few blocks from home, however, rather than in the immediate surroundings. As observed by several geographers (Plano, 1991; Rengert & Wasilchik, 1985; Rhodes & Conly, 1981; van Koppen & de Keijser, 1997), a criminal's mental map has a distance decay function. The further from home, the less detailed the map becomes and the less likely the criminal will commit a crime.

The area around rapid transit stations can become well-known to potential offenders who live elsewhere on the line. Stations are places with easy access, and riding the EL or subway is an adventure for many young teens. Travel on the rapid transit line may widen the mental map of young street criminals from other neighborhoods who are looking for attractive targets in communities with more affluent residents (Pyle, 1974). Although knowledge of an area decays with distance from home, rapid transit stations create nodes of knowledge far from home.

To understand the spatial nature of violence, and to develop successful prevention and intervention programs for this violence, we must be aware of both places and spaces. A specific situation provides the mechanism for violence, but this situation occurs at a place. Each place, in turn, is rooted in a space. A *place* is a particular small area that reflects and affects the routine activities of the participants in the short run and plays a role in the specific conflict at hand. A *space* is a larger area containing many places that modifies routine activity patterns of potential participants in conflict situations. Neither attributes of the place nor attributes of its location in space are enough by themselves to explain levels of crime. Strategies to effectively reduce crime will vary according to the different types of place-space combinations.

In the Bronx and on Chicago's Northeast Side, rapid transit stations provide both anonymity and a high density of potential targets for indigenous and commuting street robbers. Unlike more residential neighborhoods, few people on the street know each other, and the area is claimed by no one. Informal social control is difficult where intensity of use is high. Near the station, however, the potential for informal and formal social control remains high. The police may concentrate patrols in the area, and there are many eyes to see a crime. Therefore, both in the Bronx and in Chicago, street robberies are not concentrated immediately at the station but rather a few hundred feet away. In this critical intensity zone, the potential number of targets remains high, but guardianship and observability have declined.

In the areas surrounding rapid transit stations, many factors converge that create a high potential for predatory crimes. This convergence, however, also creates a potential for crime control. Changes at the New York Port Authority bus terminal inspired by the research of Ronald Clarke and coworkers (1996) demonstrate the possibility of successful prevention efforts in even the most anonymous of transit hubs. On Chicago's Northeast Side and in similar areas, proponents of problem-oriented policing could correctly argue that the general level of street robbery might be reduced by concentrating surveillance in the area surrounding rapid transit stations. The areas in which robbery concentrates are small and well demarcated. For such districts, effective street robbery reduction must focus at and near transit stations. If the areas around rapid transit station present a unique convergence of opportunities for street crime, then increased surveillance or guardianship by the community and police may decrease the overall level of violence.

NOTES

1. The original research in Chicago examined a second area on Chicago's West Side that had a very different pattern of street robbery (Block & Davis, 1996). In this area, the occurrence of street robbery was only slightly related to EL stations.

2. A standard deviational ellipse rotates two axes around the cluster of points until the variances of the X_i's are maximized along one axis and the variances of the Y_i's are maximized along the other axis.

3. Manhattan distance approximates the distance from the EL station to the street robbery location along the street grid rather than as "the crow flies." It is measured by sum-

ming the metric change in distance north-south and east-west between the station and the incident.

4. The concentration of street robberies in the southwest corner of the map probably reflects the fact that there is another rapid transit line just beyond the area boundary.

5. The STAC search for hot spots used a 125-m search radius.

6. Population-based rates were not calculated because the population living a short distance from a rapid transit station is not related to the number of patrons.

7. Often described as "the poor man's bank," currency exchanges offer check cashing and licensing services. A few exchange currency.

8. Sean Davis (Block & Davis, 1996) had to break off his observation of one area when a drug dealer's lookouts became suspicious and challenged him.

9. Of the 4,093 total street robberies, 4,010 were geocoded.

10. Part of the northeast Bronx, in which few street robberies occur, is outside the larger rectangular analysis window.

11. The Bronx map overlay for subway stations provided only the sites of the stations and not entrances and exits. For several stations, the greatest concentration of robberies is at some distance from the indicated locations of the stations. Future research should include the location of the exit or entrance to the mapped data.

12. Intensity of use of place varies by time of day, day of week, and time of year. In Chicago, few street robberies occur during rush hour, but many occur at closing times of taverns. During rush hour, rapid transit stations are heavily used, but surveillance is high. At a late hour, there are few pedestrians, but guardianship is low.

13. The curve is slightly smoother than for Chicago's Northeast Side, probably because random noise is evened out by the greater number of robberies and transit stations in the Bronx.

REFERENCES

Angel, S. (1968, February). *Discouraging crime through city planning* (Working Paper No. 75, p. 16). Berkeley: University of California at Berkeley, Center for Planning and Development Research.

Block, C. R. (1994). STAC hot spot areas: A statistical tool for law enforcement decisions. In *Proceedings of the Workshop on Crime Analysis Through Computer Mapping* (pp. 33-54). Chicago: Illinois Criminal Justice Information Authority. (Republished in 1995 as *Crime analysis through computer mapping.* Washington, DC: Police Executive Research Forum)

Block, C. R. (1998). The GeoArchive: An information foundation for community policing. In T. McCain & D. Weisberg (Eds.), *Crime prevention studies: Vol. 8. Spatial analysis and policing.* Monsey, NY: Criminal Justice Press.

Block, R., & Block, C. R. (1995). Space, place and crime: Hot spot areas and hot places of liquor-related crime. In J. E. Eck & D. Weisberg (Eds.), *Crime prevention studies: Vol. 4. Crime and place* (pp. 147-185). Monsey, NY: Criminal Justice Press.

Block, R., & Davis, S. (1996). The environs of rapid transit stations: A focus for street crime or just another risky place? In R. V. Clarke (Ed.), *Crime prevention studies: Vol. 6. Preventing mass transit crime* (pp. 237-257). Monsey, NY: Criminal Justice Press.

Chaiken, J., Lawless, M., & Stevenson, K. (1974). *The impact of police activity on crime: Robberies on the New York subway system* (Report No. R-1424-NYC). Santa Monica, CA: RAND.

Clarke, R. V., Belanger, M., & Eastman, J. A. (1996). Where angel fears to tread: A test in the New York City subway of the robbery/density hypothesis. In R. V. Clarke (Ed.), *Crime prevention studies: Vol. 6. Preventing mass transit crime.* Monsey, NY: Criminal Justice Press.

Jacobs, J. (1961). *The death and life of great American cities.* New York: Random House.

La Vigne, N. (1997). *Visibility and vigilance: Metro's situational approach to preventing subway crime* (Research in Brief, National Institute of Justice). Washington, DC: U.S. Department of Justice.

Levine, N., Wachs, M., & Shirazi, E. (1986). Crime at bus stops: A study of environmental factors. *Journal of Architectural and Planning Research, 3*(4), 339-362.

Loukaitou-Sideris, A., & Banerjee, T. (1994). *Form follows transit?: The blue line corridor's development potential.* Los Angeles: University of California at Los Angeles, Department of Urban Planning.

Plano, S. L. (1991). Transit-generated crime: Perception versus reality—A sociogeographic study of neighborhoods adjacent to Section B of the Baltimore metro. *Transportation Research Record,* No. 1402, 59-62.

Pyle, G. F. (with Hanten, E. W., Garstang Williams, P., Pearson, A. L., II, Doyle, J. G., & Kwofie, K.). (1974). *The spatial dynamics of crime.* Chicago: University of Chicago, Department of Geography.

Rengert, G. F., & Wasilchik, J. (1985). *Suburban burglary: A time and place for everything.* Springfield, IL: Charles C Thomas.

Rhodes, W. M., & Conly, C. (1981). Crime and mobility: An empirical study. In P. J. Brantingham & P. L. Brantingham (Eds.), *Environmental criminology* (pp. 167-188). London: Sage.

van Koppen, P., & de Keijser, J. (1997). Desisting distance decay: On the aggregation of individual crime trips. *Criminology, 35*(3), 505-515.

Webb, B., & Laycock, G. (1992). *Reducing crime on the London underground: An evaluation of three pilot projects* (Crime Prevention Unit Paper No. 30). London: British Home Office.

Wilcox, S. (1973). *The prevention and control of robbery: Vol. 3. The geography of robbery.* Davis: University of California at Davis, Center on Administration of Criminal Justice.

CHAPTER 12

Schools and Crime

DENNIS W. RONCEK

This chapter examines the usefulness of analyzing crime patterns by city blocks with chloropleth maps and statistical analyses. Three objectives are pursued. The first is to understand the social and environmental characteristics of crime locations. This effort links crime to communities. Such analyses help identify the limitations for affecting crime without basic alterations in areas' social structure and physical characteristics. To the extent that characteristics such as the ethnic composition and socioeconomic status of urban neighborhoods are "real" causes of crime, the impact of police activity alone will be limited. This objective also includes identifying the effects of other characteristics of high-crime places that may be changed by public agencies, such as zoning boards or social service agencies. An effort is made to estimate the effect of both fixed and malleable location characteristics on the incidence of crime.

The second objective is to illustrate crime's spatial variation within very small areas, specifically police sectors. Chloropleth maps will show the block-by-block variation in robberies. City blocks are "island blocks" for which the census reports data and are usually bounded by streets, roads, or other features. They correspond to the areas encompassed by a "walk around the block." Even in police sectors that have few blocks, crime varies substantially. Chloropleth maps of crime by blocks have several advantages. The first advantage is that they permit viewing crime variations across small areas for an entire city or borough from a letter-size transparency. Attempting to detect patterns across large areas with pin maps is virtually impossible because incident symbols can cover the underlying map and conceal variations in crime. The second advantage is that there is no software-imposed limit on the number or hotness of hot spots. The block-chloropleth approach does not require a priori constraining hot spots to a certain minimum size. Finally, this ap-

---

AUTHOR'S NOTE: All of the tables and figures to which this chapter refers can be found on the World Wide Web at http://www.urbanresearch.org

proach respects a city's physical structure. Unlike circular buffers or hot spot ellipses, a hot spot for a block-chloropleth map is a city block and does not divide a house or yard.

Chloropleth mapping, however, has disadvantages. Hot spots can be omitted. Two street sides facing each other but in different blocks might each have a moderate amount of crime but not enough to make either block a hot spot. The two-side total of crimes, however, could be enough for a hot spot. Also, this approach can conceal the precise locations of crime. If all of a block's crime is on only one or two sides, this will not be portrayed in chloropleth maps. Once "hot blocks" are identified, overlaying crime incident points on an enlarged block map remedies this problem. These maps have their uses but should not be the sole cartographic method.

The third objective is to "go beyond a pretty map" whose interpretation can vary among individuals depending on their particular perspectives. The goal is to statistically evaluate the combined and separate associations of city block characteristics with crime. The power of statistical analysis is derived from its ability to assess the controlled associations and relative importance of particular areal characteristics with crime. Buffering or hot spot ellipses might identify places with high schools (Roncek & Faggiani, 1985; Roncek & Lobosco, 1983), bars (Roncek & Bell, 1981; Roncek & Maier, 1991; Roncek & Pravatiner, 1989), or subway stops (Block & Davis, 1996) as hot spots, but such analyses cannot indicate the importance of these places for crime throughout a city. Police and other public agencies may need to justify imposing new restrictions on bars, housing types, or other facilities. One method of demonstrating the need for change is by showing that crime is associated with a facility after taking other factors into account. This is the function of statistical analyses.

Statistical analyses show that being within one block of a public high school in San Diego is associated with almost two additional Part I crimes per block per year beyond the effects of socioeconomic status, household structure, and racial composition (Roncek & Lobosco, 1983, p. 608). Such statements are difficult to make using only a map. The type of analysis used can vary. Simple analyses (Sanford, 1995) can meet short-term needs, whereas longer range and broad policy changes require more elaborate analyses.

Elaborate statistical analyses are not the sole way to extend mapping, and they have their limitations. The more elaborate an analysis, the more time it takes, the more expertise it requires, and the more difficult it is to interpret. Second, statistical analysis is continuously developing. What was sophisticated a few years ago rapidly becomes antiquated. Third, any statistical analysis requires data. The availability and timeliness of data affects the types of research and analyses.

The absence of data for a characteristic of a place requires omitting it from any analysis. Currently, identifying the influences of standard social and housing characteristics requires using census data. Several limitations follow from this. First, the data are collected only once a decade, and their usefulness declines with time. Second, the degree of information is limited due to privacy concerns, especially at small units of geography. Third, the smaller the unit of analysis, the greater the likelihood of an absence of information. For 1990 blocks, this is mostly the result of having many that are truly nonresidential (commercial or industrial) and have no residents. Fourth, the Census Bureau does not always respect a city's physical geography and can define blocks differently than would planners, geographers, or ordinary citizens. This results in the exclusion of some areas, such as parts of the Bronx's Co-op City, from the analysis.

Statistical analyses are still useful even if limited to residential areas. Statistical analyses for these areas can identify the factors associated with crime in the home areas of individual community members, a most important piece of knowledge. This does not obviate the need for analyses of places of work, business, and play, but these are beyond the scope of this chapter.

This chapter focuses primarily on robbery and its association with proximity to schools. Research shows that, after taking into account socioeconomic status, racial composition, household structure, and the housing environment, several types of crime occur at higher rates for residential blocks containing a public high school or that are within one block of one (Roncek & Benedict, 1990; Roncek & Faggiani, 1985; Roncek & Lobosco, 1983). In this chapter, I expand the range of schools to include all traditional schools from elementary to high school, and include private as well as public schools.

ANALYSES

In the Bronx, 10,175 robberies occurred from October 1, 1995, to October 31, 1996, in its 4,599 census blocks. Forty-seven percent (2,161) of all blocks had no robberies, and the most crime-ridden block suffered from 43 such crimes. The average block experienced 2.2 robberies. Figure 12.1 is a robbery chloropleth map of this block-level data. The map's wider lines represent police-sector boundaries, which are the smallest planning areas used by the New York Police Department (NYPD). When enlarged, this map shows that robbery varies substantially across the blocks in every sector.

The variation of Figure 12.1 (on web site) could be missed by a hot spot analysis of the entire city or borough because such analyses identify only the hottest spots for the larger area. A statistical spatial analysis of crime across sectors, block groups, census tracts, or precincts would also ignore it. Totaling the crime for a larger area can hide the presence of dangerous places when a larger area includes only one or a few high-crime blocks surrounded by many low-crime blocks. Identifying crime variations within sectors, however, can be important for planning and policy. Chloropleth maps easily communicate within-sector patterns, especially when supplemented with crime location pins.

As with many block-level chloropleth maps, this map shows that there are many robberies on physically large blocks. This finding can be important for law enforcement, despite its limited academic use. Police must respond to all events and will travel to these areas repeatedly. This can be useful for police patrol allocation planning (Roncek, 1981).

The frequencies of crime on city blocks are examined instead of crime rates. Creating and using meaningful city block crime rates is problematic for two reasons. First, police cannot ignore an area because of low crime/population or crime/physical area ratios. Second, except for burglaries, crime victims need not be residents of the city blocks on which the offenses occur. The resident population does not represent the population at risk of being victimized, and a crime rate based on the number of residents is likely to be inaccurate and misleading. Areas with high foot traffic, moderate amounts of crime, and few residents, such as commercial strips or industrial areas, may appear to have exorbitant high rates. Conversely, areas with large populations and many incidents can have low rates. Low rates in physically large areas do not indicate that these are safe places or that they are not a problem for law enforcement. Similar problems occur for rates based on the physical size of areas. Usefully examining the relationship between area characteristics and crime requires adjusting for resident population and the physical size. The best method for this directly extracts their influence by using these characteristics as independent variables.

Figure 12.2 (on web site) shows the Bronx's 3,480 residential city blocks, which comprise 75.6% of all Bronx blocks. For this research, a residential block is one that has data for the average value of owned housing or an average value of rent. Blocks without these data are commercial or industrial blocks or contain some type of institution, such as a jail, university, or extended care facility, and must be excluded from analyses. The large block containing Fordham University, for example, is not analyzed.

Figure 12.3 (on web site) portrays 8,780 robberies for the Bronx's residential blocks. This amounts to 86.3% of all robberies, although data appear for only 76% of all blocks. Robberies per block ranged from 0 for 1,416 blocks (41%) to 43 for the Bronx's most crime-ridden residential block. Only two blocks with more than 3 robberies per month were lost by examining only residential blocks. One of these blocks, an improperly defined large block in Co-op City, had 40 crimes, whereas the other block experienced 37 crimes. The average of 2.52 robberies per residential block is slightly higher than that for all blocks, even after excluding the Co-op City block.

The statistical analyses are for the blocks in Figure 12.3. The analyses use 22 characteristics representing household composition, ethnic composition, socio-economic status, and housing environment as well as measures of proximity to schools and the presence of urban facilities. Research and theory support using these measures (Roncek & Maier, 1991).

The household composition measures are the percentage of one-person households (% OnePer), the percentage of households without a spouse that have children under age 18 (% NoSpouse), and the percentage of persons older than 65 years of age (% 65 and Over). The ethnic composition measures include the percentage of African Americans (% Af.Am.), American Indians (% Am. Indian), Asians (% Asian), and Hispanics (% Hispanic). The census allows members of any race to define themselves as Hispanic; therefore, the percentage Hispanic cannot be added to the other categories to create a total percentage of minorities.

The best indicator of socioeconomic status from the census is the average value of owned housing in thousands of dollars (H. Value). Of the 3,480 residential blocks, 2,494 or 72% had an owned value. Blocks with rental values but no owned housing were given an estimated housing value by regressing owned housing value on rental value for all blocks with both data (Roncek & Maier, 1991).

The housing environment measures consist of the percentage of housing units in structures with 10 or more units (% Apartments) (the Census Bureau's measure of the concentration of housing in larger apartment buildings), the percentage of housing units with 1.01 or more persons per room (the traditional measure of housing unit overcrowding) (% Overcrowded), and the vacancy rate per 100 housing units (Vacancy Rate).

Each block's population in tens of people (Population in 10s) and physical area from the census are also independent variables. The division by 10 avoids statistical difficulties.

The dichotomous variables measuring facilities indicate the presence of a subway stop, a hospital, a public housing project, or a block with more than 2,000 residents. Research indicates that each of these is linked with increased crime (Block & Block, 1997; Block & Davis, 1996; Newman, 1972; Roncek, 1992; Roncek, Bell, & Francik, 1981; Roncek & Fladung, 1983; Roncek & Franz, 1988; Smith, 1987).

This research focuses on proximity to schools, incorporated into the analysis as a dichotomous variable I call primary adjacency. Blocks coded with the value of "1" have a school on them or on an adjacent block face, or they are cattycorner from a school; blocks are coded "0" otherwise. Roncek and Lobosco (1983) and Roncek and Faggiani (1985) find that the range of higher crime levels around senior public high schools extends only one block. Such measures are used for public elementary, junior high, and senior high schools as well as private grammar schools and private high schools.[1]

Figure 12.4 (on web site) is a robbery chlropleth map for all blocks around senior public high schools. Stars identify school locations. Robbery varies widely on these 302 blocks with or next to these 31 schools, referred to as primary adjacent blocks. Primary adjacent blocks had 1,426 robberies or 16.2% of all Bronx robberies, although they comprised only 6.6% of all blocks. Only 69 (23%) of these blocks did not have a robbery, which is much lower than the 47.3% rate for all Bronx blocks. Primary adjacent blocks averaged 4.72 robberies—a rate much higher than the mean of 2.2 robberies for all blocks. The worst such block had 40 robberies. As the map shows, higher levels of crime do not always occur on blocks with schools. Some distance from the school's social control may be necessary to commit crime successfully. Block and Davis (1995) explain that the robbery peak is about one block away from Chicago's subway stations, and similar processes may operate for schools.

Figure 12.5 (on web site) shows the 1,144 robberies on the 229 primary adjacent residential blocks for senior public high schools. These robberies comprise 80.2% of those for all primary adjacent blocks, whereas residential blocks constitute only 75.8% of all such blocks. The vast majority of the residential primary adjacent blocks (91.7%) do not have a school. Only 19 of 31 schools are on one of the 229 primary adjacent residential blocks. The 1,144 robberies on these 229 blocks comprise 13% of all robberies on all residential blocks, although the residential blocks near these schools comprised only 6.58% of the total. Robberies range from 0 to 26, with a mean of 4.996. This is almost twice that for all residential blocks and more than one fourth of a robbery higher than the rate for all blocks near these schools. Focusing on robbery for only the residential blocks near these schools does not ignore high-crime areas. Robbery is more severe for these blocks than for the complete group of all blocks near these schools. Using only the residential blocks near senior public high schools omits only one high-crime block—the overly large block in Co-op City.

Identifying the areas around schools and calculating their average crime levels can be done with buffers and hot spot ellipses. Evaluating the associations between crime and area characteristics with statistical analyses is fairly direct for city blocks and areas consistent with census boundaries, but it is difficult and probably inaccurate for buffers or ellipses. The following analyses relate block characteristics to the frequencies of crimes. Such analyses are problematic for buffers and ellipses because, except in rare cases, their boundaries will not match areas with available data. No precise way of identifying the composition of the subdivided part in a buffer or ellipse exists. Results from analyzing such areas depend totally on the method of assigning values to characteristics, such as the number of one-adult families, to the subdivided areas.[2] Even without such divisions, totaling the components of each area's characteristics in the buffer or ellipses to form a percentage's base is tedious. Without accurate data, meaningful statistical analyses of the links between crime and area characteristics are impossible.

Many urban crime statistical analyses begin by examining zero-order correlations to understand the uncontrolled associations of areal characteristics with each other and crime. Because 22 characteristics including robberies are used here, only the key features of these associations will be noted. The robbery correlations range from .007 for the vacancy rate to .502 for the resident population size. The correlations of primary adjacency with robberies for each of the five school types are positive: .21 for public elementary schools, .16 for public junior high schools, .15 for public senior high schools, and .06 and .03 for private grammar and high schools, respectively. Collinearity is not a problem. All variance inflation factors are below 4.0 (Fisher & Mason, 1981), and the largest condition number is below 5.0 (Belsley, Kuh, & Welsch, 1980, p. 105).

Following this technique, urban crime analysis often relies on ordinary least squares (OLS). Its ease of use and ready interpretability provide a baseline for comparison with technically more appropriate techniques that are more difficult to use and interpret. Table 12.1 lists the results of OLS analyses for all seven traditional Part I crimes.

Each block characteristic with a statistically significant effect (at the .05 level) has three entries. The first is the standardized regression coefficient for ranking the importance of these effects. The second number is the rank of each coefficient's size, and the third is the unstandardized coefficient (β) or effect of each

TABLE 12.1 Regression Results: Standardized Coefficients, Relative Importance, and Unstandardized Effects for Statistically Significant Block Characteristics

				Crime				
	Murder	Rape	Assault	Robbery	Burglary	Grand Larceny	Auto Larceny	Significant Effects
Public elementary adjacency				.062; 6; 0.820	.039; 9; 0.417			2/7; all +
Public junior high adjacency			.038; 13; 0.246			.054; 7; 0.339	.038; 11; 0.435	3/7; all +
Public senior high adjacency		.043; 8; 0.092	.070; 6; 0.801	.048; 7; 0.834			.031; 12; 0.462	4/7; all +
Private grade school adjacency			.048; 10; 0.364	.038; 12; 0.425	.039; 11; 0.444	.041; 8; 0.219		4/7; all +
Private senior high adjacency							.065; 9; 1.07	1/7; +
2,000+ housing projects	.106; 2; 0.291	.046; 4; 0.315	.095; 4; 3.49	.070; 5; 3.85	-.066; 5; -3.96		-.110; 3; -5.17	6/7; 4+, 2–
Hospital blocks		.070; 2; 0.769	.054; 9; 3.17		.064; 6; 6.29	.094; 4; 3.94	.095; 5; 7.26	5/7; all +
Subway stop blocks			.112; 3; 1.84	.170; 2; 4.22	.058; 7; 1.58	.176; 2; 2.05		4/7; all +
% OnePer								0/7
% No spouse		.059; 3; 0.002	.122; 2; 0.021			-.072; 6; -0.009	-.102; 4; -0.023	4/7; 2+, 2–
% 65 and over			-.047; 11; -0.011	-.042; 10; -0.015	-.047; 8; -0.019			3/7; all –
% African American		.045; 6; 0.0008	.059; 8; 0.006	.046; 8; 0.006				3/7; all +
% American Indian		.042; 7; 0.004						1/7; +
% Asian			.045; 12; 0.004	.035; 13; 0.024	.070; 4; 0.052		.065; 8; 0.038	4/7; all +
% Hispanic				.044; 9; 0.006	.039; 10; 0.006		-.072; 7; -0.009	4/7; 3+, 1–
Housing value in $1,000s			-.037; 14; -0.002					1/7; all –
% Apartments			.074; 5; 0.005	.101; 3; 0.010	.193; 2; 0.022	.138; 3; 0.007	.072; 6; 0.006	5/7; all +
% Crowded		.046; 5; 0.002	.061; 7; 0.013	.078; 4; 0.026	.086; 3; 0.031		.048; 10; -0.014	5/7; 4+, 1–
Vacancy rate					.030; 12; 0.021	.034; 9; 0.010		2/7; all +
Area				.039; 11; 0.004		.083; 5; 0.004	.154; 2; 0.014	3/7; all +
Population in 10s	.111; 1; 0.0005	.296; 1; 0.003	.336; 1; 0.020	.346; 1; 0.032	.405; 1; 0.041	.297; 1; 0.013	.481; 1; 0.038	7/7; all +
$R^2 \times 100$	6.1	18.2	39.7	36.3	38.5	21.5	32.5	

characteristic that gives the expected difference in crime for a one-unit difference in a block characteristic.

At the end of each column in Table 12.1 is the square of the multiple correlation multiplied by 100 of all 21 characteristics for each crime. These data are the percentage of variation explained in each crime by the characteristic. These data, which can be few for rare crimes, are typical for city block analyses. A statistically significant amount of variation, however, is explained for all the crimes. Also, the amount explained exceeds acceptable levels for the more frequent crimes, such as assaults and robberies.

Overall, the variables in the regression account for 36.4% of the variation in robbery for the residential blocks. This is respectable because the analyzed areas are small, and no direct information is available regarding the detailed activities of individuals. The strongest effects parallel those of past research. The most important characteristic is the size of the block population. This is not unusual, and it is important to plan for crimes that occur most frequently where people are located. Having a subway stop is the second most important characteristic. After adjusting for the other characteristics, a block with a subway stop is expected to have 4.21 additional robberies. Higher concentrations of the three largest minority groups— African Americans, Asians, and Hispanics—are associated with more robberies, as is lower socioeconomic status.

More interesting is that the primary adjacency measures for public postelementary schools are relatively important for robbery. Public junior high school adjacency is sixth in importance followed by public senior high school adjacency. For both, the unstandardized effect indicates that approximately one (0.8) net additional robbery per year, on average, is due to being proximate to these schools. The public senior high school results parallel those of past research, whereas the effect for junior high schools is new. Also new is that being a private grammar school primary adjacent block implies an additional 0.4 robberies per block per year.

Translating these average effects into the overall impact for all Bronx residential blocks requires multiplying the unstandardized effect by the number of adjacent blocks. Thus, public senior high school adjacency accounts for 0.829 crimes per block × 229 blocks, or approximately 190 of the robberies that occur on residential blocks after adjusting for other characteristics. This is approximately 2.2% of robberies on residential blocks. This number is much smaller than the total of 1,144 robberies on primary adjacent residential blocks that is derived from tallying the crimes on the "pretty map." Thus, the unstandardized effect illustrates how statistical analyses can provide an important restraining check on what appears to be a very strong pattern on a map. The "humbling" effect of statistical analyses is important. Overstated claims for success can produce serious problems if expectations are not met, but underestimating success usually does not.

Statistical analyses provide important information for community policing and crime prevention. They help identify problems and provide estimates of achievable change. The robbery analyses presented here imply that the expensive remedy of increased patrol near schools is unlikely to reduce robberies because there is a low number of net expected additional crimes due to school proximity.

These analyses highlight important principles. First, statistical analyses can provide objective criteria for supporting visual map interpretations. Second, they can assess whether the spatial distribution of crime is associated with specific conditions. Third, they permit estimating the average size of suggested effects. Fourth, the results inform resource allocation decisions. Combining such results with other information, pin maps, hot spot ellipses, and crime incident reports can facilitate further understanding of the underlying dynamics of crime patterns.

The results for schools show that although proximity is important, it is not the most powerful variable. Only for robbery and assault do the proximity measures rank as high as sixth in any analysis. Public senior high school adjacency and private grammar school adjacency have the largest number of statistically significant effects (four of seven), although the crimes associated with the two types of schools differ (rape, assault, robbery, and auto theft were significantly associated with public senior schools, whereas assault, robbery, burglary, and grand larceny were associated with private grammar schools). The public senior high school results parallel those of past work. The connection between private grammar school adjacency and crime, although not strong, is a new finding. New York Police Deputy Commissioner Michael J. Farrell suggests that many of the Bronx's private schools remain open and committed to their neighborhoods despite demographic change and a decline in the socioeconomic status of the average student. Simple declines in the informal social control typically associated with private school areas are also possible.

Other new findings are that public junior high school adjacency has statistically significant effects on robbery, grand larceny, and auto larceny, whereas public elementary school proximity has similar but smaller effects for assault and burglary. Youth may take advantage of opportunities for crime en route to school grounds, which may serve as convenient meeting grounds or have recreational facilities that attract young people. Paralleling past work, private senior high school adjacency has little criminogenic effect. Only for auto theft is it statistically significant, but this is ranked 13th in importance.

Among other facilities, large public housing projects have the most statistically significant effects for all four violent crimes and rank high in effect: second for murder, fourth for rape and assault, and fifth for robbery, with significant negative effects for burglary and auto theft. Hospital presence also has significant effects (Roncek & Fladung, 1983; Roncek & Franz, 1988; Smith, 1987). Only for murder and robbery are its effects not statistically significant. The effects vary in rank from second for rape to ninth for assault. Finally, having a subway stop has positive and statistically significant effects for four of seven crimes, and it is second most important with regard to robbery and grand larceny, third regarding assault, and seventh regarding burglary (Block & Davis, 1996).

The last statistical analysis is a negative binomial regression (NBR). It overcomes problems of OLS for incident count dependent variables (Greene, 1993, pp. 678-679). Specialized tests for crime data are necessary because the number of crimes cannot be less than zero. This rule is ignored by OLS. The coefficients of OLS can result in negative predicted values of crime, but those of NBR will not. The predicted values of NBR should be better than those of OLS for blocks, many of which have no crime. Because using NBR is time-consuming, the remaining analyses focus only on robbery.

Table 12.2 presents the robbery NBR results. The three columns of statistics are analogous to those in Table 12.1. The first coefficient, \bet PSCR, is a negative binomial proportional semistandardized coefficient that I developed for this work (Roncek 1997a, 1997b). Its size, ignoring sign, gives the importance of independent variables. The second is the rank of this coefficient's size and indicates its relative importance. The third, \bet \mul 100, has the result of each unstandardized NBR coefficient (\bet) multiplied by 100 to convert its value into the expected percentage change in robbery for a one-unit difference in a city block characteristic.

The last three rows present statistics for the overall robbery NBR, including the intercept, the dispersion parameter, and the "Lemeshow's R-squared." The intercept and the Lemeshow's R-squared are analogous to measures in OLS, whereas the dispersion parameter is used to determine whether NBR or Poisson regression is more appropriate. Lemeshow's R-squared is converted to a percentage and indicates that using these characteristics reduces the error in modeling robbery's distribution across blocks by 54.05%. For school proximity, all types of schools except private high schools have statistically significant effects. The relative importance of public junior and public senior high schools declines from sixth and seventh to 10th and 12th. The importance of private grammar schools increases to 11th. Public elementary school adjacency is the 14th most important characteristic and the weakest of those with statistically significant effects.

The statistically significant NBR coefficients multiplied by 100 give the additional percentage of robbery to be expected relative to comparable nonadjacent blocks. These data are as follows: 29.5% more robberies occur on blocks with primary adjacency to public senior high schools, 30.8% with adjacency to public junior high schools, 11.4% with adjacency to public elementary schools, and 21.3% with adjacency to private grammar schools. The most important effect relating to other facilities is for subway stops. Blocks adjacent to subway stops can expect an increase of 154.85% more robberies than blocks without a stop. Surprisingly, large housing projects do not have significant effects.

Several tasks remain for future research. Mapping the residuals of regression models can help identify outliers.[3] On-site investigation and incident report review can help determine why particular characteristics are associated with crime or whether other influences are responsible. Final assessments may be best accomplished through combining objective analysis techniques with mapping, taking care not to bypass hot spots due to crime across facing blocks.

DISCUSSION

This work illustrates how combining chloropleth maps of city blocks with statistical analysis allows analysts to identify factors associated with crime. Although these

TABLE 12.2 Negative Binomial Regression Results for Robberies

Block Characteristic	β_{PSCR}	Rank	$\beta \times 100$
Public elementary	.050*	14	11.398*
Public junior high	.099*	10	30.760*
Public senior high	.073*	12	29.501*
Private grammar	.081*	11	21.325*
Private high school	−.003	21	−1.310
2,000+ housing projects	.010	19	13.406
Hospital blocks	−.018	18	−37.693
Subway stops	.266*	4	154.780*
% OnePer	.146*	9	1.046
% No spouse	−.006	20	−0.034
% 65 and over	−.026	15	−0.224
% African American	.304*	3	1.004*
% American Indian	.026	16	1.304
% Asian	.154*	8	2.464*
% Hispanic	.329*	1	1.083*
Housing value in $1,000	−.067*	13	−0.098*
% Apartments	.312*	2	0.746*
% Crowded	.172*	6	1.339*
Vacancy rate	.022	17	0.320
Area	.166*	7	0.422*
Population in 10s	.228*	5	0.488*
Constant (not × 100)			−1.279*
Alpha dispersion			0.870*
Lemeshow $R^2 \times 100$		54.05%	

*Statistically significant at the .05 level.

tasks can be difficult and they are not the only methods that can be used for understanding spatial crime patterns, much can be gained by using this approach.

Chloropleth mapping city blocks makes identifying hot spots easier. It permits the identification of intra-area variation in small areas, such as police sectors and block groups. The problem of area boundaries being obscured by too many incident symbols, as occurs when using base maps, especially when trying to show intra-area variation for large areas, is avoided. If used alone, however, there is a risk of omitting some hot spots.

Statistically analyzing city block data reduces the chances of drawing faulty conclusions and can help decision makers select among alternative courses of action. When the impact of traditional crime predictors is small, creative and community-based solutions may be more valuable than simply increasing the number of police patrols. The example of school proximity and robbery used in this chapter demonstrates the feasibility of such analyses and their potential for helping to avoid incorrect inferences.

These analyses are useful for medium- and long-term evaluations and policy-making. Their value is in assessing objectively the relative importance and numerical effect of different characteristics of a place's subareas on the overall pattern of crime on maps. They permit the translation of perceived patterns into measures for evaluating and formulating policies. Due to resource constraints, such assessments are probably best conducted on a quarterly or annual basis. At these intervals, the results can provide information that solely short-term analyses cannot. They can also provide a strong evidentiary basis for changing regulations involving licensing or zoning because they take into account the effects of other influences.

In summary, effective crime analysis requires a variety of both cartographic and quantitative methods assessments. Effective crime prevention and law enforcement must operate simultaneously in the short term and the long term.

NOTES

1. Many private schools do not make the elementary-junior high school distinction, often serving students through ninth grade. Thus, only two types of private schools are used in the analyses.

2. Buffering programs claim to reaggregate and disaggregate data, but they do so under the untestable assumption that the proportion of a group residing in the buffer is the same as the proportion of the area in the buffer. There is no way to identify when this is true because census data cannot be disaggregated below the level of the city block.

3. The analyses also need adjustments for spatial autocorrelation following Roncek and Montgomery (1986, 1995). Such analyses are needed because it is important to have an initial assessment of school proximity effects before more refined analyses are done. Such analyses identify the reasons why a perceived problem could vanish under more refined analyses.

REFERENCES

Belsley, D. A., Kuh, E., & Welsch, R. E. (1980). *Regression diagnostics*. New York: John Wiley.

Block, R., & Davis, S. (1996). The environs of rapid transit stations: A focus for street crime or just another risky place? In R. V. Clarke (Ed.), *Crime prevention studies: Vol. 6. Preventing mass transit crime* (pp. 237-257). Monsey, NY: Criminal Justice Press.

Block, R. L., & Block, C. R. (1997, April). *Risky places in Chicago and the Bronx: Robbery in the environs of rapid transit stations*. Paper presented at the Workshop on the Identification and Evaluation of Methods for Measuring and Analyzing Crime Patterns and Trends with GIS, New York.

Fisher, J. C., & Mason, R. L. (1981). The assessment of multicollinearity in criminology. In J. A. Fox (Ed.), *Methods in quantitative criminology* (pp. 99-125). New York: Academic Press.

Greene, W. H. (1993). *Econometric analyses* (2nd ed.). New York: Macmillan.

Newman, O. (1972). *Defensible space.* New York: Macmillan.

Roncek, D. W. (1981). Dangerous places. *Social Forces, 60,* 74-96.

Roncek, D. W. (1992, November). *Housing projects and crimes revisited: Continuities in crime.* Paper presented at the annual meeting of the American Society of Criminology, New Orleans, LA.

Roncek, D. W. (1997a, January). *A semistandardized coefficient for negative binomial and Poisson regression* [Mimeo]. Omaha: University of Nebraska at Omaha, Department of Criminal Justice.

Roncek, D. W. (1997b, November). *A simple measure for assessing the relative importance of independent variables in one sample negative binomial and Poisson regression.* Paper presented at the annual meeting of the American Society of Criminology, San Diego.

Roncek, D. W., & Bell, R. (1981). Bars, blocks, and crimes. *Journal of Environmental Systems, 11,* 35-47.

Roncek, D. W., Bell, R., & Francik, J. M. A. (1981). Housing projects and crimes. *Social Problems, 29,* 151-166.

Roncek, D. W., & Faggiani, D. (1985). High schools and crime: A replication. *Sociological Quarterly, 26,* 491-505.

Roncek, D. W., & Fladung, C. (1983, November). *Rape: A different crime.* Paper presented at the annual meeting of the American Society of Criminology, Denver.

Roncek, D. W., & Franz, M. A. (1988, August). *The ecology of rape: A replication.* Paper presented at the annual meeting of the Society for the Study of Social Problems, Atlanta.

Roncek, D. W., & Lobosco, A. (1983). The effect of high schools on crime in their neighborhoods. *Social Science Quarterly, 64,* 598-613.

Roncek, D. W., & Maier, P. (1991). Bars, blocks, and crimes revisited: Linking the theory of routine activities to the empiricism of "hot spots." *Criminology, 29,* 725-753.

Roncek, D. W., & Montgomery, A. (1986, April). *Spatial autocorrelation: Diagnoses and remedies for large samples.* Paper presented at the annual meeting of the Midwest Sociological Society, Des Moines, IA.

Roncek, D. W., & Montgomery, A. (1995). Spatial autocorrelation revisited: Practical guidelines and the conceptual underpinnings of the use of the generalized potential as a remedy for spatial autocorrelation. In C. R. Block, M. Daboud, & S. Fregly (Eds.), *Crime analysis through computer mapping* (pp. 99-110). Washington, DC: Police Executive Research Forum.

Roncek, D. W., & Pravatiner, M. A. (1989). Additional evidence that taverns enhance nearby crime. *Sociology and Social Research, 73,* 185-188.

Sanford, R. (1995). How to develop a tactical early warning system on a small city budget. In C. R. Block, M. Daboudg, & S. Fregly (Eds.), *Crime analysis through computer mapping* (pp. 199-208). Washington, DC: Police Executive Research Forum.

Smith, L. F. (1987). *Crime in hospitals: Diagnosis and prevention.* London: Home Office Police Research Group.

PART IV

TOOLS FOR
SPATIAL ANALYSIS

Despite advances in geographic information systems (GIS), the statistical capacity of most GIS packages is severely limited. Nearly all GIS programs can produce descriptive statistics, and many contain tools for creating complex variables. For spatial statistical analysis, however, most analysts must rely on third-party add-on software.

Chapter 13, by Doug Williamson, Timothy A. Ross, Sara McLafferty, and Victor Goldsmith, evaluates software used to generate spatial statistics. There is a vital need for this review. Many spatial statistics software programs are written out of necessity by academics or other researchers as by-products of their research. The existence of various software programs and the knowledge of their capacities spread by word of mouth rather than through advertising or widespread exposure in classrooms. As GIS proliferates in law enforcement and other academic and operational areas, the demand for more robust analysis is increasing.

The main drawback of Chapter 13 is that any discussion of software in the late 1990s quickly becomes obsolete. Demand for more advanced GIS analysis, combined with intense competition between vendors, is gradually pushing commercial programmers to incrementally incorporate more spatial statistics. In addition, rapid advances are occurring in the relatively young field of spatial statistics. Each of the programs evaluated in Chapter 13 will almost certainly have undergone changes by the time this book is published.

Chapter 13, then, is not meant as a buyer's guide. It does, however, provide valuable information by explaining common spatial statistics, identifying places to start looking for software, and highlighting the advantages and disadvantages of particular programs. Until mainstream GIS packages incorporate spatial statistics, the programs examined in Chapter 13 will continue to be a primary source for advanced spatial analysis.

Evaluating Statistical Software for Analyzing Crime Patterns and Trends

DOUG WILLIAMSON
TIMOTHY A. ROSS
SARA McLAFFERTY
VICTOR GOLDSMITH

In many crime analysis settings, the maps and overlay analysis provided by geographic information systems (GIS) are not sufficient. Statistical methods are needed to test hypotheses about the causes and correlates of crime patterns. Most of the GIS packages used in this book have relatively limited capabilities for statistical and spatial data analysis. In general, they produce only simple descriptive statistics, such as frequency, mean, and standard deviation, and the packages do not reflect the most recent developments in spatial analysis and modeling. For this reason, it is important to examine other computer programs that have the ability to perform statistical analysis on spatial data. This chapter evaluates four such software packages: Stat! by Biomedware, Cluster by the Agency for Toxic Substances and Disease, S+ SpatialStats by MathSoft, and SpaceStat by Luc Anselin (1995). The packages were chosen because they address questions of interest in law enforcement and analysis, such as where crime hot spots are located and how the crime rate in one area affects the rate of crime in nearby areas.

EVALUATION OF STAT!

Stat! Version 2.0 is a statistical software program for the analysis of event or incident data that performs a variety of space-time statistical tasks. Its original applica-

---

AUTHORS' NOTE: All olf the tables and figures to which this chapter refers can be found on the World Wide Web at http://www.urbanresearch.org.

tion was for the analysis of health events to measure the spatial clustering of disease. Because the spatial characteristics of crime incidents are similar in many respects to those of disease, many of Stat!'s capabilities are applicable to crime analysis. The statistical tools available in Stat! include tests that can analyze clustering in a single time series, simultaneous clustering in several time series, spatial clustering, and methods for space-time interaction.

Dr. Geoffrey Jaquez, an expert in the analysis of the clustering of health events, developed Stat! It is distributed by BioMedware, Inc. (http://ic.net/biomware/) and costs $395.00. Stat! is a tool for exploratory data analysis (EDA) and for determining whether an observed pattern of events is significantly different from a random one.

The software runs in a DOS window and can be installed under DOS or Windows (v3.1). It can also be used in later versions of Windows, but it should be installed from the command prompt. Although Stat! is a stand-alone product, it can be used in conjunction with most GIS packages with some minor data manipulations. For example, Stat! requires that point data be in ASCII text, in the form of X1 Y1 T1, where (X1, Y1) are the spatial coordinates of event 1, and T1 is the time the event occurred (Biomedware, 1994). Although a standard text editor can transform most spatial data to this format, it is a time-consuming task.

Stat! performs a variety of statistical tests or methods. The most useful of these for crime analysis are the ones that test for space-time interaction. Specifically, they are the Direction method, Knox's method, Mantel's method, and the k-Nearest Neighbor (k-NN) method. All these statistics test to determine whether pairs of cases that are near in space occur at similar times.

Knox's method for space-time interaction is a statistical test to determine if incidents occur close to one another geographically (in space) and temporally (in time). The Knox method measures space-time interaction based on critical space and time distances. The critical distances define how close in time and space two points must be to be considered a cluster. The test statistic is a count of those pairs of cases that are separated by less than the critical space and time distances. The actual number of "close" pairs is compared to the number one would expect to find if incidents were located randomly in the study area. If the actual number of pairs is significantly greater than the expected number, the test statistic will be large, indicating clustering of incidents in space and time. The test results are sensitive to the critical distances used. An accepted rule of thumb is to use the mean distance values as critical distances, but these values are often too large.

The results for the k-NN method are slightly more complicated than those for Knox's test, but they may be better suited to the analysis of crime data. The idea behind the k-NN method is that when space-time interaction is present, nearby cases will occur at about the same time (spatial nearest neighbors tend to be temporal nearest neighbors). The test statistic is the number of pairs of cases that are k-nearest neighbors in both space and time, with the user setting the critical time and distance. When there is little or no space-time interaction, the test statistic will be small. This means that there is little or no relationship between where an event occurred and when it occurred.

As is the case with any analysis, it may be useful to have some prior knowledge about the cases being examined. For example, in Knox's method, analysts will not wish to examine a completely unrelated set of crime events. Crimes that are similar in suspect or modus operandi (MO), for example, can be analyzed. The reason for this is twofold. First, for computational purposes, it takes a considerable amount of processing power to run the test on extremely large data sets (>5,000 cases) even on modern PCs. Second, with prior knowledge about the attributes of the crimes, reasonable critical distances can be selected. If a suspect is under 17 years of age, for example, he or she cannot drive (legally). Therefore, all the traveling will be done on foot. This will limit the critical distance to a much smaller value than if the suspect has a more wide-ranging mode of transportation.

EVALUATION OF CLUSTER VERSION 3.1

Cluster v3.1 is similar to Stat! Like Stat!, it performs a variety of space-time statistical tests, and its original application was for the analysis of health events to measure the amount of disease clustering. Cluster calculates many of the same statistics as Stat! and some additional ones.

The Agency for Toxic Substances and Disease developed Cluster, and the program is distributed by the National Technical Information Service under the auspices of the U.S. Department of Commerce. The software can be purchased for $175. Like the other software packages examined in this chapter, Cluster is a tool for EDA, and as such should be used to assist in prioritizing and decision making. It cannot prove or disprove cluster reports.

Unlike Stat!, which can be installed under DOS or Windows, this software must be installed under DOS (the command prompt) and it runs in DOS mode. As is the case with the other packages, Cluster is a stand-alone product but is best used in conjunction with a GIS package. Again, for GIS data to be used in Cluster, the data must be saved as ASCII text. The format is the same as that for Stat! except that the delimiter (separating character) is a comma and a space rather than just a space.

The two most useful tests for analyzing point data are Knox's method described earlier and Barton's method. Barton's method is a test for space-time interaction in disease (crime) occurrence. The method is designed to detect changes of spatial patterns over time using an analysis of variance method. At its simplest level, Barton's method defines temporal clustering as a series of cases in which the time interval between successive cases is less than the average time interval between all cases. The test statistic in Barton's method is the ratio of the squared distances among h time periods to the mean square spatial distance between all cases (Public Health Service, 1993). If the test statistic is low (<1), a positive space-time interaction is indicated. In general, this means that the average distance in time is small relative to the average spatial distance.

As is the case with Knox's method, it is helpful to have some prior knowledge of the incidents. It is useful to use a subset of cases that are linked by a common characteristic, such as the use of a weapon or a suspect description. If all cases are used, for example, some may be close in space and time, whereas others may be widely dispersed. In such a situation, the large variability of the dispersed cases tends to wash out or hide cases that are near in space and time.

EVALUATION OF S+ SPATIALSTATS

S+ SpatialStats is an extension to the popular statistical package S+. The extension provides statistical tools designed specifically for spatial data. S+ SpatialStats is particularly useful because (a) it provides a wide assortment of exploratory data analysis tools and (b) it is linked directly to S+, which provides powerful traditional statistical tools.

MathSoft, Inc. (http://www.mathsoft.com/splus/) distributes S+ SpatialStats. The cost of a stand-alone license for S+ Professional is $1,995, and the S+ Spatial-Stats add-on is $895. Although S+ SpatialStats is best used for visualization and EDA, the direct linkage to S+ allows for robust analysis of data.

S+ SpatialStats is available for both UNIX and Windows operating systems, although only the UNIX version (v3.4) is examined here. Due to its command line interface, the UNIX version may be difficult to users accustomed to the Windows environment. Users must be extremely familiar with the syntax for each command, and the learning curve is steep. With a little patience and a lot of practice, however, the use of S+ SpatialStats becomes almost second nature.

One example of the complexity of the software is the input of data. Because S+ SpatialStats is command line driven, it is sensitive to arguments that are passed to a function. Therefore, in the case of the read.table function, the user must be specific about what exactly is going to be read. For example, S+ SpatialStats requires the following command to read a simple data set:

```
homicides <-read.table("/home/everest/dougwill/.Data/robbery.tab,"
sep = "|," col.names = ("Record," "X," "Y," "LinearTime")).
```

The first argument (in quotes) is the path and file name of the ASCII text file containing the point data. This file was not the original but rather a version modified to suit S+ SpatialStats, with column headers as the first line of the file and delimiters added. The second argument (sep = "|") tells S+ SpatialStats that the file is pipe (|) delimited as opposed to spaces or tabs or commas. The final argument tells S+ SpatialStats what the column headers should be called once read into a data frame. This is not the most intuitive process, especially for users accustomed to either PC or Mac point-and-click functionality. Specific fields can be exported from GIS packages into ASCII text files, but very often these files will need additional modifications for them to be read by S+ SpatialStats. This can be done in a variety of text editors, with scripting languages such as Perl and Awk or with native GIS scripting languages such as Avenue and MapBasic. S+ has recently released a link to S+ SpatialStats from ArcView that creates a bidirectional data bridge to the GIS pack-

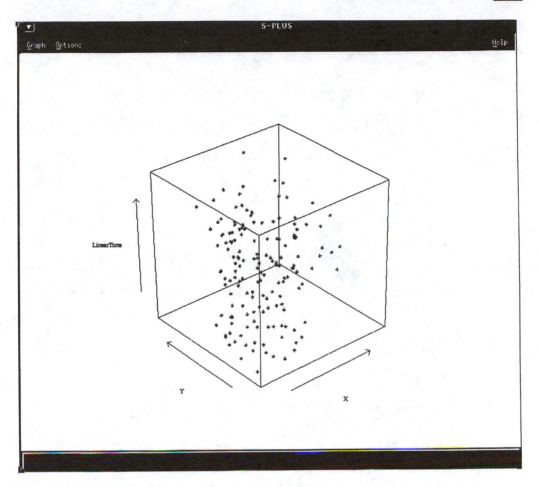

Figure 13.1. Brush and Spin Graph, With Cloud Option

age (stand-alone license is $595 in addition to S+ and S+ SpatialStats). This should greatly simplify the issue of data transfer.

S+ SpatialStats contains useful visualization tools, particularly brush and spin (with the cloud option). Brushing is a technique that allows users to evaluate multivariate data by graphing pairs of variables in an array called a scatterplot matrix. The user can then select a point in one scatterplot and see the same case highlighted in the remaining scatterplots of the matrix. The other function, spin, allows the user to create a three-dimensional point cloud from any three variables and then spin the point cloud to observe its structure. This is very useful when using time as the third dimension and examining whether or not points are close in space and time (Figure 13.1).

An interesting function in S+ SpatialStats is intensity. Intensity is a smoothing technique that describes how the mean number of points varies through space. A variety of options are available for the intensity function to determine the amount of smoothing, including kernel estimation, Gaussian estimation, and binning (MathSoft, 1996). The binning method uses a two-dimensional histogram to form

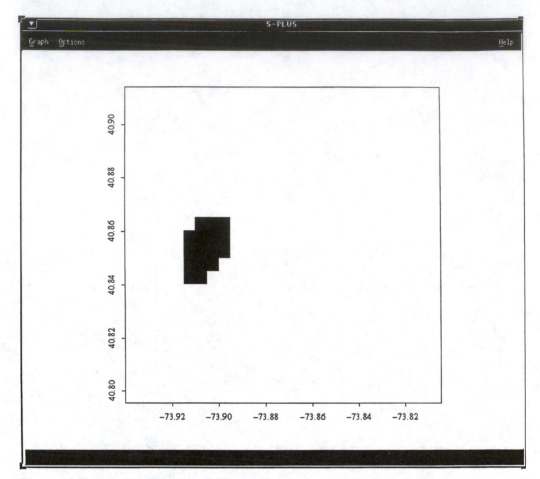

Figure 13.2. Intensity Smoothing of Bronx Homicides, With Binning Option

rectangular bins. The counts in these bins are smoothed using a loess-smoothing algorithm (MathSoft, 1995). The binning method was used to compute the intensity for a sample data set of homicides, in Bronx County, New York, provided by the New York City Police Department. Using the S+ SpatialStats plotting functions, image or wireframe, the user can visualize the intensity of incidents over an area (Figure 13.2). In Figure 13.2, S+ SpatialStats shows that the incidents of homicide are concentrated in one area, with this area centered approximately at 40.855° North latitude and 73.905° West longitude. This is in the area of 181st Street and Jerome Avenue. This suggests that the intensity of homicide is highly clustered. If the user could overlay a precinct map, this area would correspond to the 46th precinct, which had 32 homicides.

The previous functions in S+ SpatialStats are primarily visualization techniques. S+ SpatialStats also includes an array of tools that are more statistical in nature. In crime analysis, there are typically two types of data available—point data and lattice (area) data. Point data, the most common, refers to the actual location of crimes. Lattice data, however, are observations associated with regular or irregularly spaced regions. Spatial regions can be geographical areas and are not limited to a grid. In general, lattice data are aggregations or counts to some real or artificial boundary. For point patterns, S+ SpatialStats contains tests for spatial randomness, k functions, and intensity functions. For lattice data, the program calculates Geary and Moran spatial autocorrelation coefficients and spatial regression models.

An important advantage of S+ SpatialStats is that it can analyze both point and lattice data. Although most crime data are point information, often the data are aggregated over police, census, or other geographies. Many statistical methods exist for analyzing aggregated information, and although all three of the previously discussed packages allow this sort of analysis, a powerful and flexible package designed specifically for areal analysis is SpaceStat, developed by Luc Anselin.

EVALUATION OF SPACESTAT 1.80

SpaceStat 1.80 offers an impressive set of tools for spatial analysis, including multiple types of spatial regression, advanced methods for exploratory spatial data analysis (ESDA), and local indicators of spatial autocorrelation, such as Geary's c and Moran's I. Despite SpaceStat's DOS-based interface, the extension for ArcView makes the program relatively easy to use. The user's manual is well written, and computer-literate spatial statisticians should have few problems getting results. The soon-to-be-released version 1.90 promises to make the program even more user-friendly.

Luc Anselin, a regional scientist at the University of Texas, Dallas, developed SpaceStat during the past 11 years. Unlike some of the other software discussed in this chapter, SpaceStat is not a commercial product, nor is it Windows based. It intentionally does not replicate standard features found in SPSS or other statistical software packages. SpaceStat may be purchased from the SpaceStat Project run by Anselin. Prices range from $150 for students to $1,000 for private corporations. Proceeds from these purchases are used for further development of the software.

SpaceStat runs in a DOS window. Although the program can be used as a stand-alone product, SpaceStat is best suited as an add-on to ArcView. With a couple clicks, the SpaceStat extensions to ArcView let users export data in ASCII format. SpaceStat then converts the data to GAUSS. SpaceStat reports data output in comma-delimited ASCII and a number of other formats, allowing users to convert SpaceStat's ASCII output to dBase format for use in ArcView. To make learning the program easier, SpaceStat includes sample data sets and an accompanying workbook.

SpaceStat's ability to create first-order and higher-order spatial weights matrices allows researchers to see the connections among areas based on first-order and higher-order neighbors. Using a first-order spatial weights matrix with the local Moran function, for example, enables the calculation of local Moran values for each areal unit. The local Moran's I detects spatial autocorrelation.

Moran's *I* can be used as a way to identify crime clusters. Polygons that have a high local Moran for robbery either have a low number of robberies in the polygon and are surrounded by neighbors with few robberies or have a high number of robberies and are surrounded by neighbors with many robberies. Mapping local Moran scores is one way to identify crime hot spots (see Chapters 6 and 9 for more information on Moran's *I*).

SpaceStat makes mapping local Moran values simple. After creating the data set and the weights file, the output of the local Moran can be changed to dBase format and imported as a table to ArcView. Calculating local Moran values for a series of higher-order spatial weights matrices, what Anselin calls a spatial correlogram, shows how clusters can "decay" spatially as values for polygons farther away from the center of the cluster decline. SpaceStat can also identify the centroids of polygons and use distance measurements between centroids as measures of spatial association.

Once the presence of spatial autocorrelation is identified, SpaceStat offers many ways to address the problem via spatial regression. SpaceStat can create spatial lag variables, which are the average values of a variable in adjacent polygons. Using SpaceStat's spatial regression features, researchers can estimate the impact of spatial lag variables and adjust for spatial autocorrelation. SpaceStat performs a wide variety of spatial regression methods that are accompanied by a mix of diagnostics. In addition to standard regression, SpaceStat can perform maximum likelihood estimation (MLE) and instrumental variable estimation of spatial lag models, MLE for spatial error models, and estimations of heteroskedastic error models. Trend surface, spatial regimes, and spatial expansion models are also available options. Although much remains to be done in working out the intricacies of spatial regression, this is a powerful set of tools.

Deploying SpaceStat's ESDA features makes it possible to identify outliers visually. In ArcView, users can look at a map and produce a graph of local Moran or other statistical scores while moving a resizable box over the points on the graph. As the mouse-controlled box encompasses or "moves over" individual points, polygons associated with those points are selected and highlighted on the map. This makes determining the spatial distribution of both outlying and central values easy and accurate. The procedures needed to use these functions are complex but are well worth the effort—especially for people concentrating on a single map.

Users may find the following tips helpful. The ANSI character set needs to be in the right location on the hard drive and loaded in the autoexec.bat file. Otherwise, SpaceStat cannot write its menus properly. Indicator variables cannot be string variables, nor can they contain decimals, a requirement to which analysts using census tracts or blocks should be attentive. Every cell in data tables must have a value because missing values may cause errors. When using large data sets, run SpaceStat in DOS mode, and make the workspace size requested by SpaceStat as large as possible.

Users should also visit the SpaceStat Web site (www.spacestat.com). The wealth of information available here includes sample data sets, Anselin's e-mail address, and articles relating to spatial analysis. Perhaps the most useful resource is Anselin's Spatial Data Analysis and GIS course syllabus and teaching materials, which are invaluable for beginners.

For researchers, students, and statistically trained analysts, SpaceStat offers important and, in many cases, unique tools for spatial analysis. The updates to SpaceStat should make the product increasingly user-friendly and will likely provide the most recently developed statistical tools and methods for spatial analysis. It is hoped that SpaceStat will eventually be incorporated into a full-service GIS program.

CONCLUSION

Spatial analysis of crime is a complicated process. Advances in computer hardware and software have helped simplify the job of crime analysts in many ways. With the recent development of desktop GIS, analysts can "automatically" create maps of incident reports and then, using (spatial) statistical programs, compute statistics that reveal the associations among incidents in space and time. As discussed in this chapter, the quality and capability of these products are advancing every day, but the products are still far from perfect.

The obstacles to using spatial statistical programs for crime analysis include data input and verification, software limitations and compatibility, and usability. Specifically, spatial statistics programs rarely interact seamlessly with most GIS software. The transfer of data from one program to another remains difficult. There are exceptions, namely, S+ SpatialStat's link to ArcView and SpaceStat's link to ArcView. Also, most spatial statistical programs are not very user-friendly. They require knowledgeable and competent users who are well versed in computing environments and in statistics. Therefore, the use of these programs and the interpretation of their results are often challenging.

The goal should be the development of spatial statistical packages that are easily used by analysts, that are directly linked to existing GIS packages, and that require only a modest statistical background on the part of the user.

REFERENCES

Anselin, L. (1995). *SpaceStat, a software program for the analysis of spatial data, Version 1.80.* Morgantown: West Virginia University, Regional Research Institute.

Cluster, software system for epidemiological analysis instruction manual. (1993). Atlanta: U.S. Department of Health and Human Services, Public Health Service.

S-plus user's manual. (1993). Seattle: MathSoft.

S-plus guide to statistical & mathematical analysis. (1995). Seattle: MathSoft.

S+ Spatial Stats user's manual. (1996). Seattle: MathSoft.

Stat! Statistical software for the clustering of health events. (1994). Ann Arbor, MI: Biomedware.

Index

The reference locator "figure(s)*" with accompanying numbers indicates that there is material related to a particular topic on the web site www.urbanresearch.org.

About the Authors

Carolyn Rebecca Block is a senior research analyst at the Illinois Criminal Justice Information Authority. Her research interests include the use, interpretation, and analysis of criminal justice data, especially that for lethal and nonlethal violence. She is currently working on a study of lethal outcomes of intimate partner violence, and she maintains the 32-year Chicago Homicide Dataset.

Richard Block is Professor of Sociology at Loyola University of Chicago. His current research includes analysis of geographic features, such as rapid transit stations and specific housing complexes, that are likely to lead to high crime risk; the development of contour mapping for crime analysis; and the depiction of gang activity areas.

Philip Canter is Chief Statistician for the Baltimore County Police Department, of which he has been a member for 16 years. He received a master's degree in urban planning and policy analysis from Morgan State University. His research interests include crime analysis and geographic information systems (GIS).

Sanjoy Chakravorty is Associate Professor of Geography and Urban Studies and director of the GIS lab at Temple University. He spends much time studying distributions—often of income and sometimes of crime. His work has been published in *Urban Studies, Economic Geography, Urban Geography,* the *Journal of the American Planning Association,* and elsewhere.

Garth Davies is Assistant Professor of Criminal Justice at Simon Fraser University and a doctoral candidate at the Rutgers University School of Criminal Justice.

John E. Eck is Associate Professor in the Division of Criminal Justice of the University of Cincinnati, where he teaches graduate courses in policing, policy, and research methods. He has conducted research on the geography of retail drug markets for the Washington/Baltimore High Intensity Drug Trafficking Area and the Police Executive Research Forum. He has written numerous books and articles on policing, crime displacement, crime mapping, and drug control.

Jeffrey Fagan is Professor of Public Health at Columbia University and Visiting Professor at the Columbia Law School. His current research examines the social and spatial contagion of violence, situational contexts of adolescent violence, the deterrence of domestic violence, and the jurisprudence of adolescent crimes. He is past editor of the *Journal of Research in Crime and Delinquency,* and he serves on the editorial boards of *Crime and Justice, Criminology,* and the *Journal of Criminal Law and Criminology.*

Jeffrey S. Gersh is Evaluation Coordinator for the Washington/Baltimore High Intensity Drug Trafficking Area. He is currently a doctoral student at the University of Maryland at College Park. He received his master's of science degree in criminology from the University of Baltimore.

Victor Goldsmith is Acting Dean of Research and Professor of Geography at Hunter College. He also directs the Center for the Applied Study of the Environment. His research interests include three-dimensional modeling, the spatial analysis of crime patterns, and other GIS applications.

Keith Harries is a professor in the Geography and Environmental Systems Department at the University of Maryland, Baltimore County. He has a longstanding interest in geographical aspects of social issues and the geography of crime.

Eric S. Jefferis is a social science analyst with the Crime Mapping Research Center, Office of Research and Evaluation, National Institute of Justice. He is also a doctoral student in the Division of Criminal Justice at the University of Cincinnati. His research interests include the dynamics of citizen-police interactions, the influence of media on citizens' perceptions of police organizations, and the spatial and temporal analysis of crime patterns.

Thomas Kamber is a political science doctoral student at the City University of New York Graduate School. His primary research interests are in housing and political theory. He has directed a tenant ownership program for New York City and managed several campaigns for elective office.

Robert H. Langworthy is Director and Professor of the Justice Center at the University of Alaska, Anchorage. He is author or coauthor of three books, and his articles have appeared in numerous criminal justice and criminology journals. His research interests include police organization, police use of force, evaluation of police practices, and environmental criminology with particular interest in the spatial analysis of crime.

Philip G. McGuire is Assistant Commissioner for Programs and Policy in the New York City Police Department (NYPD), of which he has been a member for 24 years. He earned master's degrees from Brooklyn Polytechnic Institute and Carnegie Mellon's School of Urban and Public Affairs. He has also served as the research director of the NYPD's Crime Analysis Section.

Sara McLafferty is Professor of Geography at Hunter College of the City University of New York. Her research interests include the use of spatial analysis methods and GIS to analyze health and social problems in cities and gender and race differences in access to employment. She has published in many journals in geography, epidemiology, and urban studies and has served on the Mapping Science Committee of the National Academy of Sciences.

John H. Mollenkopf is Professor of Political Science and Sociology at the City University of New York Graduate Center, where he directs the Center for Urban Research. He has authored or edited six books on urban politics, urban policy, and New York City. His current research priorities include a large-scale study of the immigrant second generation in metropolitan New York and the use of GIS techniques to analyze the social context of crime patterns in New York City.

William V. Pelfrey Jr. is Assistant Professor in the College of Criminal Justice at the University of South Carolina and a doctoral candidate in criminal justice at Temple University. He is interested in policing, policy evaluation, and GIS.

Dennis W. Roncek is Professor of Criminal Justice at the University of Nebraska at Omaha. He is best known for his work on crime in and near public housing projects, crime near schools, and studies of bars and crime. He has also written articles on spatial autocorrelation, logistic regression, and tobit analysis.

Timothy A. Ross is a senior research associate at the Vera Institute of Justice. His writings address issues in urban politics, political participation, and public policy. He has worked with the NYPD to upgrade their crime mapping capacities, analyzed the relationship between crime and public housing, and is currently examining child welfare and juvenile justice issues in New York City.

Charles Swartz is a doctoral student in the Environmental Psychology department at the City University of New York Graduate School. His research interests include psychological responses to crime and GIS applications. His dissertation explores issues related to the fear of crime.

Charlene Taylor is a doctoral student in the Division of Criminal Justice of the University of Cincinnati. Previously, she was a research analyst with the Washington/Baltimore High Intensity Drug Trafficking Area Evaluation Section.

Doug Williamson is a doctoral candidate at the City University of New York (CUNY) Graduate School and University Center. He is a research associate for the Center for Applied Studies of the Environment of CUNY. His current research interests are the use of GIS in law enforcement, spatial statistics, and visualization.